CLEVER
cooking

PLAN AND PREPARE NUTRITIOUS
MEALS THAT WILL SAVE YOU
TIME AND MONEY

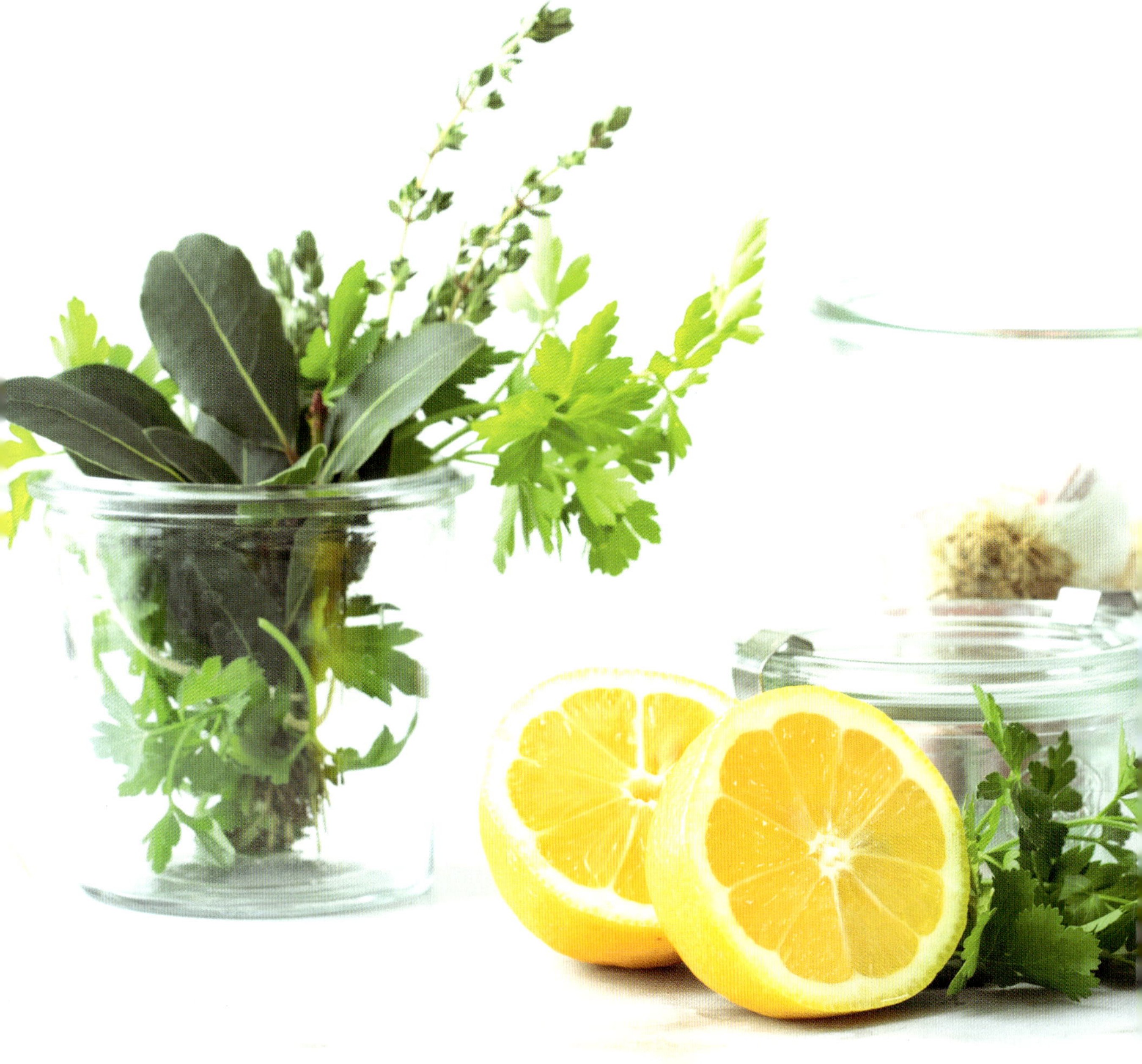

CLEVER
cooking

PLAN AND PREPARE NUTRITIOUS
MEALS THAT WILL SAVE YOU
TIME AND MONEY

VICKIE DE BEER

Published in 2023 by Penguin Books
  an imprint of Penguin Random House South Africa (Pty) Ltd
Company Reg. No. 1953/000441/07
The Estuaries, 4 Oxbow Crescent, Century Avenue,
  Century City 7441, Cape Town, South Africa
PO Box 1144, Cape Town, 8000, South Africa
www.penguinrandomhouse.co.za

Copyright © in published edition: Penguin Random House
  South Africa (Pty) Ltd 2023
Copyright © in text: Vickie de Beer 2023
Copyright © in photographs: Penguin Random House
  South Africa (Pty) Ltd 2023

All rights reserved. No part of this publication may be reproduced, stored in a retrieval system or transmitted, in any form or by any means, electronic, mechanical, photocopying, recording or otherwise, without the prior written permission of the publishers and the copyright holders.

PUBLISHER: **Beverley Dodd**
MANAGING EDITOR: **Aimee Carelse**
DESIGNER: **Helen Henn**
RECIPES, PHOTOGRAPHY AND FOOD STYLING: **Vickie de Beer**
PHOTOGRAPHY ASSISTANT: **Lucca de Beer**
EDITOR AND INDEXER: **Gill Gordon**
PROOFREADER: **Bronwen Maynier**

ISBN 978-1-48590-158-7

Reproduction by Studio Repro, Cape Town
Printed and bound by in China by
  Golden Prosperity Printing & Packaging (Heyuan) Co., Ltd

CONTENTS

MEAL PREP — 6
- ADVANTAGES OF MEAL PREP — 6
- FREEZING FOODS — 9
- COOKING WITH FLAVOUR — 14
- PLANNING AND PREPPING — 16

FLAVOUR STARTERS — 18
- FLAVOUR PASTES — 20
- SPICE MIXES — 26
- SAUCES — 28
- FLAVOURED BUTTERS — 32
- FLAVOUR BASES — 35
- MARINADES — 36
- CONFIT — 38
- COOK-IN SAUCES — 44
- FERMENTED SALADS AND SALSA — 52

BROTHS & SOUPS — 56

SLOW COOKING — 76

ONE DISH — 102

BASICS & SIDES — 140

INDEX — 158

MEAL PREP

Most of us do some form of 'prep' every time we cook or prepare a meal. In recent years, however, the term 'meal prep' has come to mean 'advance preparation', in the sense of preparing entire meals or even parts of meals ahead of time, in order to cut down on the time required to make a complete meal from scratch.

As a working mom juggling a fulltime job with raising a family, I began setting aside time over weekends to prepare meals for the week ahead. I'd make a big batch of bolognaise, and a saucepan of meaty broth, which became a winter staple in our house; we ate it for lunch, dinner, and even breakfast on cold mornings! It was good for our gut health and gave us energy for our busy lifestyle. I also baked healthy low-carb rolls or muffins for school lunches. And that would set us up for the week.

After my family immigrated to the Netherlands in 2020, I continued to do meal prep, as well as taking on the challenge of preparing nutritious meals for clients, but I was faced with new challenges, because the kitchen, fridge and stove were much smaller than I'd been accustomed to in my spacious Stellenbosch home. In order to do all the advance prep and have enough space to store meals, I had to become clever with my planning. And because I didn't want to spend *every* weekend cooking, I began to cook in bulk and freeze both complete meals and single portions, so we'd always have healthy, wholesome food to hand.

ADVANTAGES OF MEAL PREP

- You know what goes into your food and can improve the quality and/or nutritional value by preparing nutrient-dense dishes that are packed with vegetables and good fibre, and low in refined carbs, sugar and/or gluten.
- Eating home-cooked meals instead of relying on take-outs or store-bought meals is better for your nutritional health, whether you are feeding a family or cooking for one.
- Preparing meals in the freezer can save you money. By planning ahead and cooking in bulk, you can take advantage of supermarket specials on meat, seasonal vegetables and pantry staples.

HOW TO USE THIS BOOK

- Choose a flavour paste or cook-in sauce.
- Choose a broth or soup to cook on the stove.
- Choose a one-pan dish or tray bake that can go into the oven.
- Choose a slow-cooking stew or curry.
- Choose a stir-fry to go with your cook-in sauce or flavour paste.
- Choose your vegetable sides.
- Go shopping and get cooking!

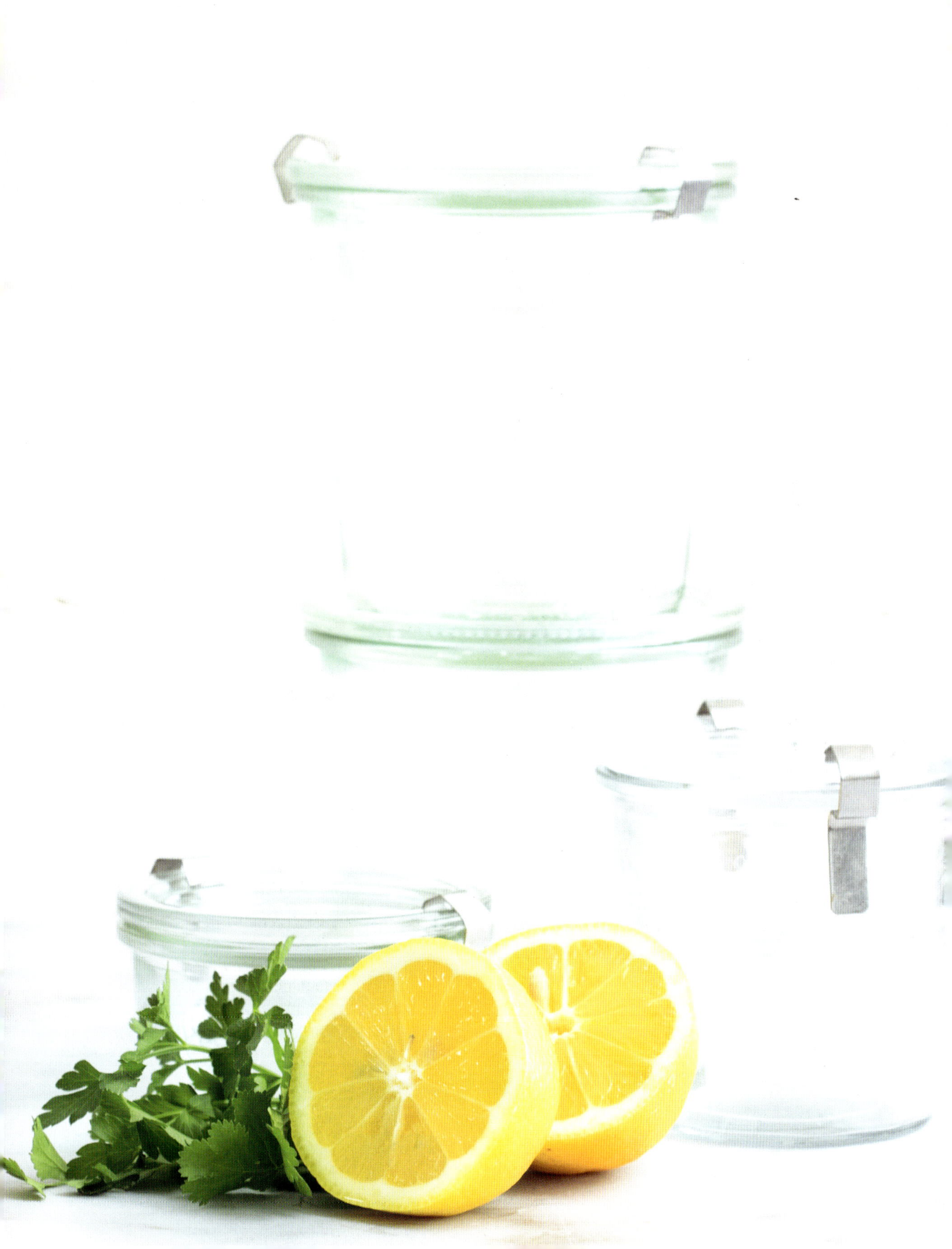

HOW DO YOU DO MEAL PREP?

The internet is full of images of neatly packaged complete meals, comprising mains, sides and salads, but this is not the sort of meal prep I do for my family. Over the years, I've found that it is more practical to freeze main dishes and prepare the sides each evening. I've also learnt that stacks of individual servings of the same meals went uneaten in the long run. However, if you prefer to freeze complete meals, simply plan your preparation so you can incorporate the main dish and your chosen sides in one container.

Meal prep doesn't mean freezing everything. If you batch cook enough for four meals, for example, you can eat one on the day, another a few days later, and freeze two. You can always change things up by adding different sides, or adapt the basic recipe to make a pie or stir-fry, for example. At first, meal prep may take time to get used to, but once you get a system going, it will become easier.

1 Start by doing an inventory of your freezer and pantry. Check expiry dates, and use up anything that has been in the freezer for a long time. Discard pantry staples that have passed their expiry date.

2 Arrange the remaining items by expiry date, placing any items that are due to expire soon at the front, so they can be used first. Place the things that you use most often at the front of the pantry or freezer. For example, I frequently use frozen tomato sauce, so I store it in the top freezer drawer, where I can quickly grab it.

3 Keep track of what meals you have in the freezer. Use a small whiteboard or a notebook to list every item as you place it in the freezer. (Note the number of portions, the portion size or total volume of the dish, as well as the date you prepared it.) Then, each time you remove something, cross it off the list. Once you get into the habit of doing this, you'll be able to see at a glance what you have on hand, what is running low, and what needs to be used up before your next batch-cooking day. (Having a whiteboard on the freezer can also remind you to take out meals in the morning so they are defrosted in time for dinner.)

4 Set aside time for cooking. Good time management is an essential part of meal prep. It's not just about setting aside enough time for batch cooking, but also about choosing meals that can be finished off in varying amounts of time. Inevitably, there'll be days when you have plenty of time to prepare a meal, and other days when what you need is a ready-made stir-fry, or a cook-in sauce that allows you to put a meal on the table in 30 minutes. Planning your food prep around your family's schedules and routines for weekdays and weekends will enable you to have meals on hand for every eventuality. Believe me, it's a great feeling to know that, at the end of a hectic day, the evening meal is sorted!

FREEZING FOODS

The size and type of containers you choose will depend on your freezer space, as well as your lifestyle, your food preferences and the quantities of food you want to prepare in advance. If you are a family with teenagers, for example, you'll need bigger containers than if you're preparing meals for two adults and a toddler.

As we are a family of four, with two teenage sons, I generally freeze meals in batches of 1–2 kg, but you might prefer to freeze smaller portions. I find that 500 g is sufficient for two, while 250 g portions are ideal for workday lunches or a lighter 'on-the-go' meal. When you are prepping and packing, you can decide whether to portion meals for family dinners as well as for individual lunches or a quick snack.

Resealable bags These are ideal when you don't have much freezer space. Fill the bags, spreading the food as flat as possible, then press out the excess air and close the seal (always make sure it is fully closed, to prevent air from getting in, or food leaking out). The bags can be stacked on top of each other, or lined up in rows (like books). Resealable bags with a broad base can stand upright, making them good for freezing liquids like soups and stocks. Eco-friendly reusable bags are available, but can be pricey and may not come in suitable sizes for your needs.

Glass containers These are eco-friendly, but they take up space and you need many containers, which can become expensive. One solution is to freeze food in 'oven to table' glass containers, or rigid plastic containers with firm-fitting lids, then turn out the frozen blocks, wrap them in cling wrap and label clearly. This way your containers are not tied up in the freezer for weeks on end. One advantage of freezing meals in ovenproof glass is that you can put the frozen block back into the same container to defrost, then put it straight into the oven or microwave for reheating. For stocks and sauces, use containers with a capacity of 500 ml or 1 litre (500 ml is enough to add to a stew, or make a creamy soup or sauce, while a litre provides a base for a brothy soup). Food expands when it is frozen, so leave room in the container for expansion. Always label containers with the meal, date of preparation and quantity (or number of portions). It is hard to tell one frozen block from another, so good labelling will ensure that you defrost the meal you want! (Instead of using adhesive labels that are hard to remove, try sticky notes, or masking tape that you can write on and peel off.)

HOW MUCH SHOULD I FREEZE?

	LIGHT MEAL FOR 1	MAIN MEAL FOR 1	2 ADULTS & 2 TODDLERS	2 ADULTS & 2 PRE-TEENS	2 ADULTS & 2 TEENS	ENTERTAINING (6+ PORTIONS)
SOUPS	250 ml	500 ml	1 litre	1.2 litres	1.5 litres	2 litres
ONE-DISH STEWS & CASSEROLES	250 g	250–300 g	700 g	800–900 g	1–1.2 kg	1.5–2 kg
MEATY MEALS	150 g	150–200 g	450–500 g	600 g	800 g	1 kg
SIDES	60 g	80 g	240 g	280 g	320 g	500 g
COOK-IN SAUCES	–	–	500 ml	500 ml	1 litre	1 litre

- Light meals are ideal for midweek lunches, either at home or work, or as a 'top-up' between activities.
- One-dish stews and casseroles are complete meals that only need a single side vegetable or salad.
- Meaty meals usually require the addition of sides, salads and/or starches to make a complete meal.
- Sides (veggies and/or carbs) can accompany either frozen or freshly made main meals.
- Cook-in sauces may be used to prepare stir-fries, or incorporated into a slow-cooked dish.

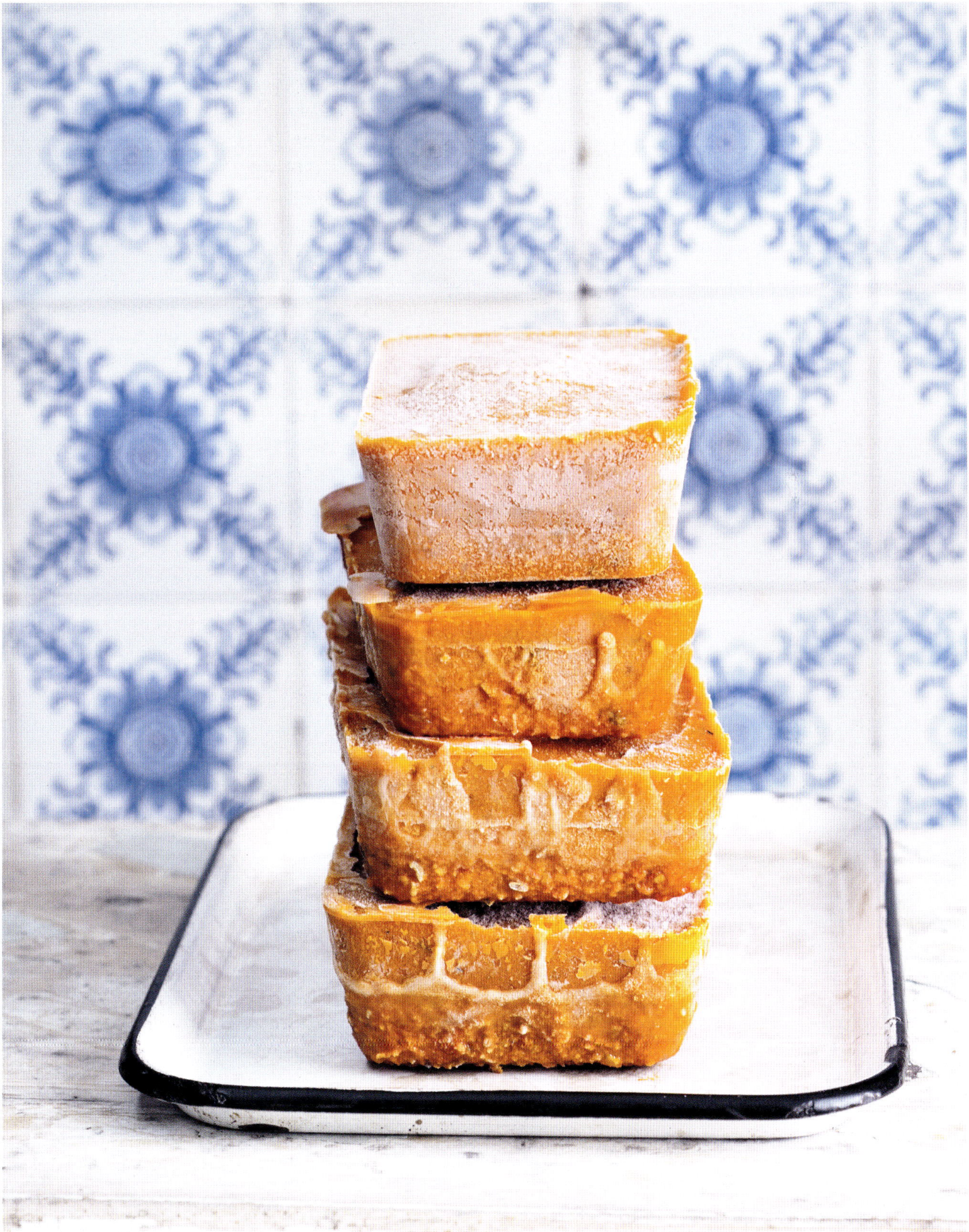

WHAT CAN BE FROZEN AND FOR HOW LONG?

You can freeze almost any food. (One thing that doesn't freeze well are eggs in their shell, but if you hard-boil and peel them, they can be frozen.) However, just because you *can* freeze almost anything doesn't mean that you *should*! Some foods, like potatoes, lose so much texture when frozen, they become unappetizing. While frozen food can generally be kept for a long time without spoiling, almost all food will lose both flavour and texture if frozen for too long. Follow your freezer guidelines for the ideal length of time to store meat, dairy and vegetables.

SAFETY TIPS FOR FREEZING FOOD

- Home freezers vary between -16°C and -18°C. Food that remains frozen at a constant -18°C is safe. Freezing causes microbes, like bacteria, fungi and yeasts, to become dormant, but it doesn't kill them, which is why food must be handled correctly both before and after freezing.

- Cool food completely before freezing. This is important, because placing warm food in the freezer causes the temperature inside the freezer to rise, possibly contaminating already frozen food. One way to cool large batches after cooking is to spread the food on oven trays to ensure even cooling before you package the food for the freezer.

- The best way to safely defrost a family meal is to remove it from the freezer the night before and place the container on a tray (to catch any water) in the fridge. If you need to defrost something in a hurry, stand the container in a basin of warm water. You can also defrost food in the microwave, using the Defrost function or the lowest heat setting, so it thaws slowly without starting to cook around the edges. If you are defrosting food bricks, remove the cling wrap and warm the food slowly in a saucepan, or transfer it to a glass container for the microwave.

- Once defrosted, food must be reheated in the oven (at 160°C) or microwave until piping hot. Cream-based sauces may split when they are reheated. To overcome this, add a little extra cream once reheated and stir well until the sauce comes together again.

- Uncooked meat which has been frozen can be refrozen after cooking.

- During limited power outages (loadshedding), items in the freezer should remain frozen for up to 24 hours, but don't open the freezer more than necessary, as this lets in warm air and will speed up the defrosting process. If loadshedding extends over longer or more frequent intervals, monitor your freezer contents and use up any items that have started to thaw.

Sterilizing containers

There is no need to sterilize containers used for freezing food. Likewise, glass containers used for fermenting foods don't require sterilization, because the fermentation process makes use of the natural beneficial bacteria contained within both the food and the container. However, when it comes to homemade preserved foods that are stored at room temperature (such as pickled vegetables, garlic in olive oil, jams or stewed fruit), all the containers and equipment must be thoroughly sterilized, because food that is improperly preserved can become contaminated by the botulin toxin, leading to food poisoning. The safest way to prevent this is by keeping all preserved (canned or bottled) foods, as well as fermented foods, in the fridge once they have been opened.

COOKING WITH FLAVOUR

Freezing does not significantly reduce the nutritional value of food, but it does cause a loss of flavour, which can be overcome by the use of fresh herbs and whole spices. I prefer to use natural flavourings rather than spice blends or processed sauces which often contain hidden starches and sugars. My fridge and pantry are usually stocked with the following:

Anchovies

Preserved in olive oil in bottles or cans, these little salty fish can boost the flavour of many dishes. They are a good source of omega-3 fatty acids, which we all need, and give a deep umami flavour to tomato-based sauces.

Bay leaves

Fresh or dried, these impart a savoury note. They are essential in a bouquet garni – a bunch of flavourful herbs (typically thyme, parsley and bay leaf, although I often add rosemary) which adds flavour to stews, soups and broths. Bay leaves also have antiviral properties.

Canned tomatoes

These come in many forms (whole or chopped, paste, passata and purée), so keep a variety on hand. I use tomato paste to deepen the colour and flavour of sauces, broths and soups, and add whole or chopped tomatoes to casseroles, curries and stews. Read the labels and opt for those without additives (often produced in Italy or labelled 'Italian style').

Fresh herbs

Herbs add flavour to most dishes. Leafy herbs like parsley, basil, coriander and chives are best added towards the end of cooking time, while hardy herbs (thyme, origanum, rosemary, sage) can stand up to longer cooking, making them ideal for adding to soups, oven bakes and slow-cooked casseroles or stews.

Garlic, ginger and chillies

Most curries, stir-fries and stews start by frying onions with garlic, ginger and/or chillies, all of which contain powerful antioxidants. For maximum freshness, buy them whole and prepare as needed. To save time, or for small quantities, buy packs of ready-chopped fresh aromatics (just enough for one or two meals).

Lemons and limes

Grated zest and freshly squeezed juice add flavour to grilled meat, bring balance to sauces, and feature in many Mexican and Asian dishes.

Paprika

This powerful antioxidant imparts a deep, often smoky, flavour to food. Sweet paprika is milder, while smoked paprika adds extra depth to meat dishes and barbecue sauces.

Salt and pepper

Freshly ground salt and pepper are essential for adding flavour to almost anything. A sprinkling of salt flakes or coarse sea salt also helps with the caramelization of meat.

Spices

These add flavour and depth. Some spices, like turmeric and cinnamon, are also powerful antioxidants. To maintain quality, buy small amounts or, if you prefer to buy in bulk, divide spices into smaller containers and freeze. For homemade spice mixes, see page 26.

Pimentón de la Vera
La Chinata
www.lachinata.com
70g
CONCENTRATO
DI POMODORO
PARMA-ITALIA

PLANNING AND PREPPING

I plan weekly menus, which I rotate and change seasonally. When we get tired of one dish, I simply swop it for something else, but the basic menu stays the same. Mondays are always hectic in our house, so I usually opt for a quick fish dish that takes under 30 minutes to prepare. Tuesdays and Wednesdays are 'normal', but by Thursday night I'm grateful to have a finished meal on standby. To accompany main dishes, I prepare a vegetable side (pages 150–151) for the freezer, and/or make my Everyday Rocket Salad (page 151). To show you what I mean, here is an example of a typical weekly menu.

SEVEN-DAY FAMILY MEAL PLAN

SUNDAY
Roast or braaied chicken with vegetables
Clever Cooking Roast two whole chickens (page 98); eat one for lunch and pull the meat off the second, setting it aside for later in the week (see Tuesday). If you're braaiing, use two spatchcocked chickens ('flatties') or two full braai packs.

MONDAY
Fish in Creamy Curry Cook-in Sauce
Clever Cooking To prepare a meal in under 30 minutes, pan-fry portions of fresh fish and add ready-made Creamy Curry Cook-in Sauce (page 48). Serve with Quick Pilaf (page 142).

TUESDAY
Chicken, Leek and Mushroom Pies
Clever Cooking Use half of the reserved chicken from Sunday to make individual pies (page 128) with pre-made frozen Basic Low-carb Pastry (page 148). If you have time, use the rest of the chicken to prepare Cheesy Chicken and Butternut Lasagne (page 122) for the freezer. Next Tuesday's meal is sorted!

WEDNESDAY
Oven-baked Bolognaise
Clever Cooking Serve precooked Oven-baked Bolognaise (page 86) with low-carb baby marrow noodles and Everyday Rocket Salad (page 151) on the side.

THURSDAY
Mexican Wraps with Chipotle Chicken
Clever Cooking Make the most of pre-prepped meals by reheating frozen Mexican Wraps (page 146) and a portion of frozen Chipotle Chicken Tray Bake (page 115). Add Hot Green Sauce (page 146) or Fermented Mexican Salsa (page 55). *Olé!* Your work is done.

FRIDAY
Burger night!
Clever Cooking I always have Low-carb Burger Buns (page 145) in the freezer. Make Burger Patties (page 133) tonight and serve with homemade Sriracha Sauce (page 28), Fermented Burger Pickle (page 52) and/or Fermented Mexican Salsa (page 55). (The patty mixture makes 12 patties, so for my family of four, I'd cook eight patties on the night, using four for the burgers, and setting four aside for next week's lunchboxes. Then I'd freeze the four uncooked patties for another meal.)

By PLANNING AHEAD and *cooking in bulk*, you can take advantage of supermarket specials on meat and pantry staples, and *make the most* of FRESH, SEASONAL VEGETABLES.

FLAVOUR STARTERS

MEAL PREP does not just mean preparing *complete meals*. Sometimes it is just as HELPFUL to have a *homemade, ready-to-use, paste, spice mix* or *cook-in sauce* in your FRIDGE OR FREEZER. The recipes in this chapter will make *weeknight* cooking EASIER, as well as more *flavourful*. Cooking 'FLAVOUR STARTERS' from scratch may require a bit more *effort*, but KNOWING exactly what goes into your *food*, and being able to ELIMINATE the preservatives, colourants or artificial flavourings that go into *processed sauces and spices*, will keep you HEALTHIER IN THE LONG RUN.

FLAVOUR PASTES

I freeze my pastes in ice-cube trays as it is easy to pop out one or two cubes to use as an instant flavour base for quick curries, stews or stir-fries.

THAI GREEN CURRY PASTE

This is my take on a traditional green curry paste. I use it to make quick curries, or add it to fishcakes and stir-fries. Roughly chopping the ingredients before processing helps to distribute them evenly, which results in a smoother paste.

- 1 onion, peeled and roughly chopped
- 2 large green jalapeño chillies (or any mild green chilli)
- 2 stalks lemongrass, roughly chopped
- 3 cloves garlic, peeled and roughly chopped
- 8 cm fresh ginger, peeled and roughly chopped
- Grated zest and juice of 2 limes
- Small bunch coriander, leaves only
- 1 small can (200 g) coconut cream
- 3–4 Tbsp peanut butter
- 2 Tbsp soy sauce

MAKES 8 FROZEN CUBES

1. Place all the ingredients in a food processor and blend to a fine, smooth paste, scraping down the sides as you go. (If necessary, add a bit of water.) Scoop the paste into an ice-cube tray (± 2 Tbsp per cube) and freeze until completely set, then pop the cubes out of the moulds and place in small resealable bags. You can add frozen cubes directly to the pan when cooking, there is no need to defrost them first. Two cubes should be enough for one meal.

Notes

When preparing lemongrass, it is important to remove any hard outer leaves and chop only the soft, inner stem.

Instead of using coconut cream, scoop the 'cream' off the top of a can of coconut milk for use in the paste and use the rest of the liquid for smoothies.

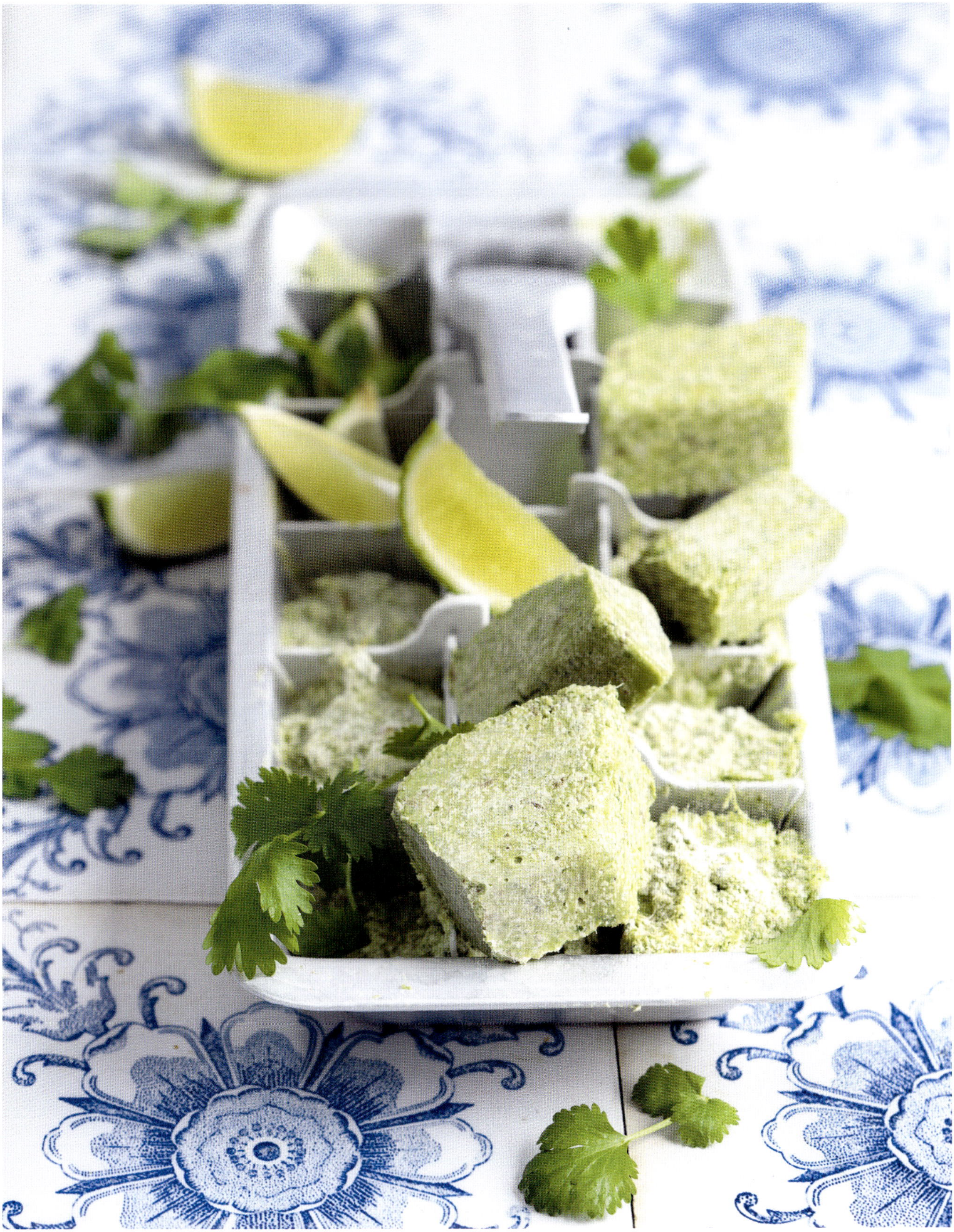

MASALA CURRY PASTE

50 g flaked almonds

2 tsp cumin seeds

2 tsp coriander seeds

2 onions, peeled and roughly chopped

3 cloves garlic, peeled and roughly chopped

6 cm fresh ginger, peeled and roughly chopped

1 red chilli, roughly chopped

4 Tbsp (¼ cup) olive oil

3 Tbsp tomato paste

3 Tbsp full-cream plain yoghurt

2 Tbsp Masala Mix (page 26) or curry powder of choice

2 tsp ground turmeric

1 tsp ground cinnamon

1 tsp salt

MAKES 8–10 FROZEN CUBES

1. Heat a small pan over medium heat and lightly toast the almonds, cumin seeds and coriander seeds until golden and fragrant. Remove from the heat and leave to cool, then add to a food processor with the remaining ingredients.
2. Blend to a fine, smooth paste, scraping down the sides as you go. (If necessary, add a bit of water.) Scoop the paste into an ice-cube tray (± 2 Tbsp per cube) and freeze until completely set, then pop the cubes out of the moulds and place in small resealable bags. You can add frozen cubes directly to the pan when cooking, there is no need to defrost them first. One or two cubes (2–4 Tbsp) should be enough for one meal.

UMAMI PASTE

This paste takes any meaty soup, broth or stew to the next level, flavourwise. Umami (often called the 'fifth taste', after sweet, sour, salty and bitter) comes from fermented foods, like soy sauce and miso, as well as from dried mushrooms, anchovies, oysters, and some dry-aged meats and cheeses.

20 g dried porcini mushrooms
4 Tbsp (¼ cup) water
1 cup grated Parmesan cheese
2 Tbsp soy sauce
2 Tbsp tomato paste
2 tsp miso paste
2 tsp balsamic vinegar
6 anchovy fillets
2 cloves garlic, peeled and roughly chopped

MAKES 12 FROZEN CUBES

1. Soak the dried mushrooms in the water for about 10 minutes, then place them in a food processor, along with the soaking water. Add the remaining ingredients and blend to a fine paste, scraping down the sides as you go. Scoop the paste into an ice-cube tray (± 2 Tbsp per cube) and freeze until completely set, then pop the cubes out of the moulds and place in small resealable bags. You can add frozen cubes directly to the pan when cooking, there is no need to defrost them. One or two cubes (1–2 Tbsp) should be enough for one meal.

Notes

If you can't get dried porcini mushrooms, use dried shiitake mushrooms instead.

To make pan gravy for roast meat or chicken, deglaze the cooking juices with water or wine, then add one cube of Umami Paste, along with 1 cup (250 ml) of Meaty Bone Broth (page 58) and simmer, stirring occasionally, until it thickens and reduces to a rich, tasty gravy.

MOROCCAN PASTE

2 red peppers
2 Tbsp ground cumin
2 Tbsp ground coriander
2 Tbsp sweet paprika
1 Tbsp ground cinnamon
1 Tbsp ground allspice
2 tsp smoked paprika
3 Tbsp tomato paste
1 Tbsp erythritol or honey
6 cm fresh ginger, peeled and finely chopped
3 cloves garlic, peeled and finely chopped
6 soft-dried apricots
½ tsp salt

MAKES 12 FROZEN CUBES

1. Place the whole peppers in a roasting pan and roast in a preheated oven at 200°C for 25–30 minutes, until blistered and soft. Set aside until completely cool before removing the skin and seeds. Chop roughly and place in a food processor along with the rest of the ingredients. Process until smooth, then taste and add more salt if necessary. Spoon into a small resealable bag and store in the fridge for up to 5 days, or freeze in an ice-cube tray (± 2 Tbsp per cube).

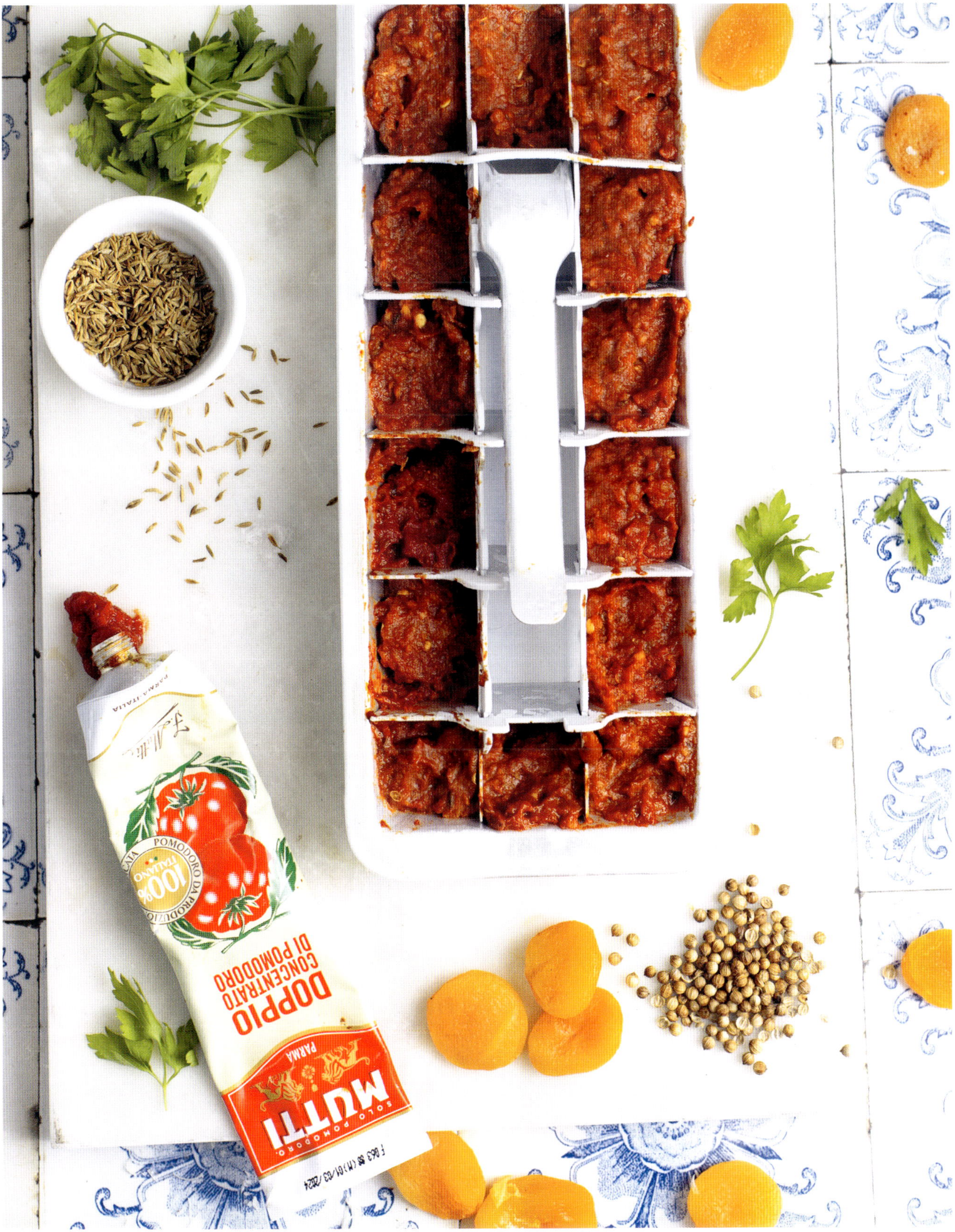
DOPPIO
CONCENTRATO
DI POMODORO
SOLO POMODORO.
MUTTI
PARMA

SPICE MIXES

Making your own spice mixes means you know exactly what they contain. Store them in the fridge to ensure freshness, and add them to curries and stews for an instant flavour boost.

SMOKY MEXICAN SPICE MIX

This is ideal for low-carb enchiladas and tacos made with chicken, pork or steak.

2 Tbsp coriander seeds
2 Tbsp cumin seeds
2 Tbsp fennel seeds
4 Tbsp smoked paprika
3 Tbsp chilli powder
2 tsp ground cinnamon
2 tsp salt
1 tsp ground black pepper

MAKES ± ½ CUP (250 ML)

1. Dry roast (toast) the whole spices in a pan over medium heat until fragrant. Combine the toasted spices with the ground spices in a bullet blender or food processor and grind to a fine powder (in batches if necessary). Store in small glass jars or resealable bags in the fridge for up to 1 month or in the freezer for up to 6 months.

CASS ABRAHAMS' MASALA MIX FOR CURRY

This makes a huge batch (enough for about 40 meals), but it will last for months.

300 g coriander seeds
250 g cumin seeds
100 g chilli flakes
50 g whole black peppercorns
5 g cardamom pods
50 g ground turmeric
50 g ground ginger
10 g ground allspice
10 g ground cinnamon

MAKES ± 800 G

Recipe reproduced with kind permission of Cass Abrahams.

1. Dry roast (toast) the whole spices in a pan over medium heat until fragrant. Combine the toasted spices with the ground spices in a bullet blender or food processor and grind to a fine powder (in batches if necessary). Store in small glass jars or resealable bags in the fridge for up to 1 month or in the freezer for up to 6 months.

Notes

To make a curry for four people, use 3 Tbsp of Masala Mix (more if you like a stronger curry). For a single dish, use 1 Tbsp coriander seeds, 2 tsp cumin seeds, 1 tsp chilli flakes, 1 tsp whole black peppercorns, 2 cardamom pods, ½ tsp each of ground turmeric and ground ginger, and a pinch each of ground allspice and ground cinnamon.

For maximum freshness, store no more than 1 cup of of Masala Mix in the fridge, and freeze the rest.

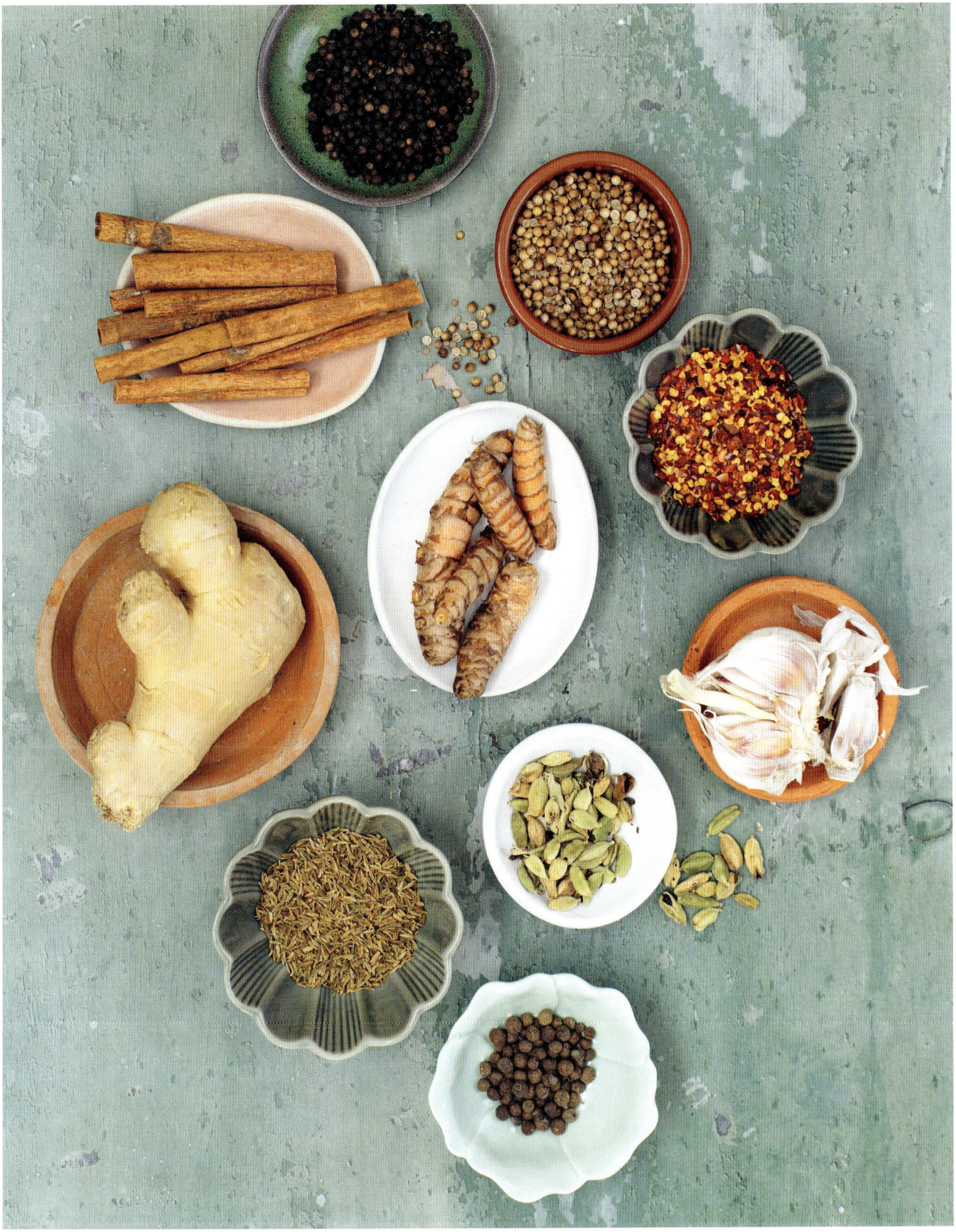

SAUCES

Store-bought sauces and condiments contain hidden sugars and starches and, because we follow a low-carb diet, I wanted to avoid them. Over the years, I've developed a number of delicious homemade low-carb alternatives that have become family favourites.

SRIRACHA SAUCE

I love the smoky, zingy flavour that sriracha imparts to dishes, particularly grilled burgers and steak. Because commercial sauces are often high in sugar and preservatives, I created my own recipe using sambal oelek, an Indonesian chilli paste.

- 2 Tbsp olive oil
- 4 cloves garlic, peeled and finely chopped
- 6 cm fresh ginger, peeled and finely chopped
- 200 g sambal oelek (chilli paste)
- 1 can (400 g) whole peeled tomatoes
- 2 cups water
- 1 cup apple cider vinegar
- ½ cup (125 ml) soy sauce
- 6–7 Tbsp powdered erythritol or granulated sugar
- 3 Tbsp smoked paprika
- 1 Tbsp xanthan gum or Maizena (cornflour)

MAKES 1½ CUPS (± 375 ML)

1. Heat the olive oil in a saucepan over medium heat. Add the garlic and ginger and cook for 2–3 minutes until soft and flavourful. Add the sambal oelek and stir through.
2. Crush the whole tomatoes with a fork and add to the saucepan, along with the juice from the can. Add all the remaining ingredients, except the xanthan gum, and stir to combine. Lower the heat and simmer for 10–15 minutes, until the sauce has reduced slightly and has developed flavour.
3. Add the xanthan gum and whisk vigorously to prevent any lumps from forming. Remove from the heat and leave to cool. (Do not allow xanthan gum to boil, as it will lose its ability to thicken the sauce.) Scoop into glass jars or resealable bags. Store in the fridge for up to 1 week, or in the freezer for up to 1 month.

Notes

Xanthan gum can become a bit slimy after freezing; if the texture bothers you, rather use Maizena (cornflour). You'll find xanthan gum at Dis-Chem, Clicks or Wellness Warehouse, as well as at most health stores and pharmacies.

For convenience, I keep one 125 ml jar in the fridge and freeze two 125 ml portions.

Some chilli pastes contain glucose, so if sugar is an issue for you, read the labels carefully.

BARBECUE BASTING SAUCE

I use my version of a typical American smoky BBQ sauce for basting ribs, sosaties or burger patties, or when making slow-cooked pulled pork or brisket.

2 Tbsp olive oil
2 onions, peeled and finely chopped
3 cloves garlic, peeled and finely chopped
6 cm fresh ginger, peeled and finely chopped
1 jalapeño chilli, finely chopped
3 cups (750 ml) tomato passata
1 cup (250 ml) apple cider vinegar
½ cup (125 ml) bourbon
4 Tbsp (¼ cup) soy sauce
3 Tbsp smoked paprika
4 tsp cumin seeds
4 tsp fennel seeds
2 tsp coriander seeds
Salt to taste

MAKES 2 CUPS (± 500 ML EACH)

1. Heat the olive oil in a saucepan over medium heat. Add the onion, garlic, ginger and jalapeño chilli and fry until soft and translucent.
2. Add the remaining ingredients and stir through. Reduce the heat to low and simmer the sauce for 15–20 minutes, until it thickens and becomes almost caramelly. Remove from the heat and leave to cool before decanting into glass jars or resealable bags. I fill four small jars (± ½ cup each), keep one in the fridge for 1 week and freeze the others. Remember to label the jars clearly.

Note

Instead of bourbon, you can use Tennessee whiskey or South African brandy, but don't use Scotch or Irish whisky, as the flavour profiles are different. If you don't consume alcohol, leave it out and add ½ cup water instead.

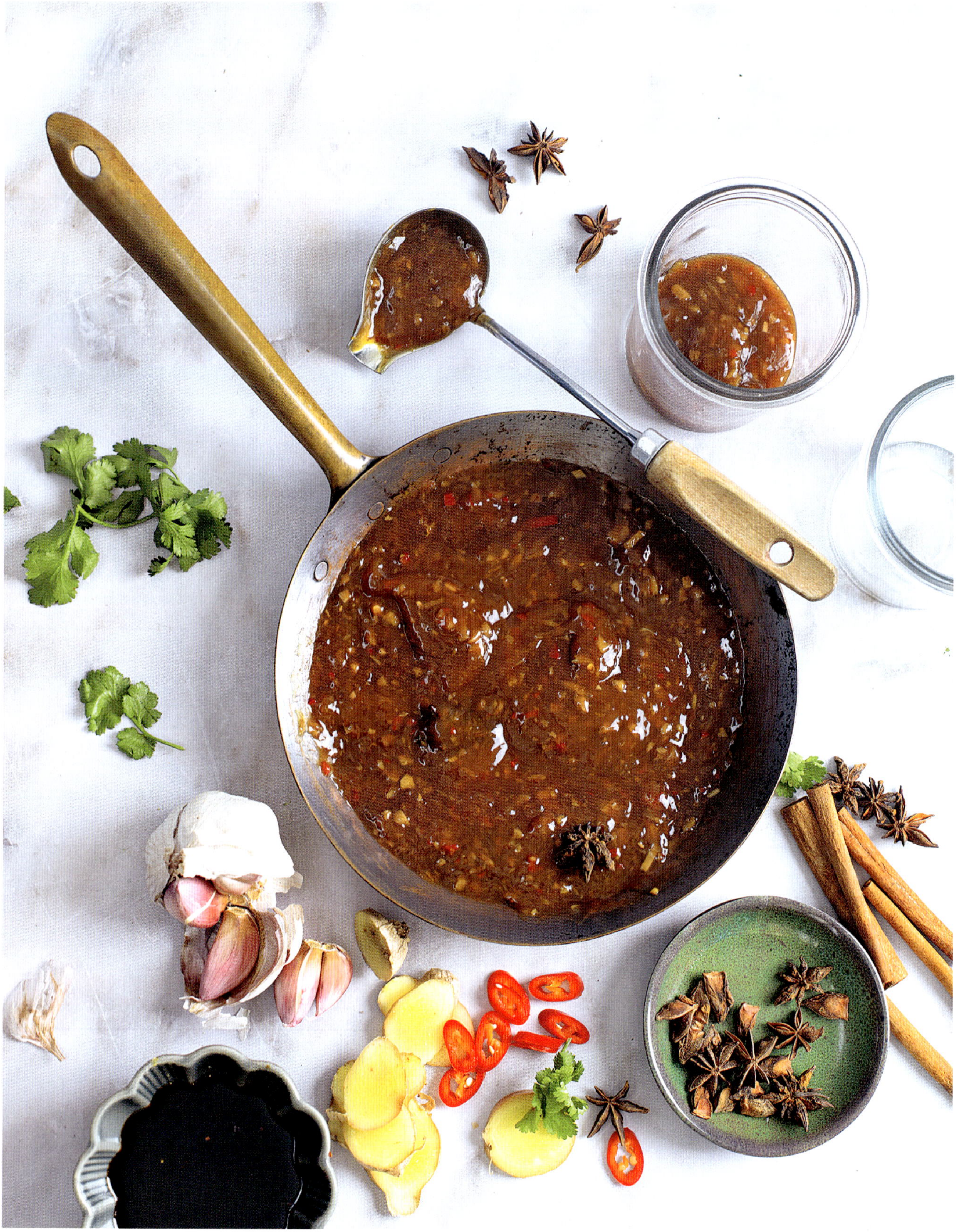

BASIC STIR-FRY SAUCE

4 Tbsp (¼ cup) sesame seeds
2 Tbsp olive oil
1 medium onion, finely chopped
4 cloves garlic, peeled and finely chopped
8 cm fresh ginger, peeled and finely grated
1 red chilli, finely chopped
1½ cups (375 ml) Chicken Broth (page 62) or chicken stock
4 Tbsp (¼ cup) soy sauce
4 Tbsp (¼ cup) erythritol or honey
3 Tbsp apple cider vinegar
2 tsp sesame oil
Finely grated zest and juice of 1 orange
2 star anise
1 cinnamon stick
½ cup coriander leaves and stalks, roughly chopped
2 tsp xanthan gum or Maizena (cornflour)

MAKES 2 CUPS (± 500 ML EACH)

1. Toast the sesame seeds in a dry pan until golden (take care not to let them burn). Set aside to cool.
2. Meanwhile, heat the olive oil in a saucepan over medium heat. Add the onion, garlic, ginger and chilli and fry until the onion is soft and translucent.
3. Add the toasted sesame seeds and the remaining ingredients (except the xanthan gum) and stir to combine. Reduce the heat to low and simmer for 15–20 minutes, until the sauce thickens. Add the xanthan gum and whisk vigorously to prevent any lumps from forming (don't allow xanthan gum to boil, as it will lose its ability to thicken the sauce). Remove from the heat and set aside to cool before decanting into glass jars or resealable bags. I fill four jars (± ½ cup each), keep one in the fridge for 1 week and freeze the others. Remember to label the jars clearly.

Note

If you don't have homemade chicken stock, use good-quality store-bought liquid stock.

FLAVOURED BUTTERS

Flavoured butters are great for everything from frying eggs and fish fillets to rubbing under the skin of chicken before roasting or grilling. They are quick to prepare and last for ages in the freezer. The quantities below each make ± 250 g, which I divide into two rolls, placing one in the fridge for immediate use, and the other in the freezer (remember to label them).

LEMON AND GARLIC

250 g butter, at room temperature
3 cloves garlic, peeled
Finely grated zest and juice of 1 lemon
Large handful flat-leaf parsley
Salt and black pepper to taste

SUNDRIED TOMATO AND HERBS

250 g butter, at room temperature
100 g soft sundried tomatoes in oil, drained
3 cloves garlic, peeled
4 sprigs thyme, leaves only
2 sprigs rosemary, leaves only
Large handful flat-leaf parsley
Salt and black pepper to taste

MAKES ± 250 G EACH

1. Combine all the ingredients in a food processor and process briefly, until smooth. (Alternatively, finely chop the ingredients before combining them in a bowl, and use a fork to mash everything to a smooth paste.) Divide the butter between two pieces of baking paper, wax paper or cling wrap and roll it into a smooth log. Chill in the fridge until firm enough to slice or freeze for future use.

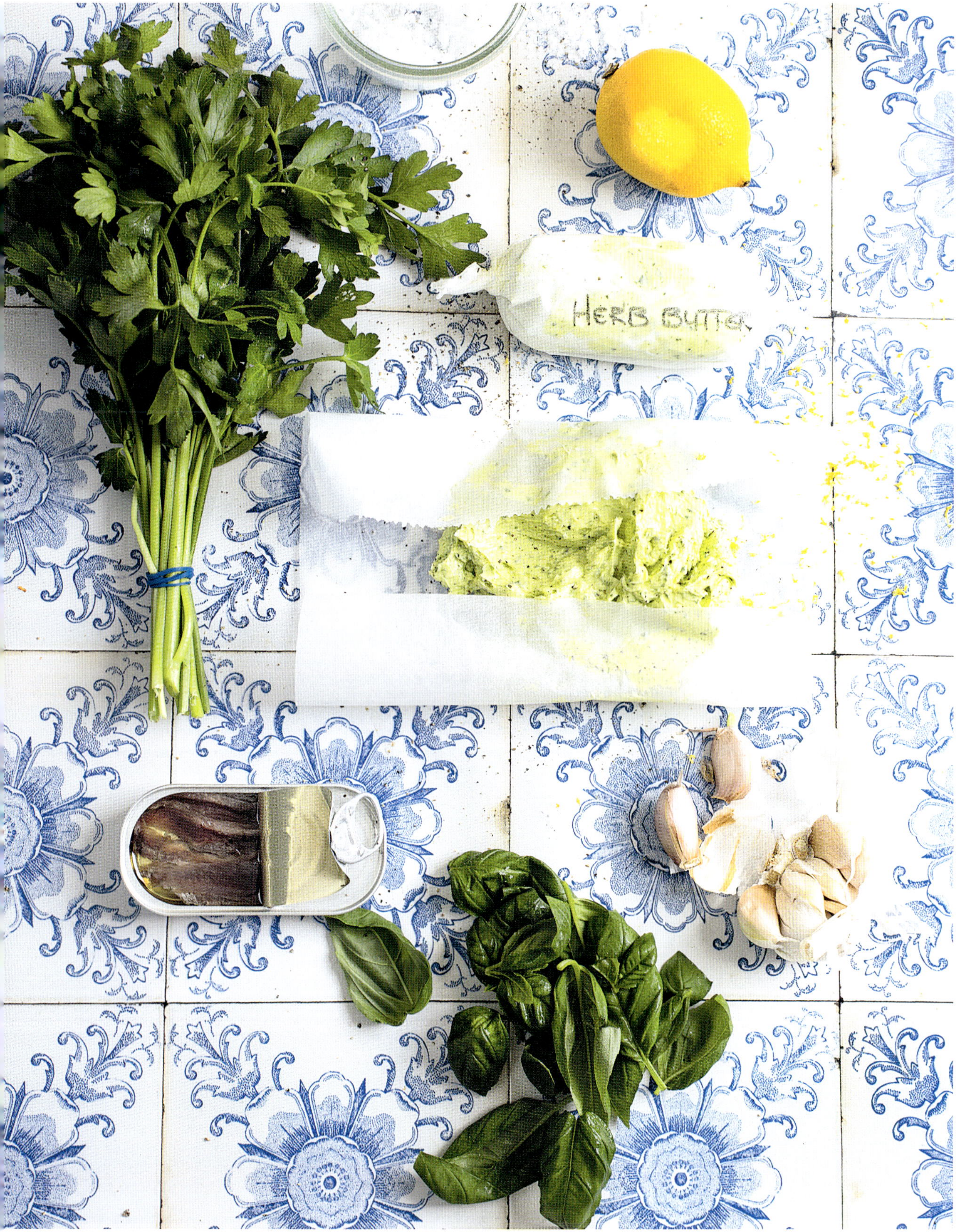
HERB BUTTER

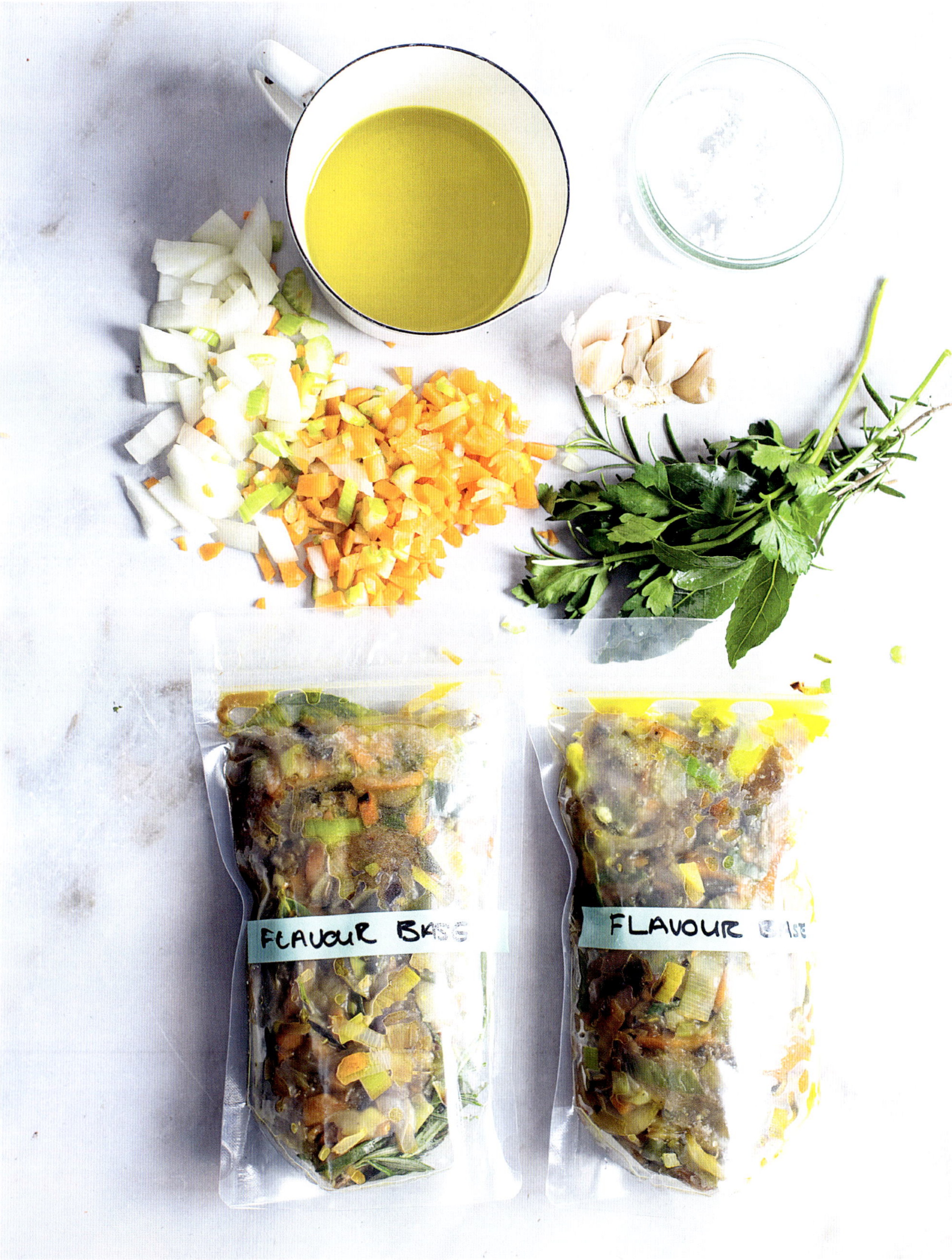
FLAVOUR BASE
FLAVOUR BASE

FLAVOUR BASES

'Mire poix' is a French term used to describe a flavour base made from finely diced vegetables, which is used in all classic stocks, soups and stews. Because fish is more delicate than meat, a 'white mire poix' (made with fennel instead of carrot) is often used when making fish broths or soups. I usually make my flavour base a day or so before I start a big meal prep; it's amazing how much time that saves. Freezing the flavour base in 'recipe portions' makes it easier to prepare dishes when you don't have time to cook from scratch. The quantities below each make about 2 cups (500 ml) in total, which is enough for two portions.

FLAVOUR BASE FOR MEATY STEWS AND BROTHS

4 Tbsp (¼ cup) olive oil
4 medium onions, peeled and finely chopped
8 cloves garlic, peeled and finely chopped
4 anchovy fillets, finely chopped
4 medium carrots, peeled and finely chopped
4 leeks, finely chopped
4 short celery sticks, finely chopped
4 fresh or dried bay leaves
4 sprigs thyme
4 sprigs rosemary

FLAVOUR BASE FOR SEAFOOD AND FISH DISHES

4 Tbsp (¼ cup) olive oil
4 medium onions, peeled and finely chopped
8 cloves garlic, peeled and finely chopped
4 anchovy fillets, finely chopped
1 large fennel bulb, finely chopped
4 leeks, finely chopped
4 short celery sticks, finely chopped
4 fresh or dried bay leaves
4 sprigs parsley

MAKES 2 CUPS (500 ML EACH)

1. Heat the olive oil in a large saucepan over medium heat. Add the onion, garlic and anchovies and cook, while stirring, until soft and translucent.
2. Add the rest of the vegetables and cook for a further 5 minutes, stirring occasionally. Add the herbs and cook until the vegetables soften and start to caramelize. Remove from the heat and set aside until completely cool. Divide into resealable bags (±1 cup each) and label clearly. Keep in the fridge for up to 3 days or freeze for up to 1 month. (There is no need to thaw the flavour base before use. Just place it in a saucepan over low heat while you prepare the rest of the ingredients.)

MARINADES

Making marinades in advance allows you to quickly put together a stir-fry or tray bake, or marinate meat overnight for use the next day or to freeze.

SPICY INDIAN MARINADE FOR BEEF CURRY

2 Tbsp olive oil

3 cloves garlic, peeled and finely chopped

6 cm fresh ginger, peeled and finely chopped

3 Tbsp Masala Mix (page 26) or curry powder of choice

1 cup full-cream plain yoghurt

½ tsp salt

MAKES ±1 CUP, ENOUGH TO MARINATE 800 G CUBED BEEF

1. Combine all the ingredients in a large bowl. Add the meat, season lightly with salt and use your hands to massage the marinade into the meat.
2. Spoon the marinated meat into a large resealable bag, pressing down with your hands to distribute the marinade evenly and remove any air that might be trapped between the pieces of meat. Keep in the fridge for up to 3 days or freeze for up to 2 months.

JALAPEÑO AND LIME MARINADE FOR STIR-FRY

4 Tbsp (¼ cup) olive oil

2 Tbsp soy sauce

3 cloves garlic, peeled and finely chopped

6 cm fresh ginger, peeled and finely chopped

1 jalapeño chilli, finely chopped

Grated zest and juice of 2 limes (±4 Tbsp)

Small handful coriander leaves, chopped

Salt and black pepper to taste

MAKES ± ⅓ CUP, ENOUGH TO MARINATE 500 G CHICKEN STRIPS OR BEEF STRIPS

1. Combine all the ingredients in a large bowl. Add the meat, season lightly with salt and use your hands to massage the marinade into the meat.
2. Spoon the marinated meat into a large resealable bag, pressing down with your hands to distribute the marinade evenly and remove any air that might be trapped between the pieces of meat. Keep in the fridge for up to 3 days or freeze for up to 2 months.

FLAVOUR STARTERS

HONEY AND MUSTARD MARINADE

1 cup (250 ml) buttermilk
2 Tbsp olive oil
2 Tbsp Dijon mustard
2 tsp honey or erythritol
3 cloves garlic, peeled and finely chopped
2 sprigs rosemary
Salt and black pepper to taste

MAKES ± 1 CUP, ENOUGH TO MARINATE 800 G DEBONED, SKINLESS CHICKEN THIGHS

1. Combine all the ingredients in a large bowl. Add the meat, season lightly with salt and use your hands to massage the marinade into the meat.
2. Spoon the marinated meat into a large resealable bag, pressing down with your hands to distribute the marinade evenly and remove any air that might be trapped between the pieces of meat. Keep in the fridge for up to 3 days or freeze for up to 2 months.

SPICY CHIPOTLE MARINADE

1 can (± 260 g) chipotle chillies in adobo sauce
2 Tbsp olive oil
3 cloves garlic, peeled and finely chopped
Grated zest and juice of 1 lime (± 2 Tbsp)
2 tsp smoked paprika
1 tsp ground cumin
Salt to taste

MAKES ± ½ CUP, ENOUGH TO MARINATE 500 G DEBONED, SKINLESS CHICKEN THIGHS OR PORK CUBES

1. Combine all the ingredients in the bowl of a food processor and process until smooth.
2. Place the meat in a bowl and season lightly with salt. Pour over the marinade and use your hands to massage it into the meat.
3. Spoon the marinated meat into a large resealable bag, pressing down with your hands to distribute the marinade evenly and remove any air that might be trapped between the pieces of meat. Keep in the fridge for up to 3 days or freeze for up to 2 months.

FLAVOUR STARTERS | 37

CONFIT

In classic French cooking, 'confit' is a technique where ingredients are cooked low and slow in olive oil or duck fat. This preserves all the flavour and also gives you a fragrant oil to cook with. I love this method, because I can cook things like onions, garlic and tomatoes without being too involved. Just pop them into the oven and forget about them for a while.

GARLIC CONFIT

Peeling individual cloves of garlic takes a long time, but you will end up with enough oozy, soft garlic flesh for a number of dishes, as well as a delicious garlic-flavoured oil that can be used for cooking.

6 whole heads garlic
6 sprigs thyme
3 sprigs rosemary
4 fresh or dried bay leaves
1 cup (250 ml) good-quality olive oil

MAKES ONE 375 ML JAR

1. Cut off the tops of the garlic heads to expose the tops of the cloves. Place the garlic heads in a small deep oven tray. Add the herbs and pour over enough olive oil to completely cover the garlic. Cover the tray with foil and place in a preheated oven at 160°C for 1½ hours, or until the garlic is completely soft. Remove from the oven and set aside until completely cool.
2. Pour the olive oil into a glass jar with a tight-fitting lid. Press the garlic cloves out of the heads and place in the jar, along with the herbs, making sure everything is submerged in the oil. Seal and keep in the fridge for up to 2 weeks, making sure the confit garlic remains covered in oil.

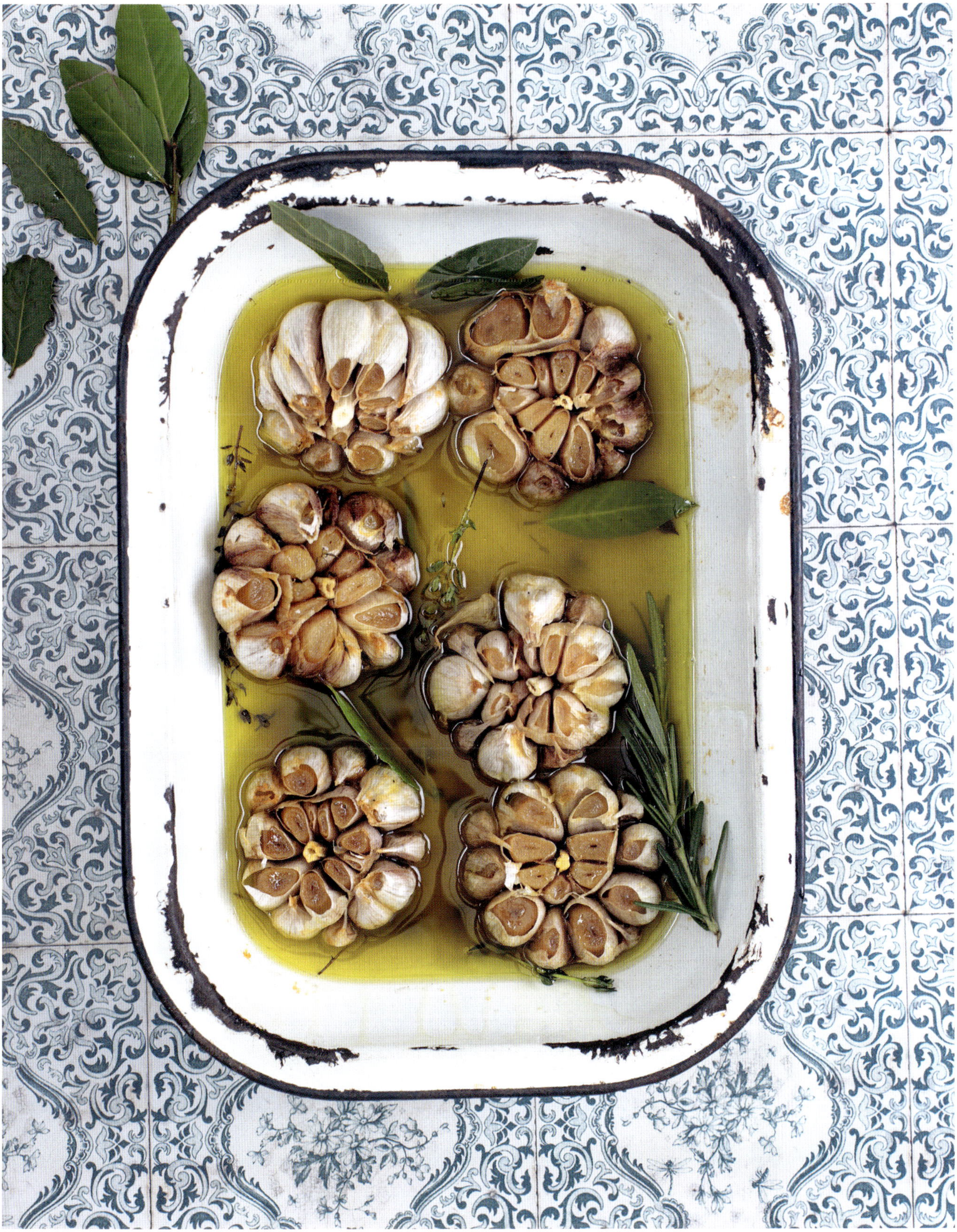

TOMATO CONFIT

These are delicious on bruschetta (toasted bread rubbed with garlic) or with low-carb noodles or pasta. I also use them to make Tomato Cook-in Sauce (page 44).

6 large, ripe tomatoes or 500 g cherry tomatoes
1½ tsp salt flakes
3 cloves garlic, peeled and roughly chopped
3 sprigs rosemary
6 sprigs thyme
1 Tbsp balsamic vinegar
2 cups (500 ml) olive oil

MAKES TWO 375 ML JARS

1. If you are using whole tomatoes, slice them in half. (Leave cherry tomatoes whole.) Place the tomatoes in a deep oven tray or roasting dish. Season with salt flakes and add the garlic cloves and herbs, tucking them among the tomatoes. Sprinkle with balsamic vinegar and pour over enough olive oil to submerge the tomatoes. (Don't worry if the tomatoes are not completely submerged; as they cook and soften, they will become covered.) Cover the tray with foil and place in a preheated oven at 160°C for 1½ hours, or until the tomatoes are completely soft. Remove from the oven and set aside until completely cool.
2. Pour the olive oil into glass jars with tight-fitting lids. Spoon the confit tomatoes into the jars, pressing down to ensure that everything is submerged in the oil. Seal and keep in the fridge for up to 2 weeks, making sure the tomatoes are always covered in oil.

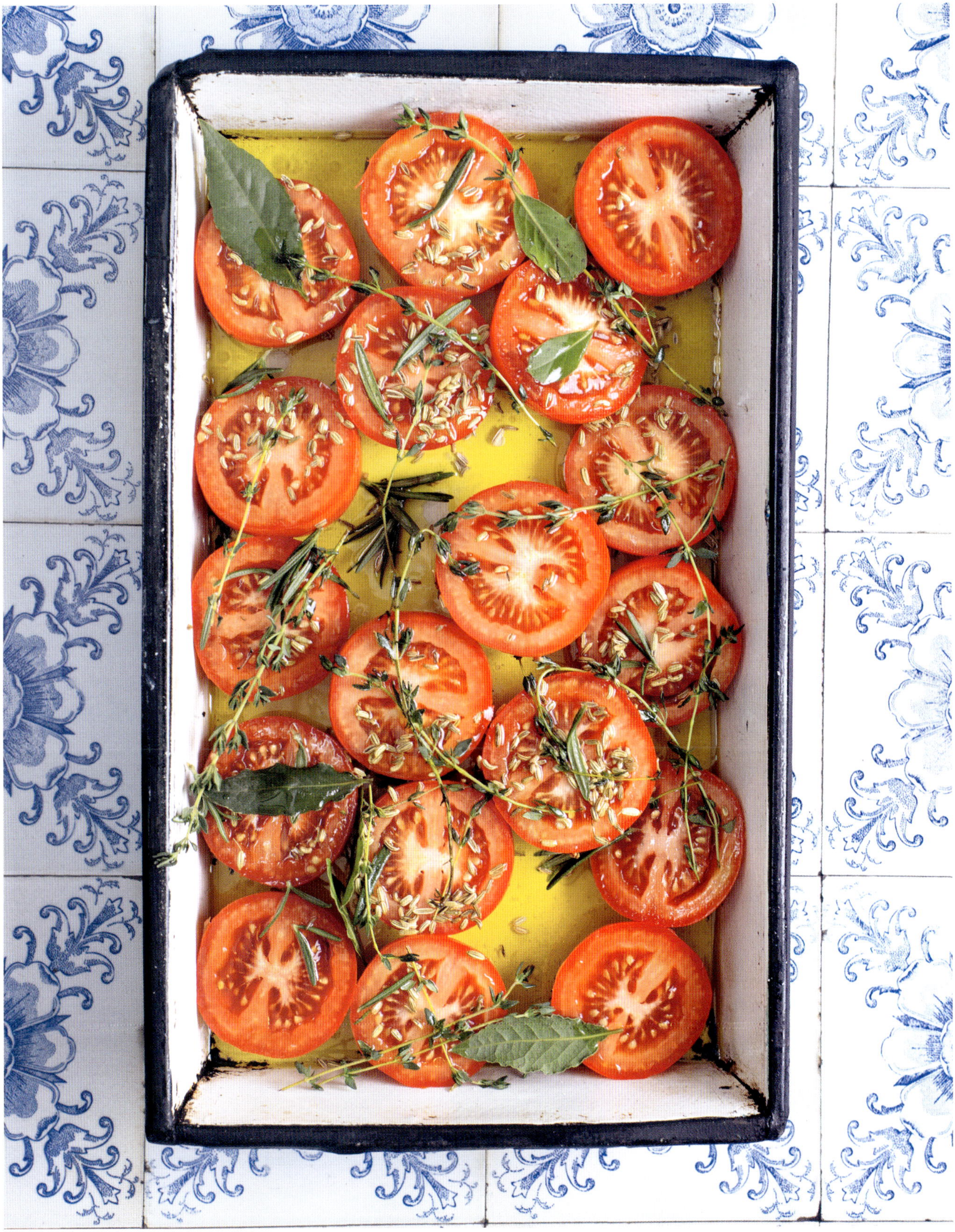

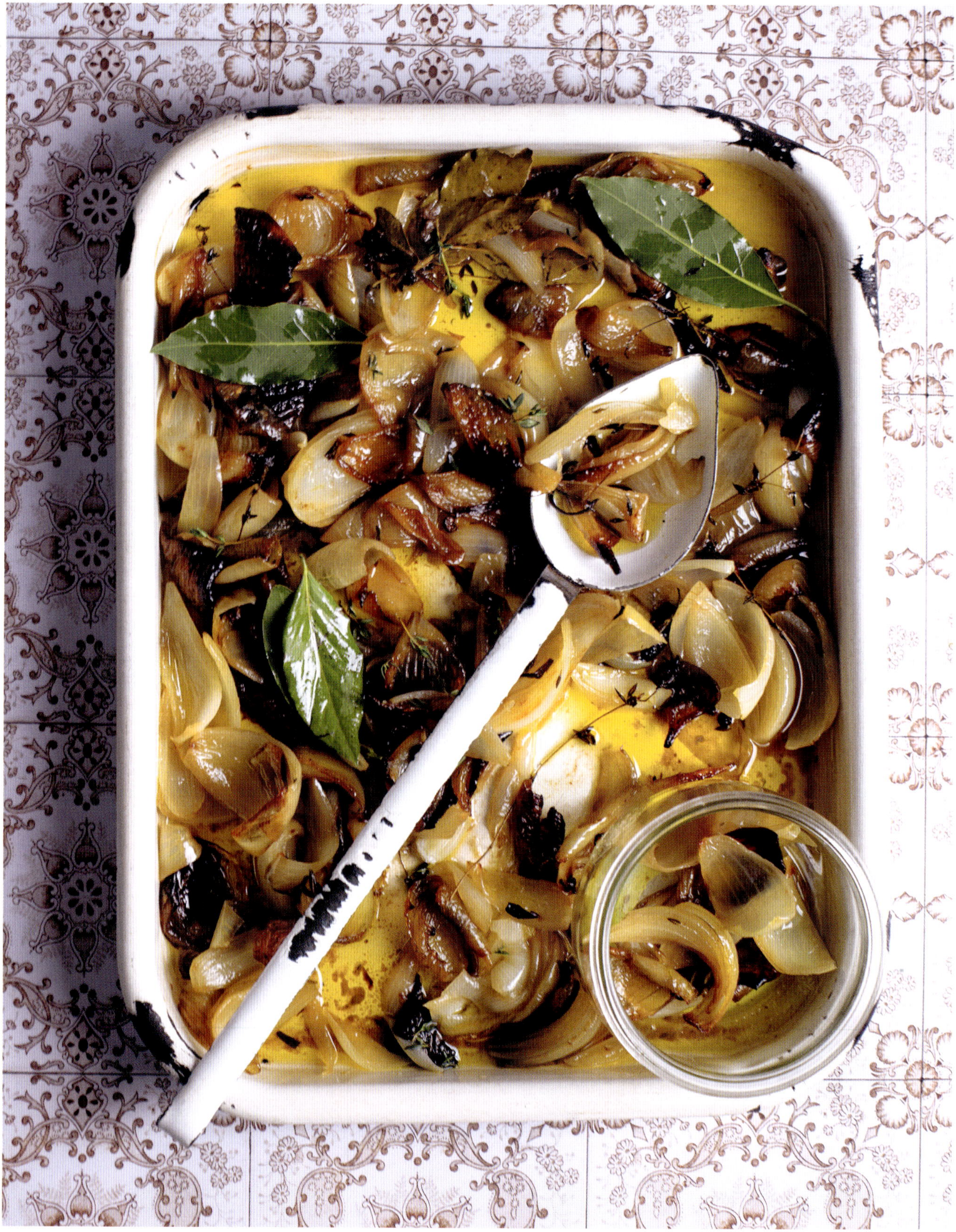

ONION CONFIT

6 medium onions, peeled and thickly sliced
½ tsp salt flakes
4 anchovy fillets, chopped
3 cloves garlic, peeled and coarsely chopped
3 sprigs rosemary
6 sprigs thyme
1 Tbsp balsamic vinegar
1½ cups (375 ml) olive oil
Fresh bay leaves, optional

MAKES ONE 375 ML JAR

1. Place the sliced onions in a small oven tray or roasting dish and season with salt flakes. Add the anchovies, garlic and herbs. Drizzle over the balsamic vinegar and enough olive oil to just cover the onions. Cover the tray with foil and place in a preheated oven at 160°C for 1 hour, or until the onions are completely soft. Remove the foil and continue cooking for about 30 minutes, to allow the onions to caramelize. (Keep an eye on them, as they burn easily.) Remove from the oven and set aside until completely cool.
2. Pour the olive oil into a glass jar with a tight-fitting lid. Spoon the onions into the jar, pressing down to ensure that everything is submerged. Add 1–2 bay leaves. Seal and keep in the fridge for up to 2 weeks, making sure the confit onion remains covered in oil.

COOK-IN SAUCES

Flavourful cook-in sauces are a great option for advance meal-prepping, as they can be made in big batches. All you have to do is add your choice of protein and, in no time, you'll have a delicious meal. The versatile tomato and mushroom sauces can also be served with pasta or noodles, turned into soups, or served with grilled or roasted chicken or meat.

TOMATO COOK-IN SAUCE

Using different types of tomatoes creates a delicious sauce. Instead of roasting fresh tomatoes, add 1 cup Tomato Confit (page 40) along with the passata.

6 large, ripe tomatoes

3 sprigs rosemary

3 sprigs thyme

2 dried bay leaves

4 Tbsp (¼ cup) olive oil, divided

2 tsp salt flakes or sea salt

3 cloves garlic, peeled and finely chopped

3 anchovy fillets, chopped

1 onion, peeled and finely chopped

4 small celery sticks, roughly chopped

2 carrots, peeled and roughly chopped

4 Tbsp tomato paste

1 can (400 g) Italian chopped tomatoes with juice

1 bottle (750 ml) Italian tomato passata

1 cup (250 ml) red wine or Chicken Broth (page 62)

1 bouquet garni

Salt to taste

½ cup fresh basil leaves, chopped

MAKES 4 JARS (± 500 ML EACH)

1. Place the tomatoes in a oven tray with the rosemary, thyme and bay leaves. Drizzle with 2 Tbsp olive oil and season with salt. Roast in a preheated oven at 200°C for 30 minutes or until the tomatoes start to blister.
2. While the tomatoes are roasting, heat 2 Tbsp olive oil in a large saucepan over medium heat. Add the garlic, anchovies, onion, celery and carrots and cook, stirring occasionally, for 5 minutes until soft. Stir in the tomato paste, then add the chopped tomatoes, tomato passata, red wine or chicken broth and the bouquet garni. Stir to combine, then reduce the heat to low and simmer for 30 minutes.
3. Remove the roasted tomatoes from the oven. (Discard the herbs, bouquet garni and any stems.) Add the tomatoes to the sauce, along with any pan juices, gently squashing them with a fork. Cook for 15 minutes, until the sauce is thick and flavourful. Season to taste and stir in the basil. Set aside until cool before spooning into jars or resealable bags. Cool completely and store in the fridge for up to 4 days, or in the freezer.

Notes

To make a bouquet garni, tie together 4 sprigs fresh thyme, 2 sprigs fresh rosemary and 2 fresh bay leaves.

Italian tomatoes contain less sugar and additives than regular canned tomatoes.

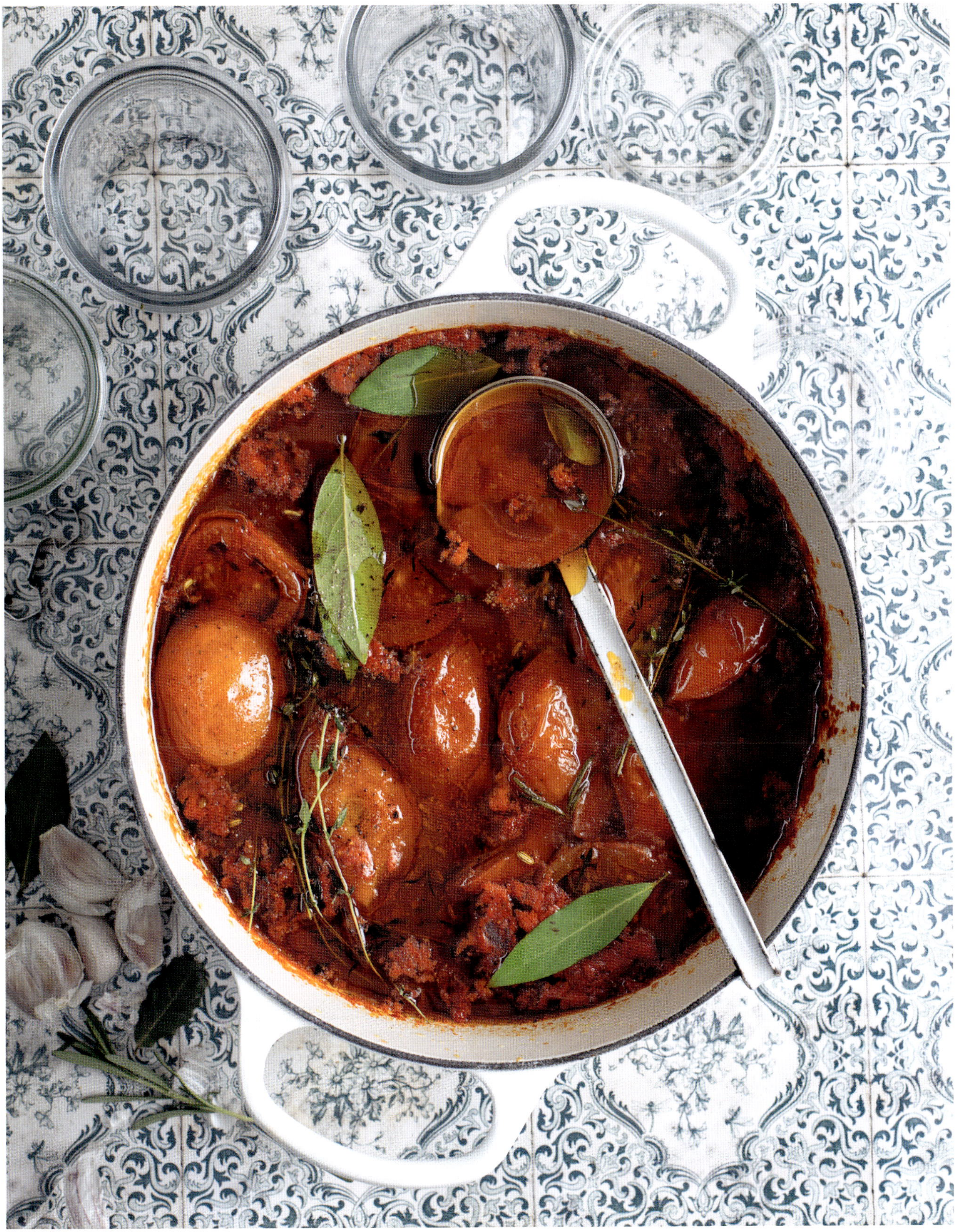

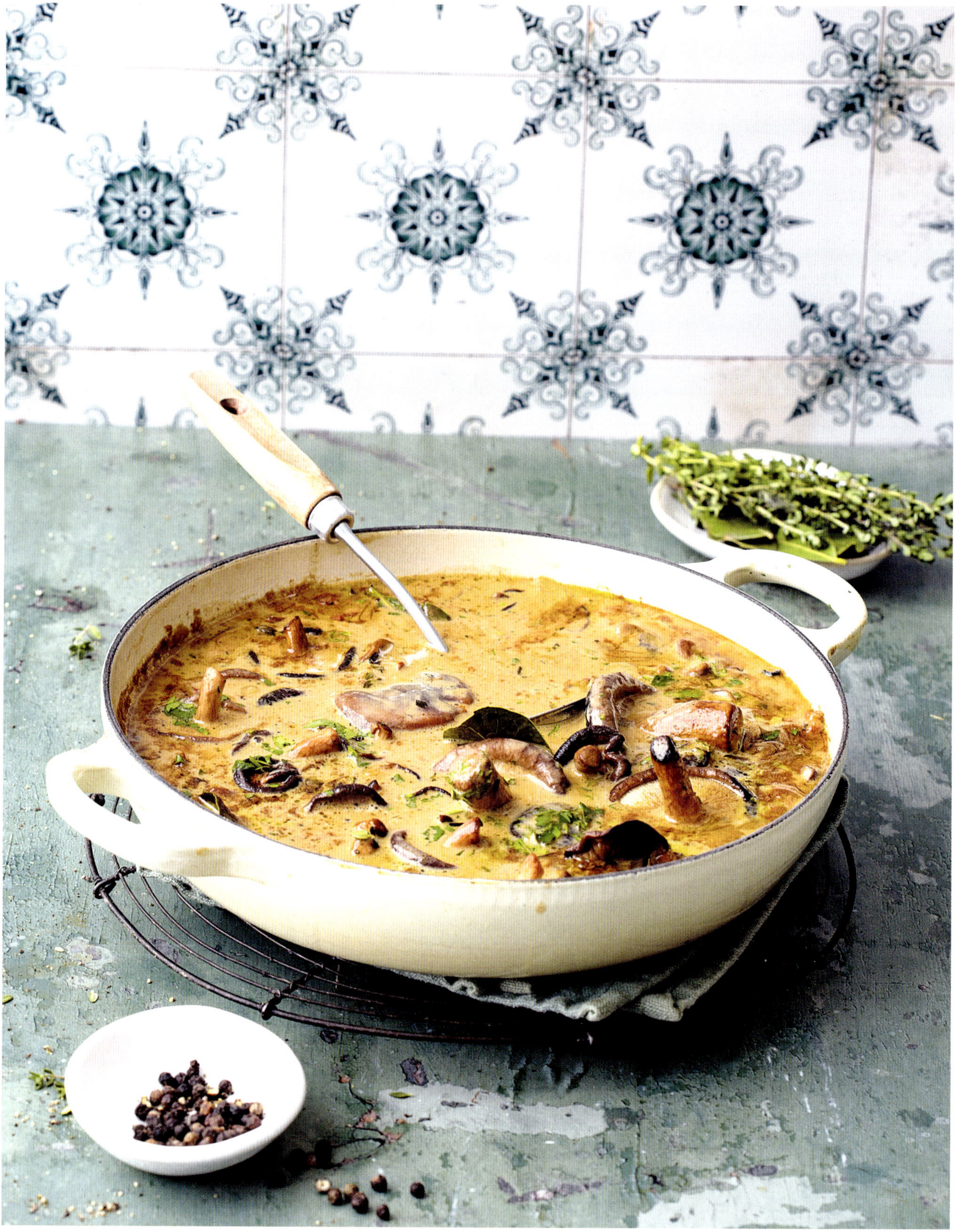

CREAMY MUSHROOM COOK-IN SAUCE

This sauce goes well with baby marrow noodles, pasta, and grilled steak or chicken. I roast chicken thighs in the oven and pour over the sauce for the last 15 minutes. To make a quick beef stroganoff, pan-fry strips of rib-eye steak, add the sauce to the pan and heat through. Serve with green beans and rocket salad.

2 Tbsp olive oil

1 Tbsp butter

1 onion, peeled and finely chopped

3 cloves garlic, peeled and finely chopped

150 g streaky bacon, chopped

250 g portabellini or brown mushrooms, roughly chopped

500 g shiitake mushrooms, roughly chopped (leave some whole)

4 sprigs thyme

½ cup (125 ml) white wine

1 Tbsp Dijon mustard

1 cup (250 ml) Chicken Broth (page 62) or chicken stock

2 cups (500 ml) cream

2 Tbsp soy sauce

Salt and black pepper to taste

MAKES 2 JARS (± 500 ML EACH)

1. Heat the oil and butter in a medium saucepan. Add the onion and garlic and cook for 3–4 minutes, until soft. Add the chopped bacon and cook for 7–8 minutes, until crisp.
2. Add the mushrooms and thyme in batches, cooking each batch for 4–5 minutes before adding the next. This gives the sauce more texture than if all the mushrooms were cooked for the same amount of time. When all the mushrooms have been added, deglaze the pan with white wine.
3. Add the mustard and stir through, then stir in the chicken broth and cream. Reduce the heat to medium-low and simmer, stirring occasionally, for 7–10 minutes, until the sauce starts to thicken and reduce slightly. Add the soy sauce and stir through. Adjust the seasoning by adding salt and pepper and/or more soy sauce to taste.
4. Remove from the heat and set aside until cool before spooning into jars or resealable bags. Keep in the fridge for up to 4 days or in the freezer for up to 1 month.

Note

If you don't consume alcohol, you can deglaze the pan with a little water and then add an extra ½ cup (125 ml) of chicken broth or cream.

CREAMY CURRY COOK-IN SAUCE

2 Tbsp olive oil

3 onions, peeled, halved and cut into thick half moons

6 cloves garlic, peeled and finely chopped

8 cm fresh ginger, peeled and finely chopped

2 red chillies, finely chopped

3 Tbsp Masala Mix (page 26) or curry powder of choice

2 cinnamon sticks

4 cardamom pods

2 fresh or dried bay leaves

2 fresh or dried curry leaves

1 can (400 g) whole peeled tomatoes

2 cans (400 g each) coconut milk

1 cup (250 ml) Chicken Broth (page 62) or chicken stock

MAKES 4 JARS (± 375 ML EACH)

1. Heat the oil in a medium saucepan and fry the onions, garlic and ginger until soft and translucent. Add the chillies, masala mix, spices, and bay and curry leaves, and cook for 3 minutes until fragrant.
2. Add the tomatoes, plus the juice from the can, crushing them lightly. Then add the coconut milk and chicken broth or stock. Stir through and simmer for 20 minutes, until the sauce has reduced and thickened.
3. Remove from the heat and leave until cool before spooning into jars or resealable bags. Place in the fridge for up to 4 days, or freeze.

Note

To prepare a quick fish curry, pan-fry individual portions of salmon or any firm-fleshed fish for 5–6 minutes, until just cooked through (don't overcook the fish, as it will continue to cook in the sauce). Add the sauce and simmer over medium heat for 7–8 minutes, stirring once or twice, until the sauce is warm and the fish flakes easily.

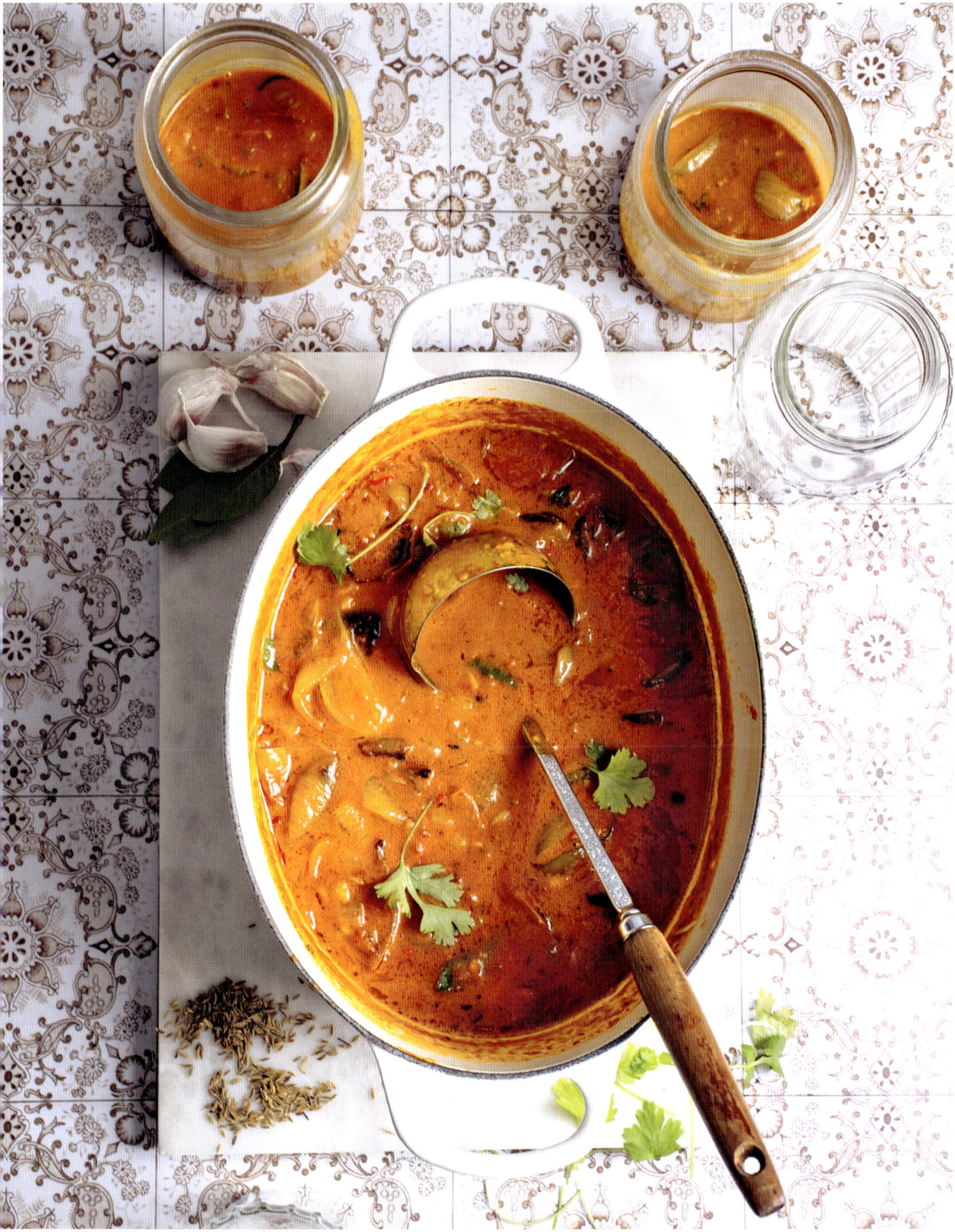

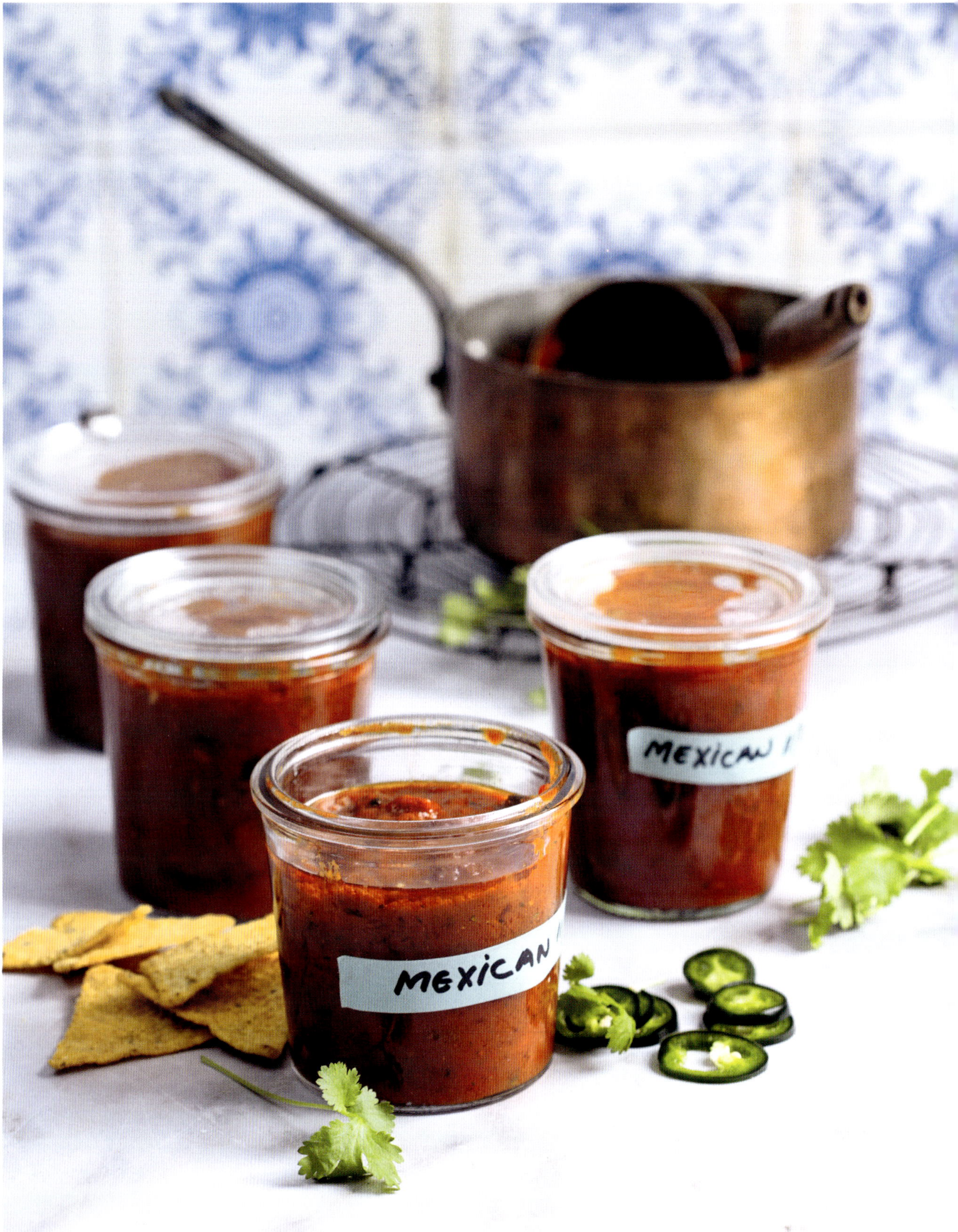
MEXICAN
MEXICAN

MEXICAN COOK-IN SAUCE

This chunky sauce is great with burgers, burritos or nachos.

2 red peppers, halved and seeds removed

2 Tbsp olive oil

2 green peppers, seeds removed and roughly chopped

2 onions, peeled and finely chopped

3 cloves garlic, peeled and finely chopped

1 jalapeño chilli, finely chopped

1 Tbsp cumin seeds

2 tsp coriander seeds

2 tsp fennel seeds

2 Tbsp smoked paprika

2 cans (400 g each) whole peeled tomatoes

1 can (± 260 g) chipotle chillies in adobo sauce

1 cup (250 ml) Chicken Broth (page 62) or chicken stock

Fresh coriander leaves, chopped

MAKES 4 JARS (± 250 ML EACH)

1. Place the red pepper halves on a baking sheet and roast in a preheated oven at 200°C for 15–20 minutes, until soft. Remove from the oven, set aside until cool, then roughly chop.
2. Heat the olive oil in a saucepan over medium heat. Add the green peppers, roasted red pepper, onions, garlic, jalapeño chilli and spices and cook for about 7 minutes, until soft and fragrant.
3. Add the tomatoes, plus the juice from the cans, crushing them lightly. Roughly chop the chipotle chillies in adobo sauce, before adding to the saucepan, along with the chicken broth or stock. Reduce the heat and simmer for 15–20 minutes, until the sauce reduces and thickens slightly. Add the fresh coriander leaves and stir for about 2 minutes, until wilted.
4. Remove from the heat and set aside until cool before spooning into jars or resealable bags. Keep in the fridge for up to 4 days or freeze for up to 1 month.

FERMENTED SALADS AND SALSA

Fermented salads add zingy flavours to food. Natural fermentation allows good bacteria, called probiotics, to populate salads or salsas. Probiotics are beneficial for your gut health and immune system. During fermentation, the natural sugars in vegetables are broken down by micro-organisms. When vegetables are submerged in a salty brine, good bacteria begin to turn the sugars into natural yeast and bacterial growth when oxygen is not present. Finely slicing the vegetables speeds up the fermentation process, while adding salt prevents bad bacteria from developing before the good bacteria can do their work.

FERMENTED BURGER PICKLE

- 1½ cups (375 ml) still mineral water
- 1 Tbsp Himalayan pink salt or coarse sea salt
- 8 radishes, thinly sliced
- 6 snacking cucumbers, thinly sliced
- 2 red onions, peeled and thinly sliced
- 2 cloves garlic, peeled and finely chopped
- 1 jalapeño chilli, thinly sliced
- 1 Tbsp Himalayan pink salt
- 2 tsp fennel seeds
- 2 tsp coriander seeds
- 1 tsp mustard seeds
- 1 tsp whole black peppercorns
- 4–5 sprigs fresh dill

MAKES ONE 375 ML JAR

1. To make a brine, pour the water into a jug or bowl. Add the salt, stir until dissolved, and set aside.
2. Combine the remaining ingredients in a bowl, then ladle into a jar. Fill the jar with the brine, pressing down on the vegetables to ensure they are completely submerged (you may not need all the brine). Place a piece of cabbage leaf or green pepper on top of the vegetables to keep them covered. (If they are not submerged, mould will form on the surface.) Tightly seal the jar and leave it at room temperature, away from direct sunlight.
3. Small bubbles should appear after the first day. This means fermentation has started. Leave the jar at room temperature for another 24 hours before storing in the fridge. (Stand the jar on a plate because some liquid will overflow during fermentation; this is normal and will not stop the process.) The pickle will be ready after 3 days, but can be kept in a sealed jar in the fridge for up to 2 months. Once opened, consume within 1 week.

Note

You can use any jar with a tight-fitting lid. Jars do not have to be sterilized, just washed with soapy water and rinsed well. Keep pickled vegetables in the fridge door (where it is slightly warmer) for up to 2 months, ensuring they remain submerged in brine. They should have a fresh, sour smell; if they develop an 'off smell', discard them.

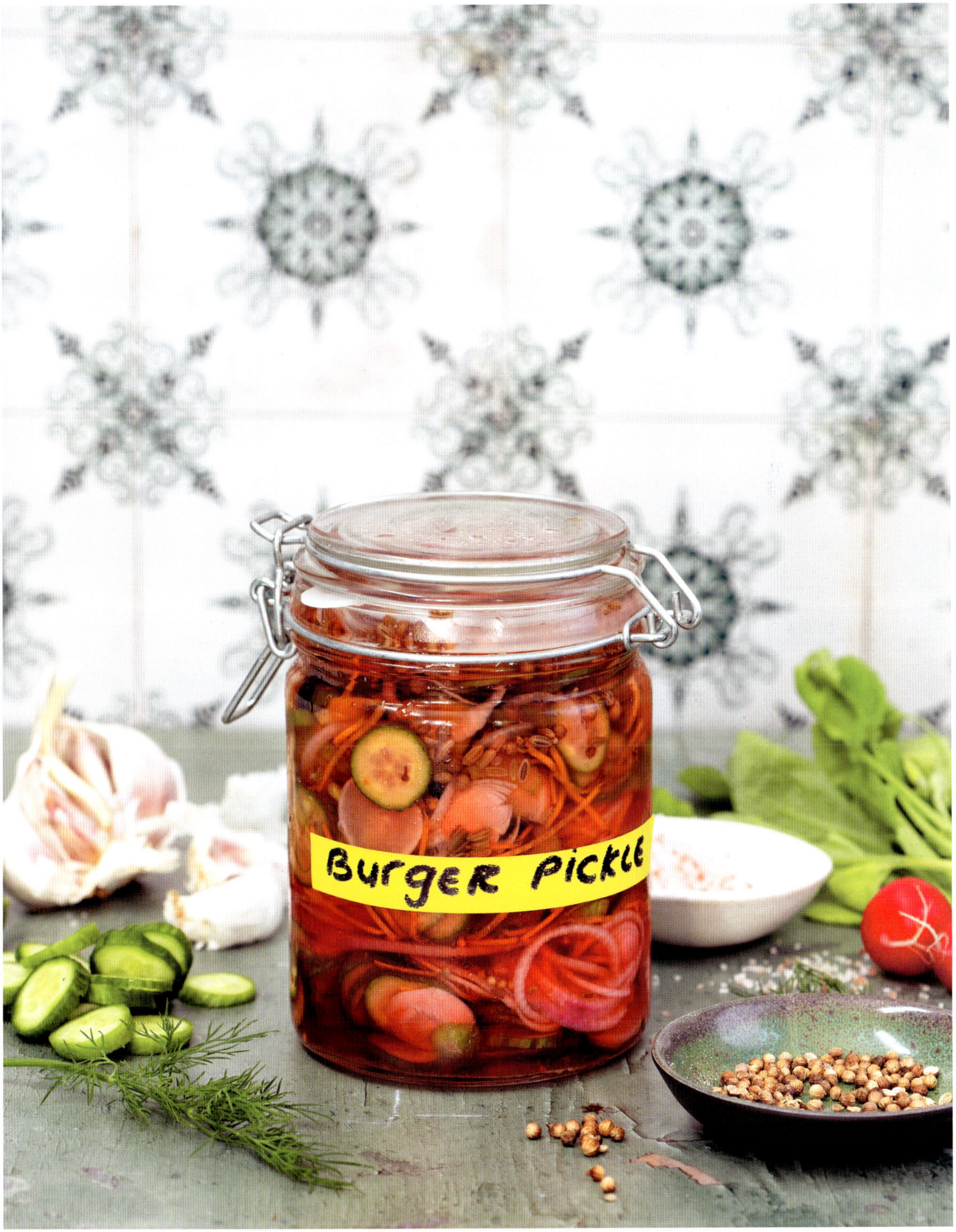
Burger Pickle

MEXICAN SALSA

FERMENTED MEXICAN SALSA

I like to use a combination of cherry (cocktail) tomatoes and salad tomatoes, because they contribute different textures and flavours.

1 kg tomatoes, roughly chopped

2 red onions, peeled and finely chopped

1 green pepper, seeds removed and finely chopped

2 jalapeño chillies, finely chopped

4 cloves garlic, peeled and finely chopped

1½–2 cups finely shredded red cabbage

1 cup roughly chopped coriander leaves

2 tsp fennel seeds

2 tsp coriander seeds

1 tsp mustard seeds

1 tsp whole black peppercorns

1 Tbsp salt, or to taste

MAKES ONE 500 ML JAR

1. Combine all the ingredients in a bowl, squashing them gently with your hand. Taste, and add more salt if necessary (you should be able to taste the salt). Salt kills the bad bacteria, so it is important to add enough to taste it.

2. Spoon the salsa into a jar, pressing down hard to release some liquid. The vegetables should be submerged, so add any liquid left in the mixing bowl to the jar. (If you don't have enough liquid to cover the veggies, add some water.) Place a piece of cabbage leaf or green pepper on top of the vegetables to keep them covered. (If they are not submerged all the time, mould will form on the surface.) Tightly seal the jar and leave it at room temperature, away from direct sunlight.

3. Small bubbles should start to appear in the jar after the first day. This means fermentation has started. Leave the jar at room temperature for another 24 hours before storing in the fridge. (Stand the jar on a plate because some liquid will overflow during fermentation; this is normal, and will not stop the process.) The salsa will be ready to eat after 3 days, but can be kept in a sealed jar in the fridge for up to 2 months. Once opened, consume within 1 week.

BROTHS & SOUPS

BROTH-BASED SOUPS freeze really well and are *highly nutritious* and *comforting*. My family EATS *bone broth* on a daily basis as part of our HEALTH REGIME. I usually *drink* a mug of BROTH in the late morning for my *breakfast*, the boys have it for *lunch* and, if I RUN OUT OF TIME in the evenings, it *becomes dinner*. MY RECIPES for *bone broth*, *chicken broth* and *fish broth* have wonderful GUT-HEALING PROPERTIES, because the *extraction* of *natural collagen* and *gelatine* is ENHANCED by the addition of APPLE CIDER VINEGAR. I call them 'BROTHS' because they contain both MEAT and VEGETABLES and are not strained, making them more *cloudy* than *clear stocks*. SLOW COOKING a broth for an extended period of time allows *more gelatine* and *minerals* to be EXTRACTED from the BONES. Some people cook bone broths for up to 48 HOURS, but even 3 HOURS of cooking will *result* in a FLAVOURFUL BROTH that is *packed* with HEALTH BENEFITS.

MEATY BONE BROTH

4 meaty beef shin bones (± 200–250 g each)
4 beef marrow bones (± 400 g in total)
Salt to taste
3 Tbsp olive oil, divided
1 onion, peeled and roughly chopped
3 short celery sticks, roughly chopped
2 carrots, roughly chopped
2 Tbsp tomato purée
3 fresh or dried bay leaves
4 sprigs thyme
2 Tbsp apple cider vinegar
1 can (400 g) whole peeled tomatoes
4 litres water

MAKES 3–4 LITRES

1. Season the meaty shin bones and marrow bones with salt. Heat 2 Tbsp olive oil in a large saucepan (± 5-litre capacity) over high heat and brown the bones on all sides. (Don't omit this step, as the depth of flavour comes from the bones.) Remove the bones and set aside.
2. Reduce the heat to medium-high and add the remaining olive oil. Add the onion, celery, carrots and tomato purée and brown for 5–6 minutes.
3. Return the bones to the saucepan and add the herbs (tied together with string), apple cider vinegar, whole peeled tomatoes and the water. Bring to a boil then lower the heat to low and simmer for 6–8 hours. Check the broth after 3 hours and add more warm water (up to 500 ml extra) if it reduces too much.
4. Remove the broth from the heat and leave to cool slightly, then lift out the shin bones and use two forks to pull the meat from the bones. Return the meat to the saucepan and discard the bones. Lift the marrow bones out of the broth, press out any remaining marrow and return it to the saucepan, discarding the bones. Season to taste with salt and set aside to cool before decanting into containers for the fridge or freezer. (If you intend to use the broth for making sauces or as a base for soups, strain out the meat and vegetables, retaining just the clear liquid.)

Notes

To make a thicker soup, add 3 cups coarsely grated baby marrows and 1 cup thickly sliced cabbage after about 3 hours of cooking.

The broth can be frozen for up to 3 months in a rigid container or resealable freezer bag.

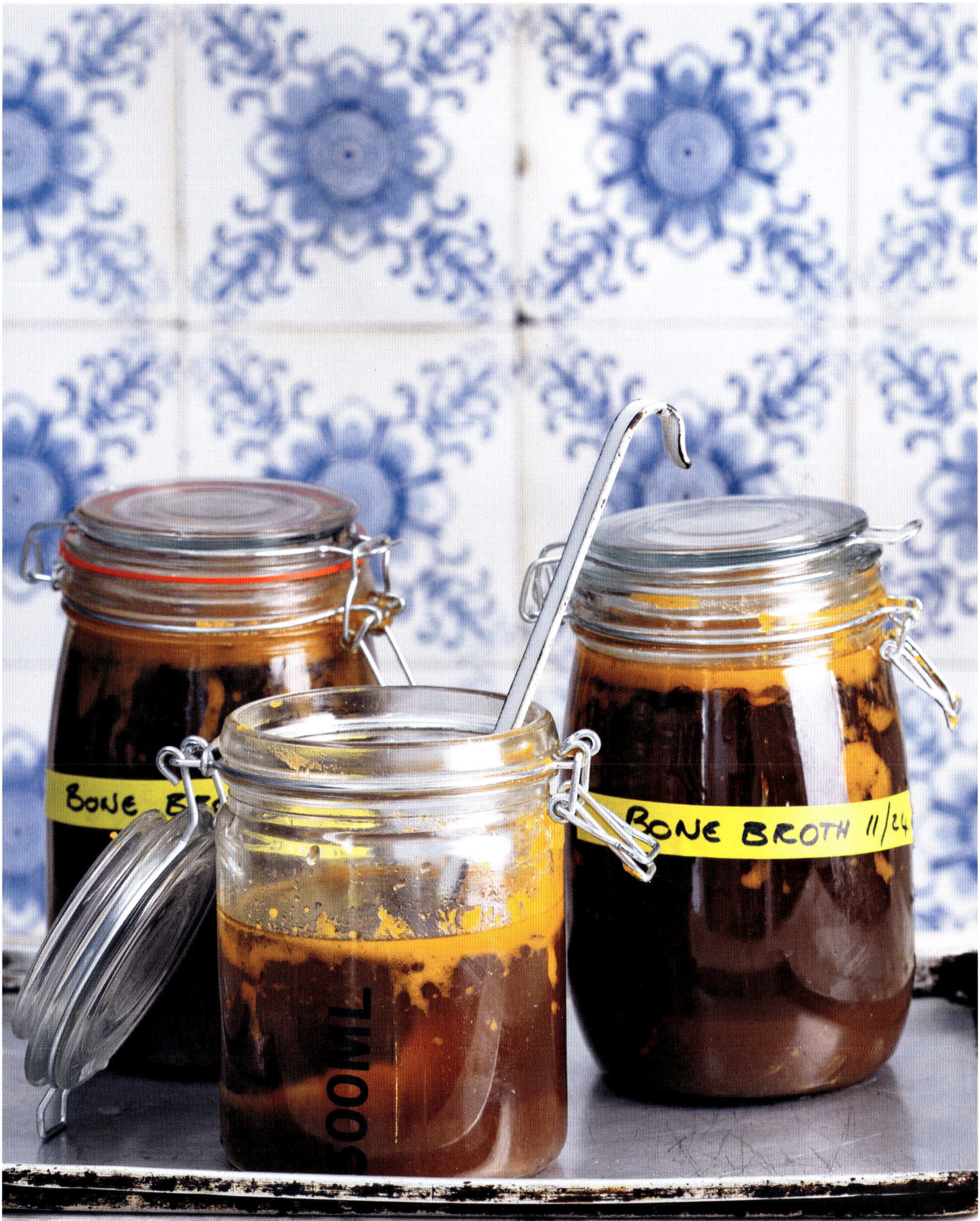
BONE BROTH 11/24
500ML

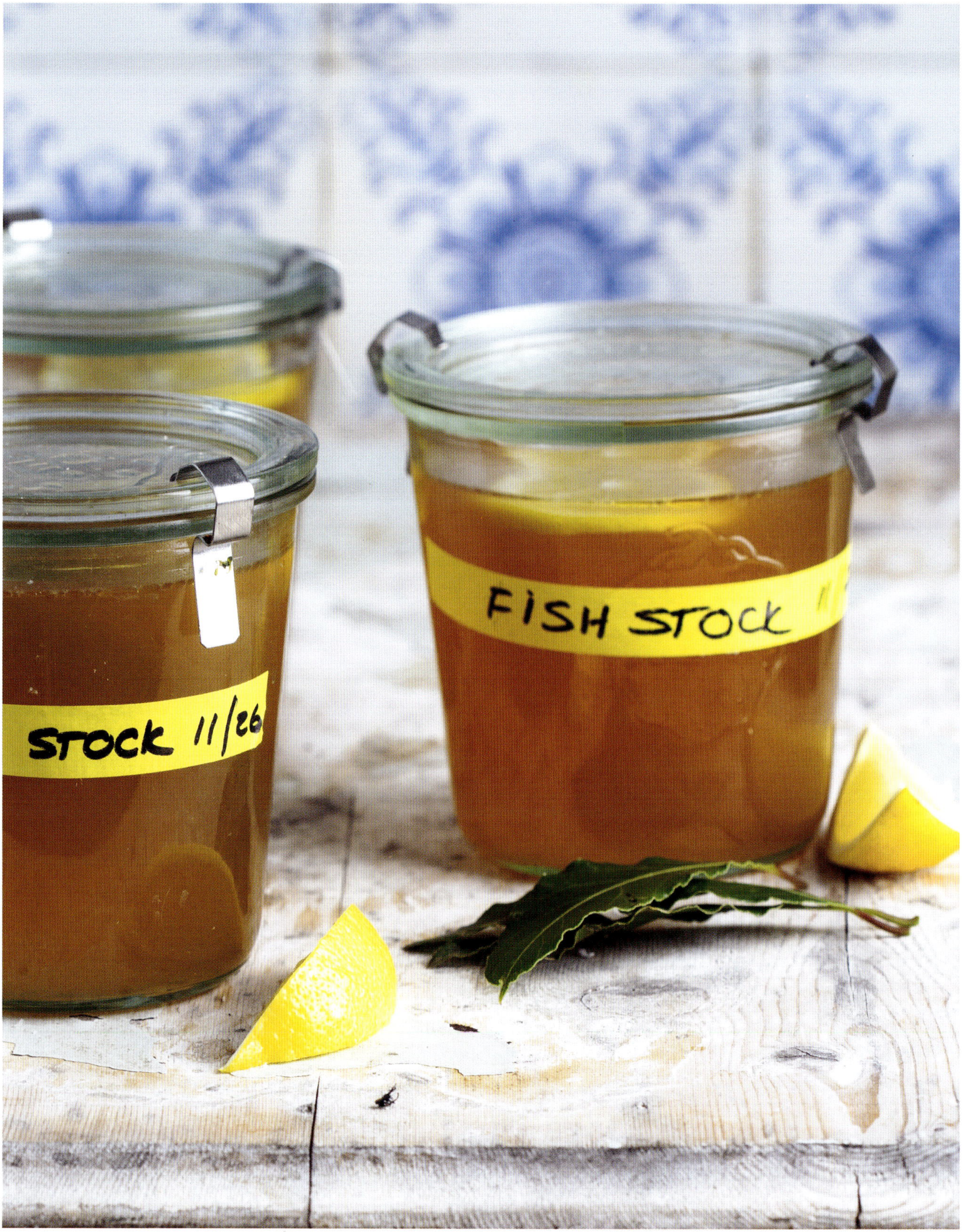
FISH STOCK
STOCK 11/26

FISH STOCK

2 Tbsp olive oil
1 leek, white parts only, roughly chopped
1 long stick celery, roughly chopped
1 small fennel bulb, roughly chopped
1 onion, peeled and roughly chopped
1.5 kg fish backbones
200 g prawn shells (optional)
6 sprigs parsley
2 fresh or dried bay leaves
3–4 slices lemon
6 white peppercorns
1 cup (250 ml) white wine
2 litres water

MAKES ± 2 LITRES

1. Heat the oil in a large saucepan over medium heat. Add the leek, celery, fennel and onion, and cook for about 5 minutes, until fragrant.
2. Add the fish bones and prawn shells (if using), herbs, lemon slices and peppercorns, and cook for about 5 minutes, to bring out the flavours.
3. Add the white wine and cook for 5 minutes, until reduced by about a third.
4. Add the water and bring to a boil, then reduce the heat to low and simmer for 25 minutes. Remove the saucepan from the heat and set aside until completely cool. Remove the fish bones and prawn shells (if using) before decanting the broth into containers. Label clearly with the recipe name and date and store in the fridge for up to 2 days or in the freezer for up to 2 months.

Notes

Fish bones are not always easy to come by, so when we cook whole fish over the braai, I retain the backbone and freeze it. You can ask your supermarket fish counter for bones. Most types of fish are suitable, although oily fish can result in a cloudy broth. If you prefer a clear liquid, stick to white fish. Make sure the bones are clean, with no visible blood. It is important to keep the backbone intact. This not only makes it easier to remove later, but reduces the risk of small bones falling off and remaining in the broth, which can be very dangerous. Fish stock does not need to cook as long as meat-based stock.

If you do not consume alcohol, replace the wine with the same quantity of water.

When I cook whole prawns, I peel them and freeze the shells; they add so much flavour to fish stock.

CHICKEN BROTH

4 chicken legs
4 chicken thighs
Salt to taste
2 Tbsp olive oil
1 onion, peeled and roughly chopped
3 short celery sticks, roughly chopped
2 carrots, peeled and roughly chopped
3 fresh or dried bay leaves
4 sprigs thyme
2 Tbsp apple cider vinegar
3 litres water

MAKES 3 LITRES

1. Season the chicken with salt. Heat the oil in a large saucepan over high heat and brown the chicken on all sides. (Don't omit this step, as the flavour comes from the browning.)
2. Add the onion, celery and carrots and cook, stirring, for 3–4 minutes, until tender. Add the herbs, apple cider vinegar and enough water to completely cover the chicken (you may not need the full 3 litres).
3. Bring to a boil, then reduce the heat to low and simmer for 2 hours. (Check halfway and top up with a little more water if necessary.)
4. Remove the saucepan from the heat and set aside until cool enough to lift the chicken from the broth. Pull the meat off the bones (use two forks to do this), taking care to remove any small bones. Discard the bones and skin and return the meat to the broth. Season to taste with salt. Leave until completely cool before decanting into containers. Label with the recipe name and date and store in the fridge for up to 4 days or in the freezer for up to 2 months.

Note

To make a clear stock, don't return the chicken meat to the broth. Instead, shred it (taking care to remove any small bones) and freeze for use in pies or lasagne. Strain the liquid before decanting into containers.

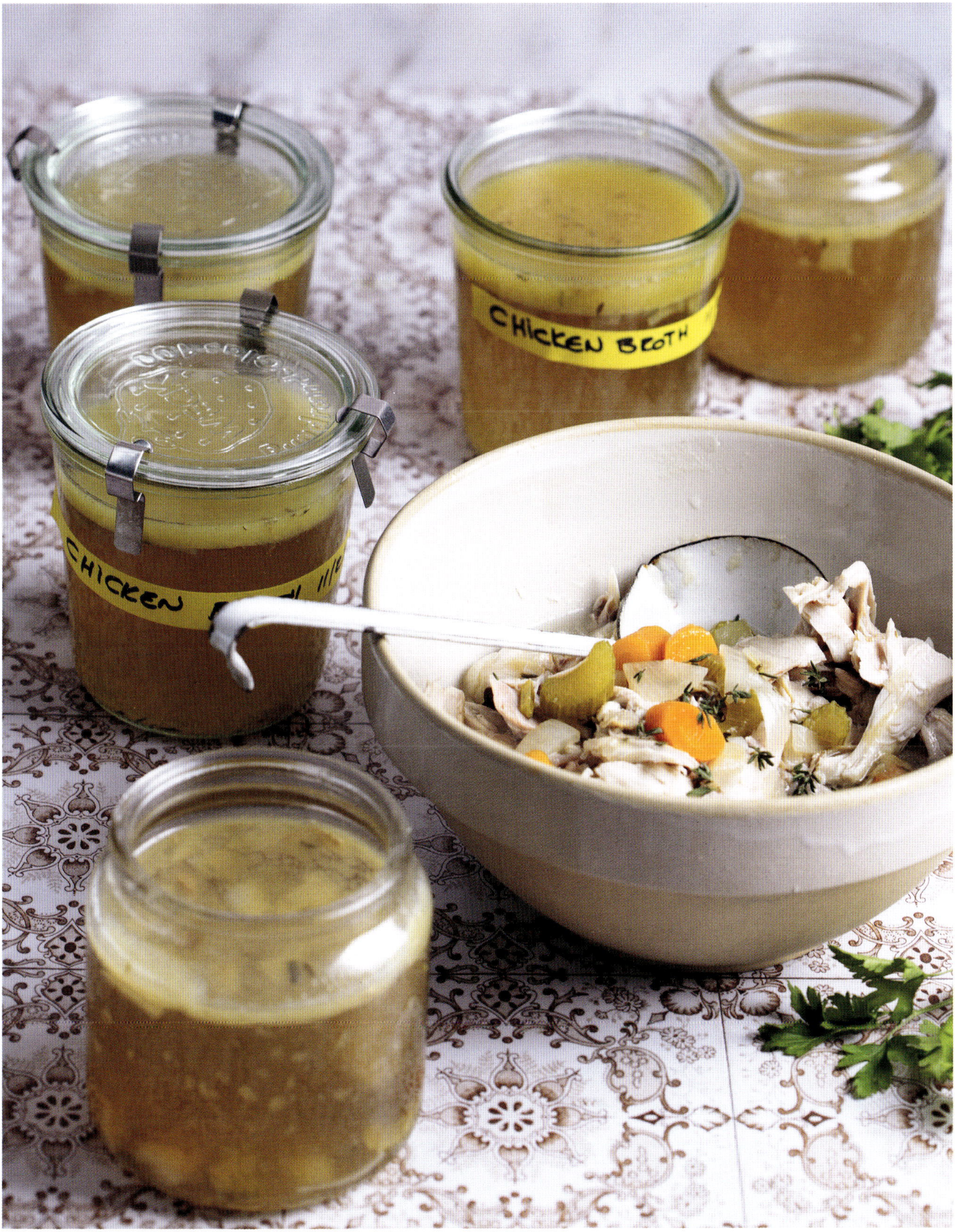
CHICKEN BROTH
CHICKEN

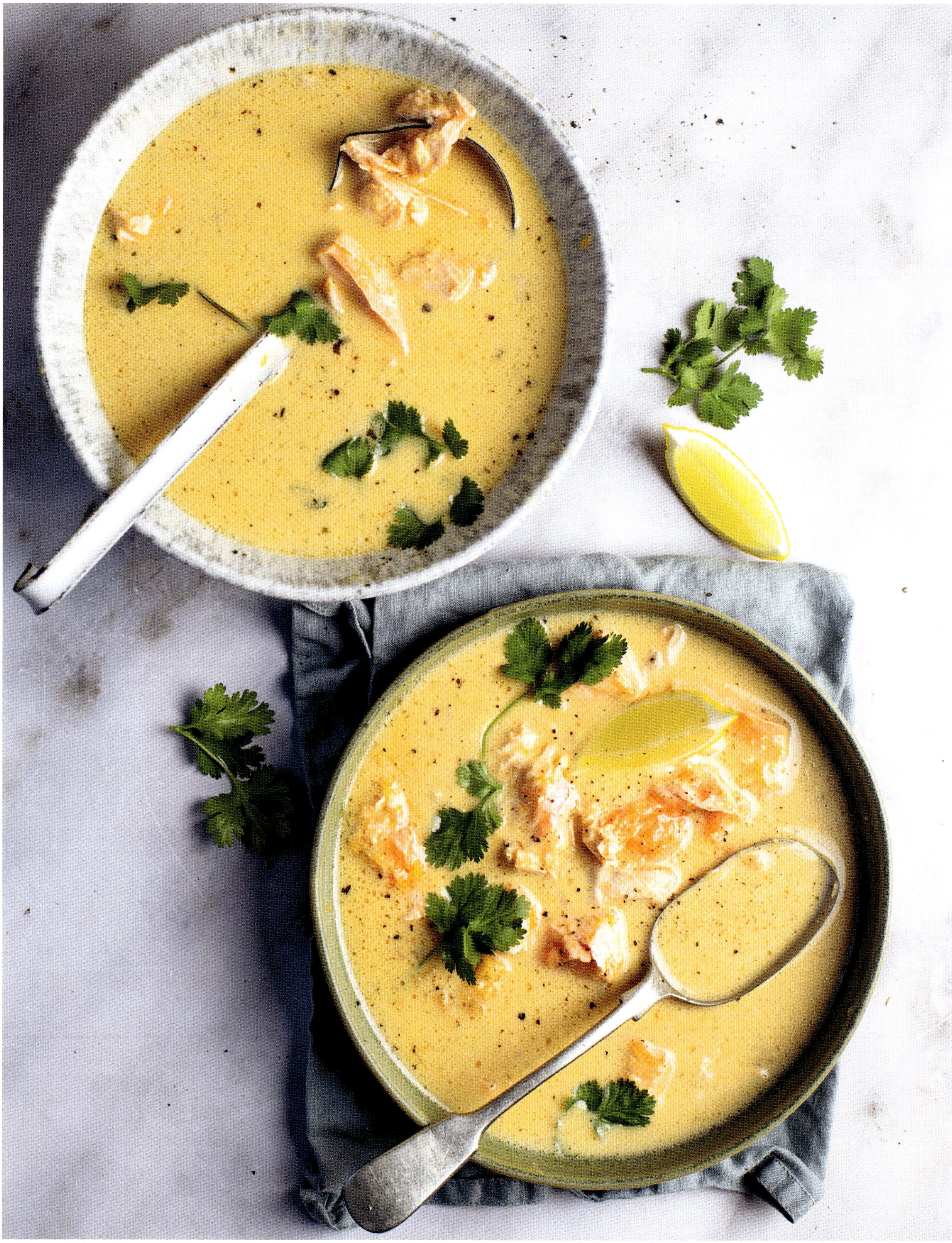

CREAMY PUMPKIN AND SALMON SOUP

Oily fish is a great source of essential fats, including omega-3 fatty acids, which boost brain health and help protect us against heart disease, strokes and inflammation. Because our bodies can't make essential fats, we have to obtain them from our food. Salmon is the best source of omega-3 fatty acids, but rainbow trout, sardines, tuna and mackerel are other options. Although you can use pumpkin or butternut for the soup, I prefer pumpkin because of its lower carb count.

2 Tbsp butter

1 onion, peeled and finely chopped

2 cloves garlic, peeled and finely chopped

500 g pumpkin or butternut, peeled and cut into chunks

Salt to taste

2 fresh or dried bay leaves

4 sprigs thyme

1 litre (4 cups) Fish Stock (page 61)

1 can (400 g) coconut milk

1 can (400 g) salmon

2 Tbsp olive oil

1 fillet (± 100 g) fresh salmon or rainbow trout, skin on,

Juice of 1 lemon

MAKES ± 1.5 LITRES

1. Heat the butter in a large saucepan over medium heat. Add the onion and garlic and cook for 5–6 minutes, until soft and translucent.
2. Season the pumpkin lightly with salt and add to the saucepan, along with the bay leaves and thyme. Cook, stirring, for about 10 minutes, until the pumpkin starts to caramelize.
3. Add the fish stock, coconut milk and canned salmon and cook for 20 minutes, or until the pumpkin is tender. Remove the bay leaves and thyme and purée the soup using a stick blender. Lower the heat to a simmer.
4. Heat the olive oil in a pan over medium heat. Season the fresh salmon or trout with salt and place in the pan, skin-side down. Cook for 2 minutes, then turn and cook for 1 minute on the other side, until just cooked through. Flake the fish, discarding the skin, and add to the soup, along with the lemon juice. Remove from the heat and serve immediately, or leave to cool completely before decanting into containers. Label clearly with the recipe name and date and store in the fridge for up to 2 days or in the freezer for up to 2 months.

RICH OXTAIL RAMEN

You can use beef shin, but oxtail imparts a really delicious flavour and is a rich source of both gelatine and collagen. The cabbage ribbons serve as a low-carb, gluten-free alternative to traditional wheat-based noodles in this ramen-type dish.

1 large oxtail (±1.5 kg), sliced into 6 pieces
Salt to taste
3 Tbsp olive oil
1 onion, peeled and roughly chopped
2 cloves garlic, peeled and finely chopped
6 cm fresh ginger, peeled and finely chopped
2 celery sticks, roughly chopped
1 large carrot, peeled and roughly chopped
6 sprigs thyme
3 fresh or dried bay leaves
2 cinnamon sticks
5 allspice berries
2 star anise
1 cup (250 ml) red wine
2–3 Tbsp tomato paste
3 Tbsp soy sauce
3 litres chilled Meaty Bone Broth (page 58) or beef stock
3 cups thickly sliced green cabbage
200 g shiitake mushrooms
200 g Tenderstem® broccoli, halved lengthways
Coriander leaves, for serving
Sesame seeds, for serving

MAKES ±3 LITRES

1. Season the oxtail all over with salt. Heat the oil in a large heavy-based saucepan over medium heat and brown the pieces on all sides. Remove with a slotted spoon and set aside.
2. Add the onion, garlic, ginger, celery and carrot and cook until soft and caramelized. Tie the thyme and bay leaves together with string and add to the saucepan, along with all the spices, and cook for 4 minutes, until fragrant.
3. Add the wine and simmer for 2 minutes, scraping any residue off the bottom of the saucepan.
4. Return the oxtail to the saucepan. Add the tomato paste, soy sauce and beef broth or stock. Lower the heat and simmer, with the lid off, stirring occasionally, for 3–4 hours, or until the meat falls off the bone. Check after about 2 hours, and add a little warm water if it has reduced too much. Remove the oxtail from the soup, cool slightly, then use two forks to pull any remaining meat from the bones. Return the meat to the saucepan and discard the bones.
5. Add the cabbage ribbons, mushrooms, and broccoli and simmer for 15 minutes, until cooked. Add the coriander leaves and sesame seeds and stir through. Serve immediately or leave to cool completely before decanting into containers for freezing.

Note

If you do not consume alcohol, replace the wine with an additional cup (250 ml) of beef broth or water.

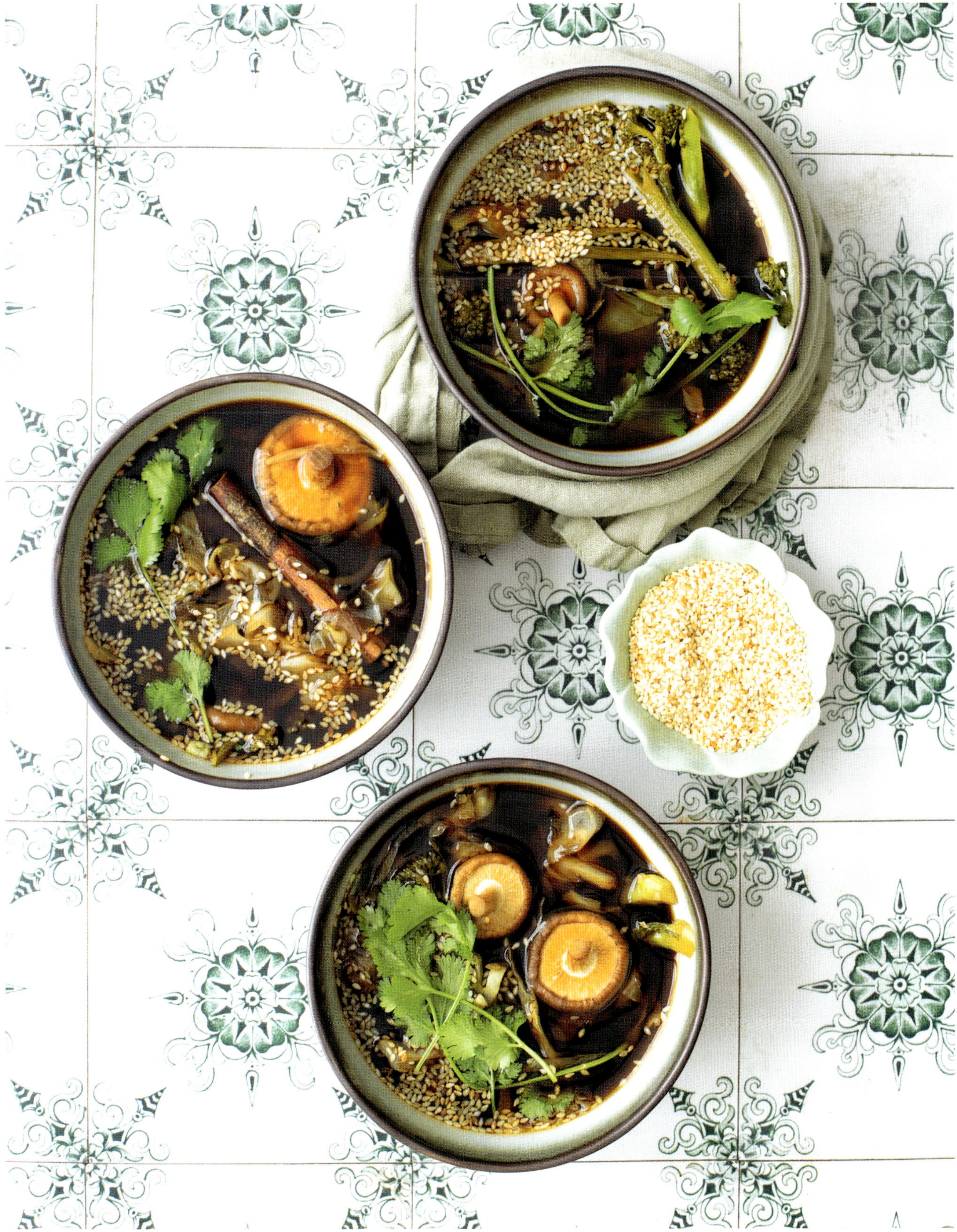

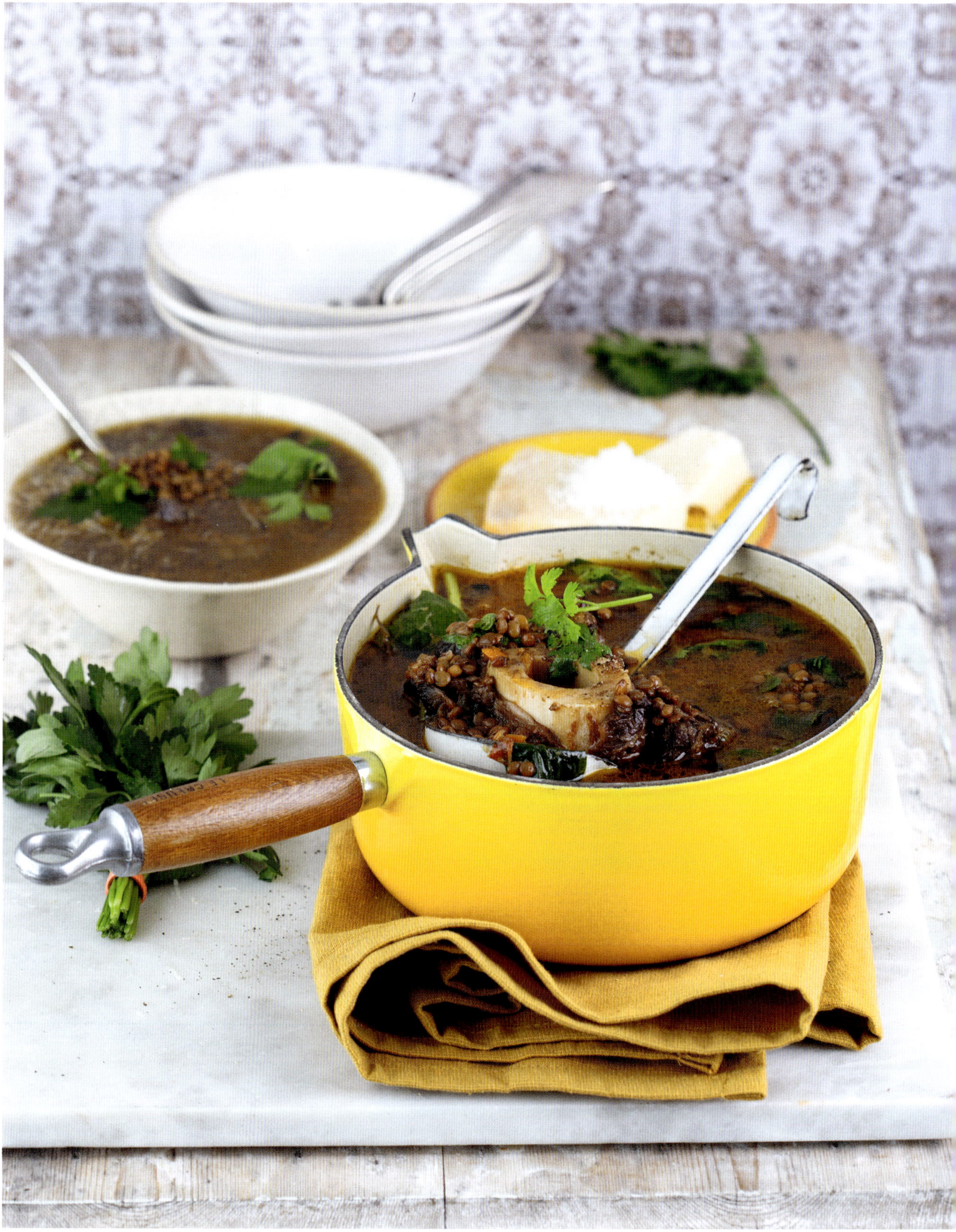

BEEF AND LENTIL SOUP

6 beef shins (± 200 g each)
Salt to taste
2 Tbsp olive oil
2 large onions, peeled and roughly chopped
4 cloves garlic, peeled and finely chopped
2 carrots, peeled and chopped
2 sticks celery, chopped
2 litres Meaty Bone Broth (page 58)
2 litres water
2 cups (400 g) brown lentils
4 fresh or dried bay leaves
4 sprigs thyme
2 sprigs rosemary
2 Tbsp soy sauce
Ground black pepper to taste
Fresh parsley, for serving

MAKES ± 3 LITRES

1. Season the beef shins with salt. Heat the oil in a large saucepan over medium-high heat and brown the meat in batches, then remove and set aside. Add the onions, garlic, carrots and celery and cook, stirring, for 5 minutes, until lightly browned.
2. Return the meat to the saucepan along with the broth, water, lentils and herbs. Bring to a boil, then reduce the heat to low and simmer, with the lid off, for 2–3 hours, stirring occasionally. Garnish with fresh parsley. Season to taste with soy sauce and ground black pepper, and additional salt if required.
3. Serve the soup with the shin bones. If not serving immediately or within 24 hours, leave the soup to cool completely, then remove the bones before decanting into containers for freezing.

GREEN CURRY BROTH

I use homemade Thai Green Curry Paste and Chicken Broth for this flavourful soup. Good-quality store-bought curry pastes are a handy standby, but they are likely to contain sugar, so rather make your own if you follow a low-carb or sugar-free diet. If you prefer a meatier soup, add 10–12 cooked meatballs before serving (see Note).

1 Tbsp olive oil

1 Tbsp sesame oil

1 onion, peeled and finely chopped

3 Tbsp Thai Green Curry Paste (page 20)

2 litres Chicken Broth (page 62)

1 can (400 g) coconut milk

3 cups baby spinach leaves

3 cups thinly sliced green cabbage leaves

6 spring onions, thinly sliced

2 Tbsp soy sauce

1 Tbsp fish sauce

Salt to taste

Coriander leaves, for serving

2 Tbsp sesame seeds, lightly toasted

MAKES ± 2 LITRES

1. Heat the olive oil and sesame oil in a large saucepan over medium heat. Add the onion and green curry paste and cook for 2–3 minutes, until soft and fragrant. Add the chicken broth and coconut milk, reduce the heat to low and simmer for 10 minutes.
2. Add the baby spinach leaves, cabbage ribbons, spring onions, soy sauce and fish sauce. Simmer for 15 minutes, then check the seasoning, adding a pinch of salt if needed. (If adding meatballs, add them after about 10 minutes.)
3. If serving immediately, top with the coriander leaves and toasted sesame seeds. Otherwise, leave to cool completely before decanting into containers for freezing.

Notes

Add precooked meatballs (page 134) near the end of the cooking time and simmer for 6–7 minutes, until heated through. When serving, make sure each portion contains a few meatballs.

Trim the cabbage to remove any hard white stalks, as these won't soften during the cooking process.

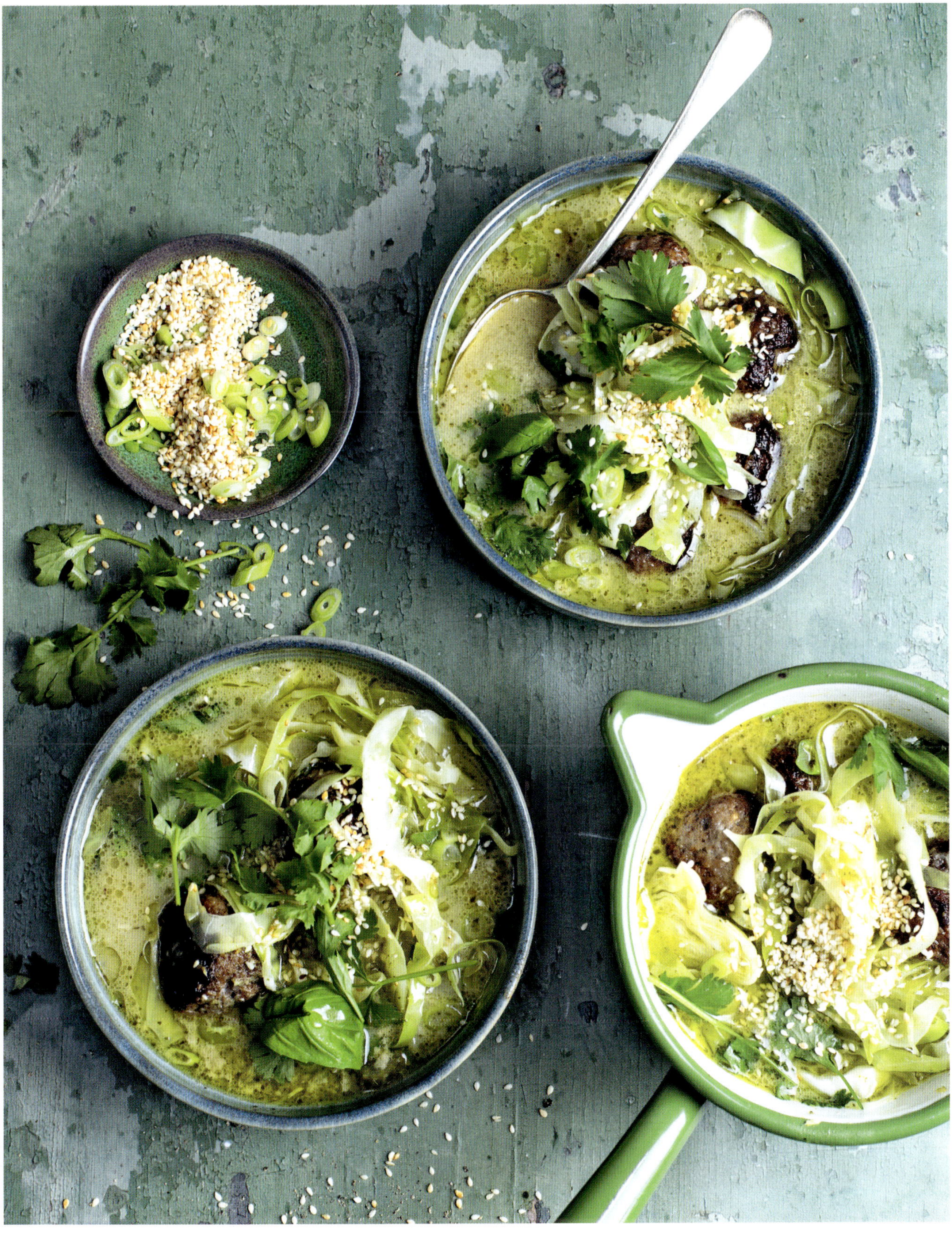

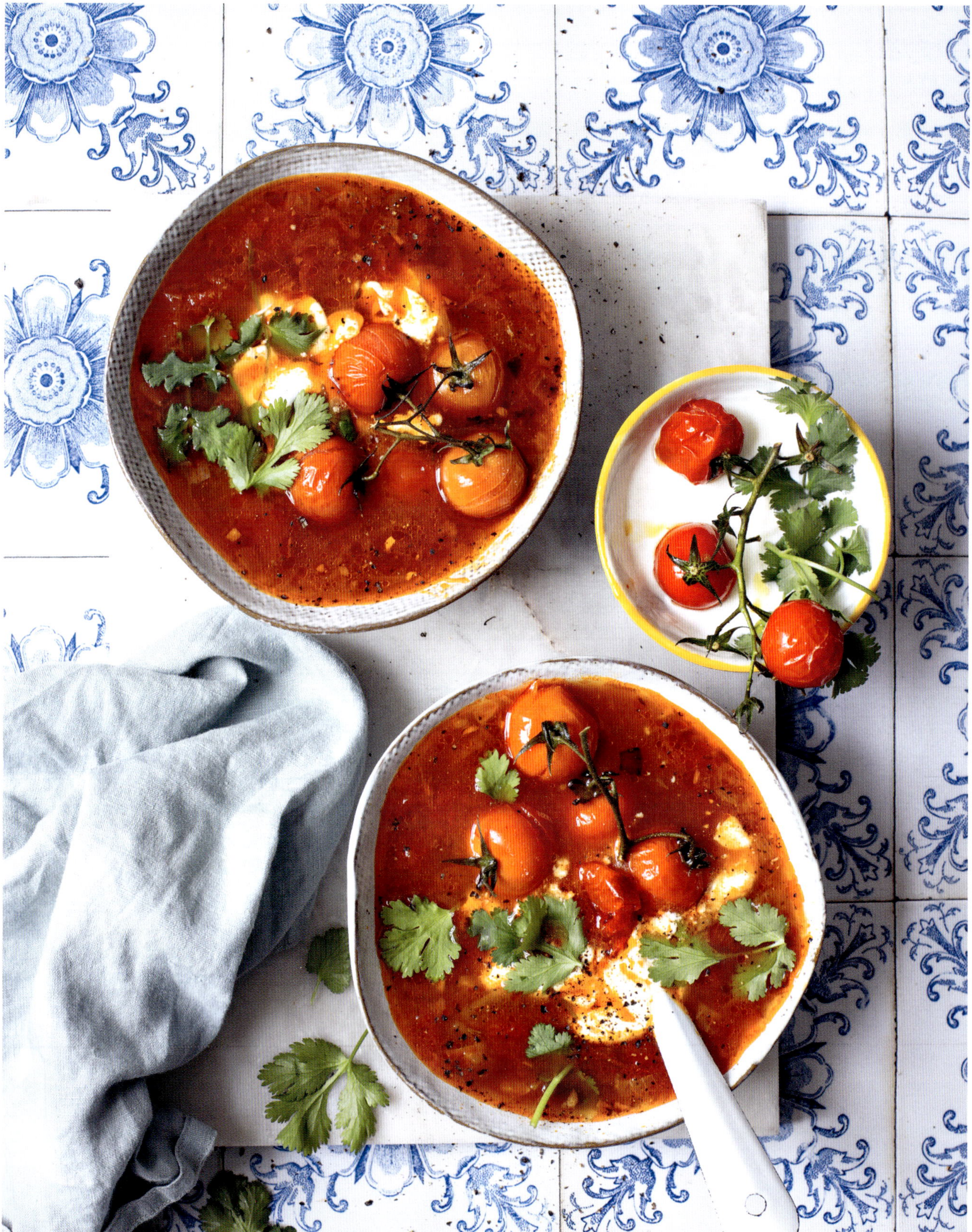

MOROCCAN TOMATO SOUP

This is a good basic tomato soup with lots of flavour, but you can pimp it by adding a swirl of yoghurt and some roasted cherry tomatoes, or crispy bacon and basil pesto.

- 2 tsp cumin seeds
- 2 tsp coriander seeds
- 2 Tbsp olive oil
- 1 large onion, peeled and finely chopped
- 5 cloves garlic, peeled and finely chopped
- 3 Tbsp Moroccan Paste (page 24)
- 1 cinnamon stick
- 1 can (400 g) whole peeled tomatoes
- 1 can (400 g) chickpeas, drained and rinsed
- 1.5 litres Chicken Broth (page 62)
- Grated zest and juice of 1 lemon
- 1 cup coriander leaves or basil leaves
- Salt to taste
- ½ cup full-cream plain yoghurt, optional, for serving
- Roasted cherry tomatoes, optional, for serving

MAKES ± 1.5 LITRES

1. Lightly toast the cumin seeds and coriander seeds in a dry pan, then crush in a mortar and pestle.
2. Heat the oil in a large saucepan over medium heat. Add the onion and garlic and cook for 5–6 minutes, until soft and translucent. Add the Moroccan paste, crushed cumin and coriander seeds and cinnamon stick and cook for a further 2 minutes, until fragrant.
3. Add the canned tomatoes, crushing them lightly, along any juice from the can. Add the chickpeas and Chicken Broth and stir through. Reduce the heat to low and simmer for 20 minutes.
4. Add the lemon zest and juice, and the coriander or basil leaves (reserving some for garnish). Season to taste with salt, then remove from the heat. If serving immediately, add some yoghurt, roasted cherry tomatoes (*see Note*) and coriander or basil leaves to each bowl. Omit the toppings if you intend to freeze the soup.

Notes

If preferred, replace homemade Moroccan paste with 3 Tbsp store-bought harissa paste.

Instead of homemade Chicken Broth, you can use the same quantity of good quality chicken stock.

To roast cherry tomatoes, place 200 g cherry tomatoes (on the vine if possible) in a small roasting dish. Season with salt and drizzle with 2 Tbsp olive oil. Roast in a preheated oven at 200°C for 15 minutes, until the skins start to blister.

BOUILLABAISSE WITH ROUILLE

This rich, wholesome seafood broth, traditionally served with rouille (a delicious sauce made from red peppers), is probably best reserved for special occasions and celebrations.

3 Tbsp olive oil

2 medium onions, peeled and chopped

2 leeks, washed and chopped

4 cloves garlic, peeled and finely chopped

1 can (400 g) whole peeled tomatoes, crushed

2.5 litres Fish Stock (page 61)

2 fresh or dried bay leaves

2 sprigs thyme

2 long strips orange peel

2 tsp saffron filaments, dissolved in 4 tsp water

Salt and black pepper to taste

450 g large prawns, uncooked and peeled

450 g hake or firm white fish, cut into chunks (5–7 cm)

450 g black mussels

Fresh parsley, for serving

MAKES ± 3.5 LITRES

ROUILLE

1 red pepper

1 mild red chilli or ¼ tsp ground cayenne pepper

1 Tbsp fresh lemon juice

1 clove garlic, peeled

2 Tbsp ground almonds or almond flour

4 sprigs parsley, leaves only

Salt to taste

4 Tbsp extra-virgin olive oil

MAKES ± ½ CUP

1. Heat the oil in a large saucepan over medium heat. Add the onions and leeks and cook until soft and translucent. Add the garlic and cook for a minute, until fragrant, then add the crushed tomatoes, fish broth, herbs, orange peel and saffron. Season to taste with salt. Bring to a boil, then reduce the heat to low and simmer for 15 minutes.
2. Add the prawns and cook for 1–2 minutes, until they turn pink. Add the fish and black mussels, cover and simmer for 5–6 minutes, until the fish is cooked through and the mussels are open. Taste, and season with salt and/or black pepper if needed. Top each serving with fresh parsley and a spoon of rouille.

ROUILLE

1. Halve the red pepper and the chilli, if using, and remove the seeds. Place on a baking sheet and roast in a preheated oven at 200°C for 20 minutes, until the skin is blistered and soft. Remove from the oven and leave to cool completely before pulling the skin from the pepper (discard the skin).
2. Place the roasted pepper and chilli, together with the rest of the ingredients, except the olive oil, in the bowl of a food processor and pulse until smooth. Slowly add the olive oil, while pulsing, to form a paste. Spoon into a bowl and set aside until required. You can make this ahead and store in the fridge, covered with a thin layer of olive oil, for up to 4 days.

Note

Clean fresh mussels thoroughly beforehand to remove any beards and/or traces of sand or grit. Frozen black mussels have usually been cleaned, but check them anyway.

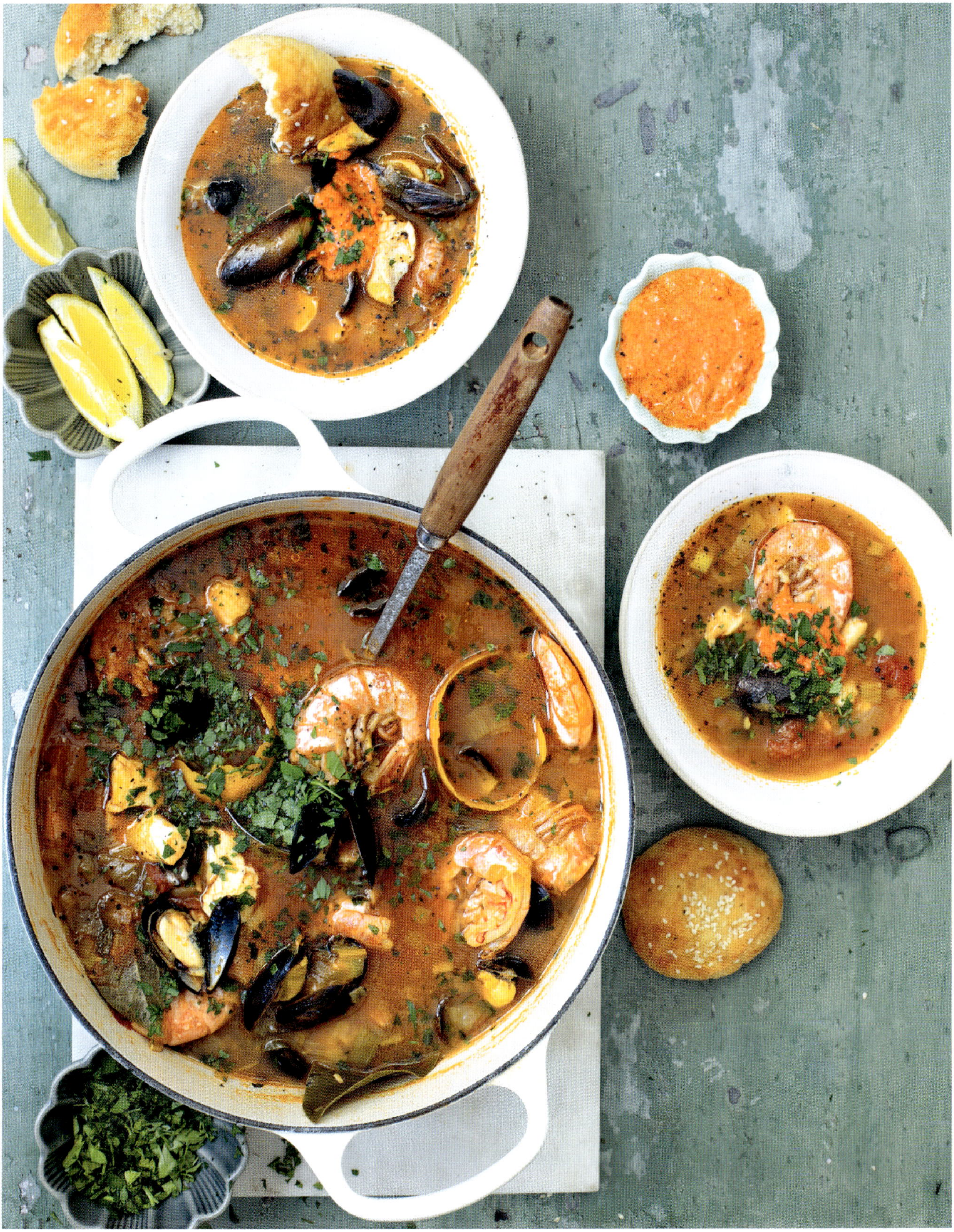

SLOW COOKING

SLOW COOKING really *intensifies* the *flavour* of stews. The *secret* lies in BROWNING the MEAT well from the start (a *combination* of *butter* and *olive oil* gives the best results). I PREFER not to *cook* with flour, because of the carbs and gluten, so I don't dust meat with flour before browning, as many recipes suggest.

I also use LESS LIQUID than normal, which creates a thick, *rich stew*. I prefer COOKING in the *oven*, but some dishes can be slow-cooked on the *stovetop*, which is handy if you want to PREPARE *two* or *three* meals at once. It is IMPORTANT to check *oven-cooked stews* every 30 MINUTES or so, because they can *dry out* very quickly. Both slow-cooked STEWS and roasted PULLED MEAT freeze very well. Most of the recipes in this chapter are 'BIG-BATCH', which means you can have ONE MEAL that day, and FREEZE ENOUGH for another meal. They will also *keep* in the *fridge* for up to *3 days*, so you can *make meals ahead*, perhaps over a weekend, for serving later in the week.

PORK NECK COOKED IN MILK

Pork braised in milk, or maiale al latte, is a traditional Italian dish. The milk solids separate during cooking, which does not make it the prettiest dish, but it is delicious. Because there isn't a lot of sauce, this is not ideal for freezing, but it keeps very well for about 4 days in the fridge, making it a good dish to enjoy later in the week.

1 deboned pork neck (± 2.2 kg)
Salt to taste
3 Tbsp olive oil
2 Tbsp butter
3 leeks, thinly sliced
2 heads of garlic, cut in half crossways
1 fennel bulb, roughly chopped
16–20 sage leaves
3 fresh or dried bay leaves
1–2 strips lemon peel
1.5 litres full-cream milk

MAKES 8 PORTIONS

1. Slice the pork neck into 8 steaks (± 5–7 cm thick), season with salt and set aside for 30–60 minutes. Heat the oil in an ovenproof casserole over high heat. Brown the meat on all sides, then remove and set aside.
2. Reduce the heat to low. Add the leeks, garlic and fennel and cook for 3–4 minutes, stirring, until soft and flavourful. Add the sage leaves, bay leaves and lemon peel.
3. Return the meat to the casserole, along with the milk. Cover with a lid and place in a preheated oven at 160°C for 2 hours, turning the meat every 30 minutes. After 2 hours, remove the lid and continue cooking for another 20 minutes, or until the meat is tender and the milk has reduced. Serve with Creamy Vegetable Mash (page 150) or Soft Polenta (page 150).

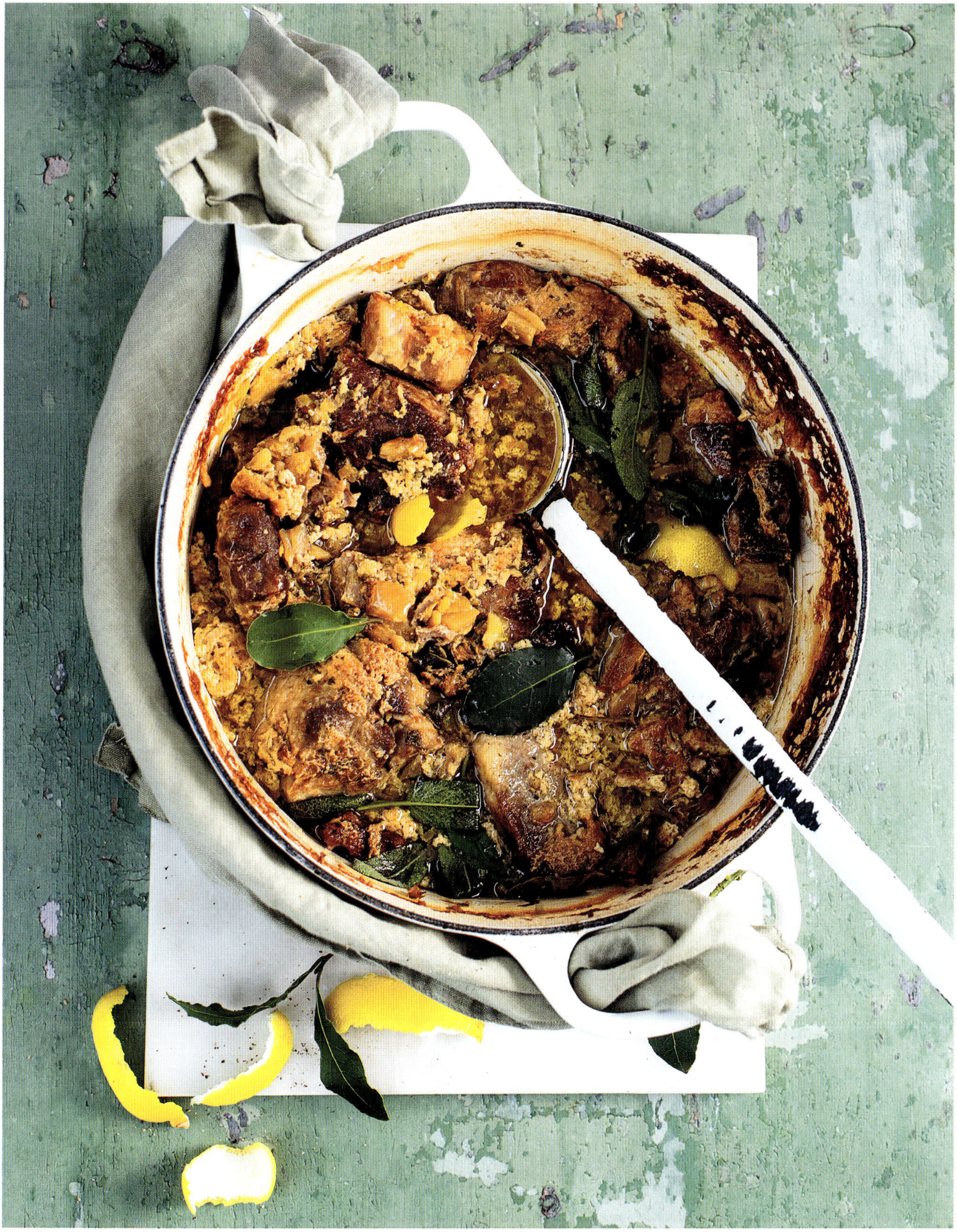

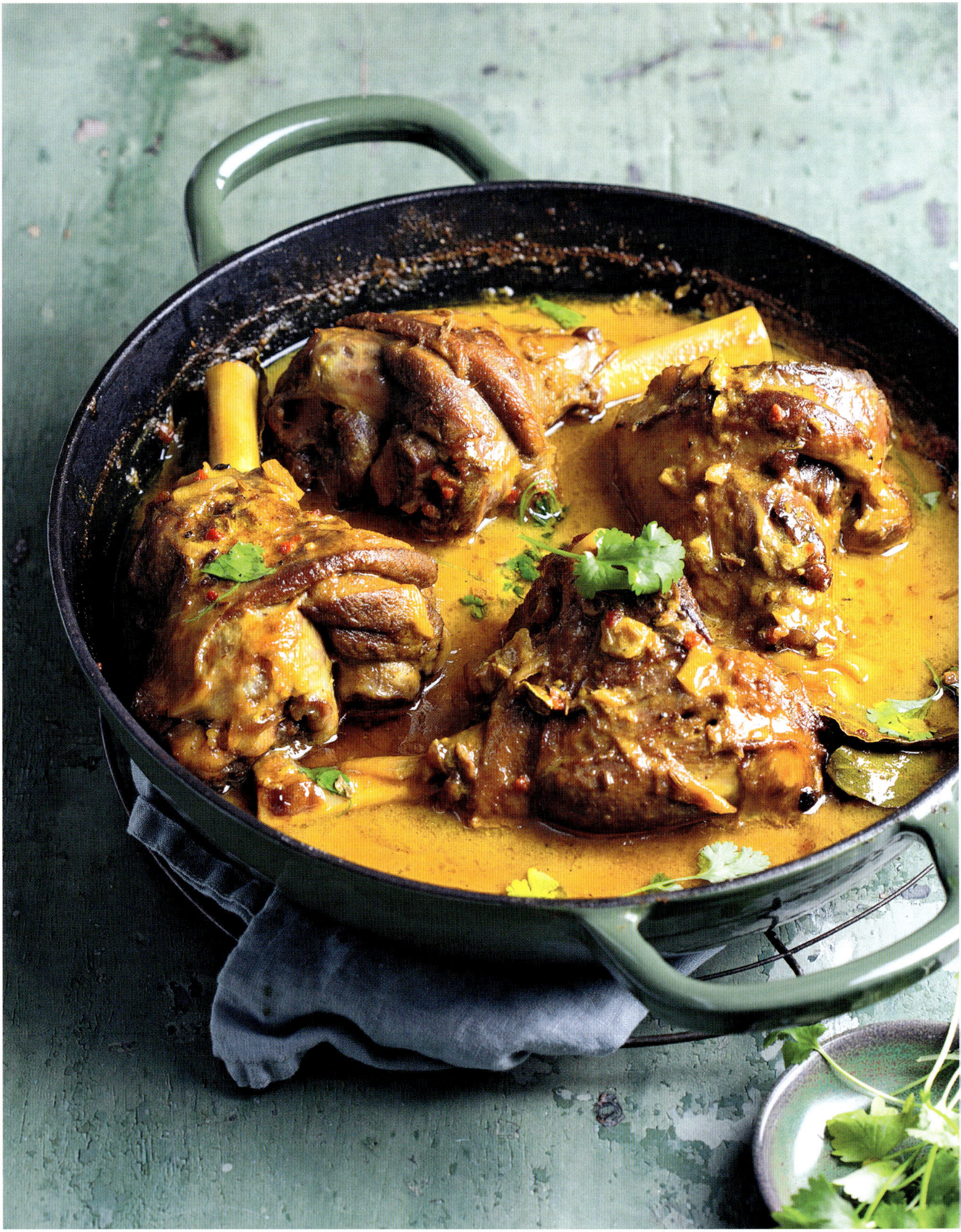

FRAGRANT LAMB SHANK CURRY

This dish freezes well. You can either freeze the shanks whole or pull the meat off the bones before freezing.

2 Tbsp olive oil
2 Tbsp butter
4 lamb shanks
Salt and black pepper to taste
2 onions, peeled and roughly chopped
4 cloves garlic, peeled and finely chopped
6 cm fresh ginger, peeled and finely chopped
1 red chilli, finely chopped
3 Tbsp Masala Mix (page 26) or curry powder
1 tsp coriander seeds
1 tsp cumin seeds
1 tsp fennel seeds
2 cinnamon sticks
4 cardamom pods
3 fresh or dried bay leaves
1 can (400 ml) coconut milk
Coriander leaves, for garnish

MAKES 4 PORTIONS

1. Heat the oil and butter in an ovenproof casserole over medium-high heat. Season the lamb well with salt and pepper and brown well on all sides (do this in batches, if necessary), then remove and set aside.
2. Reduce the heat and add the onions, garlic, ginger and chilli. Cook, stirring, for 5 minutes, until soft and fragrant. Add the Masala Mix or curry powder, whole spices and bay leaves and cook for a further 5 minutes. Stir in the coconut milk.
3. Return the meat to the casserole. Cover with a lid or foil and place in a preheated oven at 160°C for 2½–3 hours, or until the meat is tender (stir it once or twice during cooking). Remove from the oven, garnish with coriander leaves and serve with Quick Pilaf (page 142).
4. If not using immediately, set aside until completely cool before dividing into portions and spooning into resealable bags (flatten the bags to push out excess air before sealing). Label clearly with the name and date, and freeze for up to 3 months.

DAL MAKHANI

Slow-cooked lentils are easy to prepare in the oven. Dal is delicious as is, or served with your favourite curry. We rarely eat pulses because of their high carb count (100 g brown lentils contains 61 g carbs), but when we do, this flavourful, comforting dish is the one we choose.

200 g dried brown lentils

1 litre water

2 Tbsp butter

2 Tbsp olive oil

2 large onions, peeled and finely chopped

6 cloves garlic, peeled and finely chopped

5 cm fresh ginger, peeled and finely chopped

3 Tbsp Masala Mix (page 26) or curry powder

4–5 dried chilli rings or 1–2 tsp chilli flakes

2 cardamom pods, lightly crushed and husks removed

2 whole cloves

1 cinnamon stick

1 fresh or dried bay leaf

1 tsp coarse sea salt

¼ tsp ground black pepper

2 cans (400 g each) whole peeled tomatoes

160 g tomato paste

Salt to taste

½ cup (125 ml) cream or coconut cream

2–3 Tbsp cold butter, diced

Coriander leaves, for garnish

MAKES 6–8 PORTIONS

1. Place the lentils and water in a saucepan. Bring to a boil, then lower the heat, cover with a lid and simmer for 1 hour, stirring occasionally, until tender.
2. Heat the butter and oil in a pan over medium heat. Add the onions and cook for about 15 minutes, stirring occasionally, until soft and caramelized. Add the garlic and ginger and cook for 1–2 minutes, until soft. Add the Masala Mix or curry powder, chilli rings or flakes, whole spices, bay leaf, salt and pepper. Cook, stirring, for 2–3 minutes, until fragrant, then remove from the heat.
3. Drain the lentils, reserving the cooking water, and transfer to an ovenproof casserole. Add the whole tomatoes, plus any juice from the can, the tomato paste and salt to taste. Mash half of the mixture finely with a fork.
4. Add the onion mixture to the casserole, along with any reserved cooking water from the lentils. Cover with a lid and place in a preheated oven at 160°C for 2–3 hours, stirring occasionally. If the mixture gets too dry, add warm water (up to ½ cup). Remove from the oven and stir in the cream and butter. Garnish with coriander and serve in bowls. If not using immediately, leave until completely cool, then spoon into resealable bags (flatten the bags to push out any excess air before sealing). Freeze for up to 1 month. Defrost fully before reheating over medium heat.

Note

To make a quick curry, brown a pack of chicken thighs and legs in a little olive oil. Add the dal makhani and a can of coconut milk. Stir through, season to taste and simmer for 45 minutes, until the chicken is cooked and the sauce is thick.

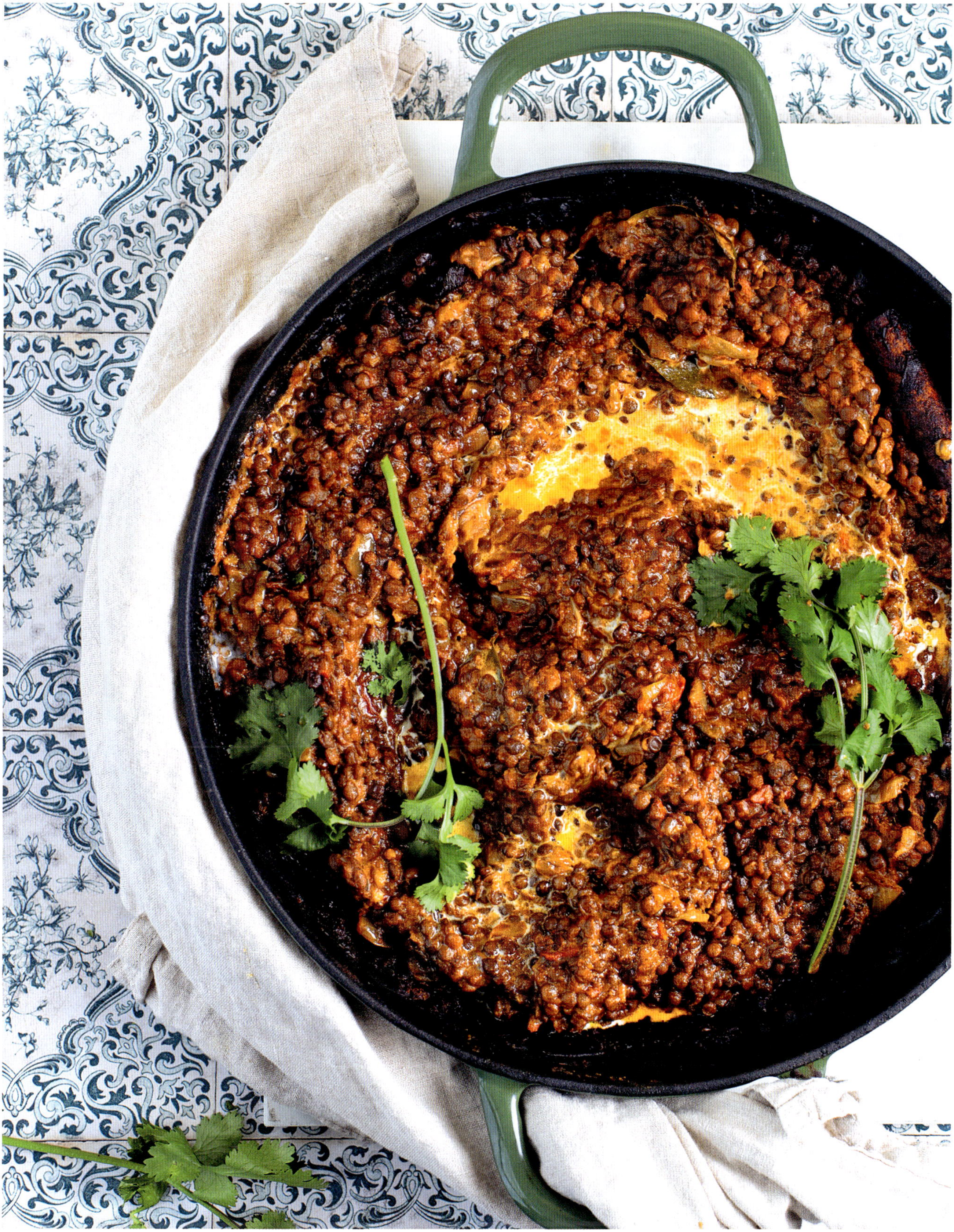

LAMB SHANK BOBOTIE

My version of this perennial favourite is made with lamb shanks, cooked slowly until the meat falls off the bone, which takes it to the next level. If you intend to make the bobotie ahead and freeze it, use a dish that can go from freezer to oven to table.

4 lamb shanks
Salt and black pepper to taste
2 Tbsp olive oil
2 Tbsp butter
2 onions, peeled and thickly sliced
1–2 cloves garlic, peeled and finely chopped
6 cm fresh ginger, peeled and finely grated
2 tsp Masala Mix (page 26)
3 tsp ground turmeric
1½ Tbsp coriander seeds
1½ Tbsp cumin seeds
3 whole cloves
5 allspice berries
½ tsp ground black pepper
½ cup (125 ml) Meaty Bone Broth (page 58) or liquid beef stock
2 Granny Smith apples, peeled and grated
½ cup flaked almonds
4 eggs
1 cup (250 ml) cream or coconut cream
12 fresh or dried bay leaves

MAKES 6 PORTIONS

1. Season the lamb shanks with salt and ground black pepper. Heat the oil and butter in a heavy-based casserole over medium heat. Brown the shanks on all sides, in batches if necessary, then remove and set aside.
2. Add the onions and fry for 2–3 minutes, until translucent. Add the garlic, ginger, Masala Mix, 1 tsp turmeric, coriander seeds, cumin seeds, cloves, allspice berries and black pepper, and cook for a further 2–3 minutes, until fragrant.
3. Return the shanks to the casserole, along with any juices. Add the bone broth or stock, cover with a lid, reduce the heat to low, and simmer for about 2 hours, until the meat starts to pull away from the bone. Check every now and then, and top up with a little extra hot water or broth if it starts to get too dry.
4. Remove the casserole from the heat. Using forks, pull the meat off the bones, shredding it into bite-sized pieces (discard the bones). Spoon the meat into an ovenproof dish and stir in the grated apples. Spread the mixture evenly and scatter over the flaked almonds.
5. Crack the eggs into a bowl and whisk lightly. Add the cream and 2 tsp turmeric and whisk to combine. Season to taste with salt. Pour the custard over the meat mixture to cover the surface. Arrange the bay leaves on top.
6. Place in a preheated oven at 200°C for 20–30 minutes, until the custard is golden and set and the lamb is heated through. Serve with Quick Pilaf (page 142).
7. To freeze, set aside until completely cool, then cover with a double layer of foil or cling wrap. To freeze individual portions, scoop into small rigid containers. Label clearly and freeze for up to 3 months.

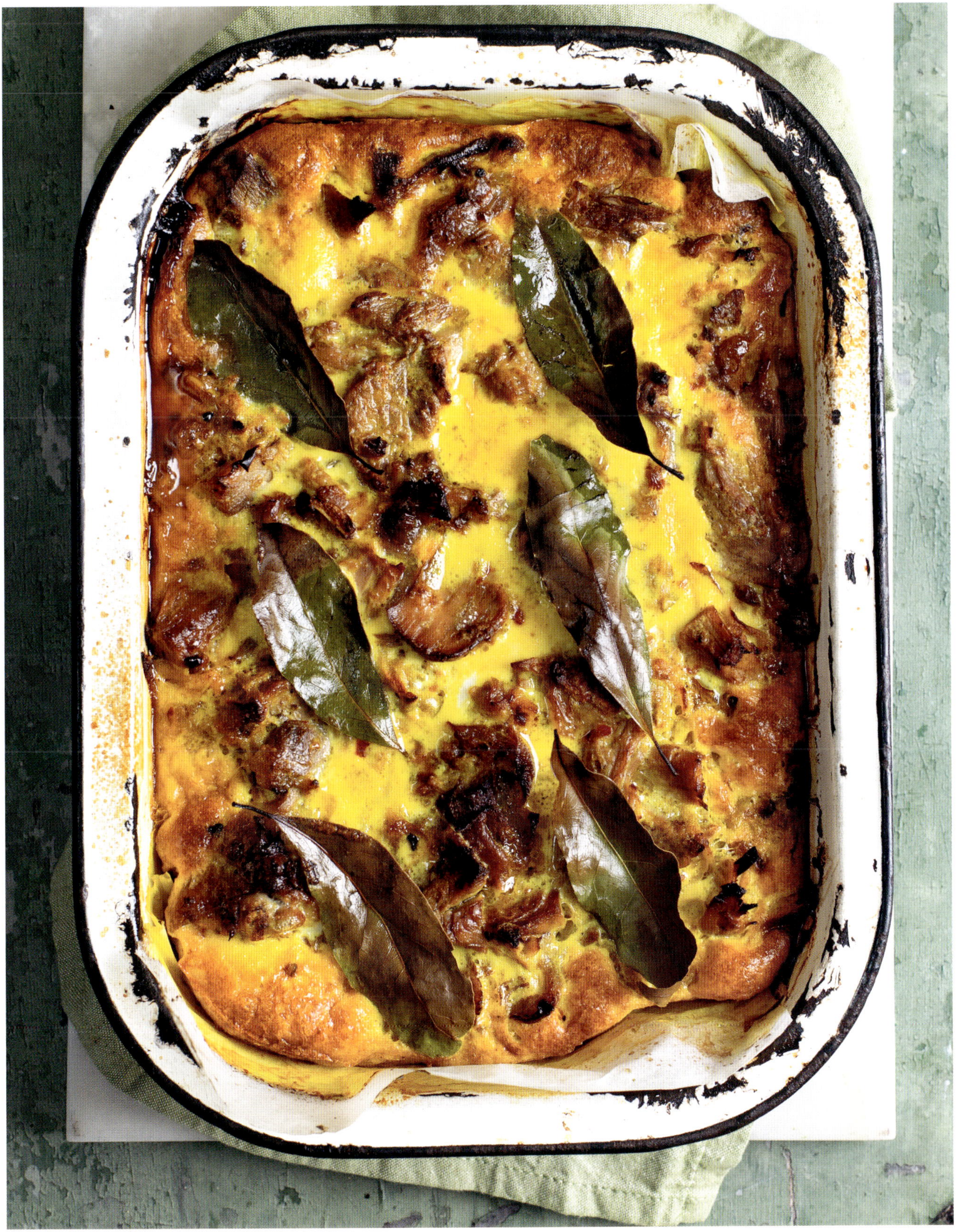

OVEN-BAKED BOLOGNAISE

Adding chicken livers is a good way to increase your intake of organ meat, and makes the sauce flavourful and rich.

5 Tbsp olive oil

1 kg beef mince

1 kg pork mince

Salt and black pepper to taste

2 onions, peeled and finely chopped

3 celery sticks (±10 cm each), finely chopped

2 carrots, peeled and finely chopped

4 cloves garlic, peeled and finely chopped

4 anchovy fillets, chopped

4 chicken livers, finely chopped

150 g pancetta or streaky bacon, chopped

¾ cup (185 ml) red wine

3–4 Tbsp tomato paste

4 fresh or dried bay leaves

4 sprigs thyme

1 cup (250 ml) Meaty Bone Broth (page 58) or liquid beef stock

1 bottle (700 g) Italian passata

1 can (400 g) whole peeled tomatoes

MAKES 8 PORTIONS

1. Heat 3 Tbsp olive oil in a large ovenproof casserole over medium heat. Brown the mince in batches, seasoning with salt and pepper, and stirring to break up any lumps. Remove the mince with a ladle and set aside, retaining any cooking juices.
2. Add the remaining olive oil, along with the onions, celery, carrots, garlic and anchovies. Cook, stirring, for 5 minutes, or until the vegetables soften and start to caramelize. Add the chicken livers and the pancetta or bacon and cook, stirring, until golden.
3. Add the red wine, tomato paste and herbs and bring to a boil. Reduce the heat to low and simmer for 5 minutes, until the liquid reduces slightly.
4. Add the broth or stock, the passata and the whole peeled tomatoes, plus any juice from the can, crushing the tomatoes lightly with a fork. Simmer over low heat, stirring occasionally, for 5 minutes.
5. Return the mince, plus any juices, to the casserole. Taste for seasoning and add a little more salt if needed. Cover with a lid and place in a preheated oven at 160°C for 2 hours, until the meat is rich and flavourful. Check every 30 minutes and top up with a little extra stock or water if it starts to get too dry. Serve with baby marrow noodles, your choice of pasta, or blanched fine green beans, with Everyday Rocket Salad (page 151) on the side.
6. To freeze, set aside until completely cool before spooning into rigid containers or resealable bags (flatten the bags to push out any excess air before sealing). A large bag (±2 litres) will hold enough for 4 servings.

Note

If you don't consume alcohol, replace the wine with the same quantity of beef stock or broth.

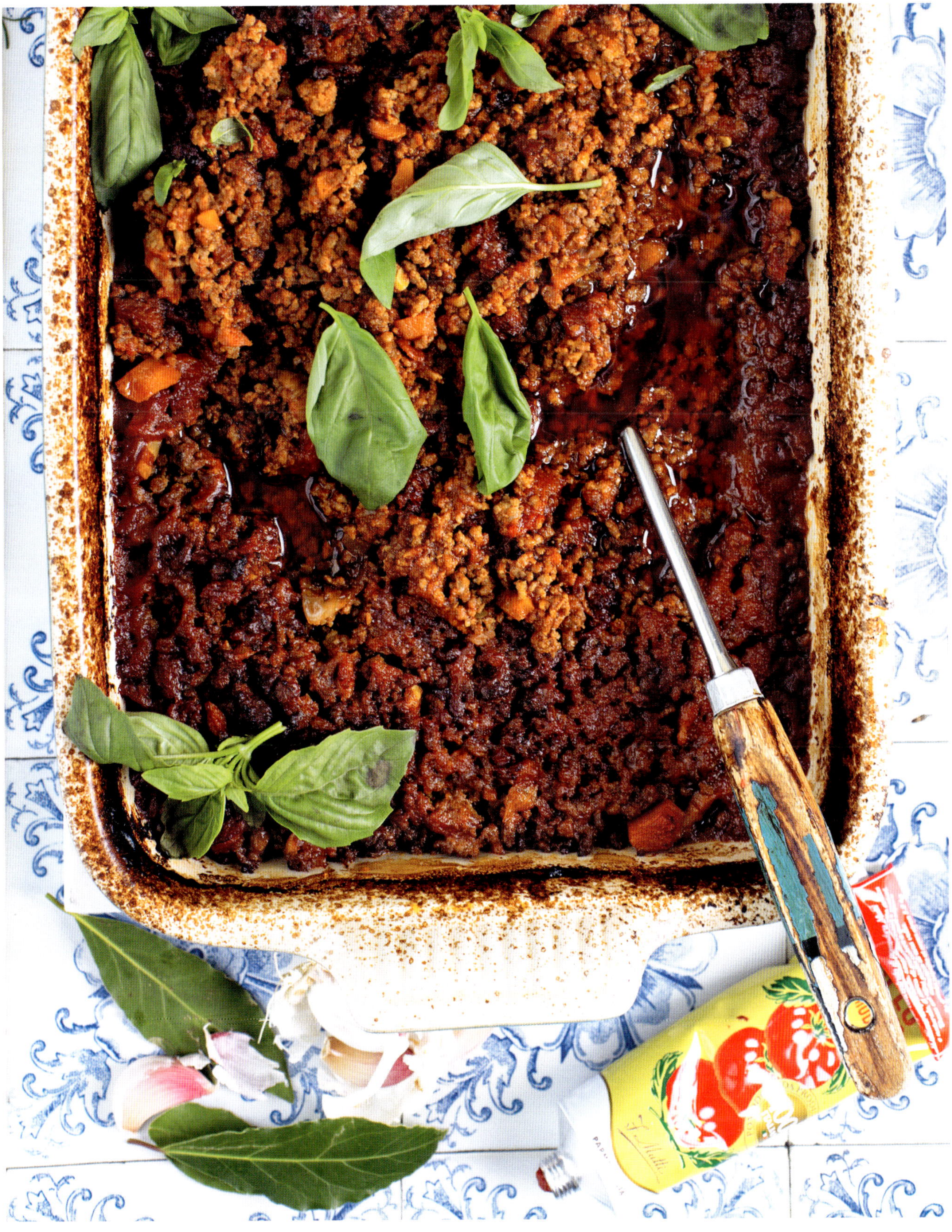

BEEF AND RED WINE STEW

This is a winter staple in my house; the only thing that changes is the cut of meat. I mostly use short ribs, but the stew can be made with any stewing beef.

2 kg beef short ribs
Salt to taste
2 Tbsp olive oil
2 Tbsp butter
1 onion, peeled and finely chopped
2 celery sticks, finely chopped
1 carrot, peeled and finely chopped
2 cloves garlic, peeled and finely chopped
3 anchovy fillets, chopped
1 cup (250 ml) red wine or beef stock
1 cup (250 ml) Meaty Bone Broth (page 58) or liquid beef stock
1 can (400 g) whole peeled tomatoes
3 fresh or dried bay leaves
3 sprigs rosemary
3 sprigs flat-leaf parsley
4 sprigs thyme

MAKES 8 PORTIONS

1. Cut the ribs into smaller pieces (± 8–10 cm) by slicing between the bones. Season all over with salt. Heat the oil and butter in a large ovenproof casserole over medium-high heat. Brown the meat on all sides (in batches if necessary), then remove with a slotted spoon and set aside on a shallow plate, to catch any juices.
2. Add the onion, celery, carrot and garlic and cook for 4–5 minutes, until soft. Add the anchovies and cook for 1–2 minutes, until dissolved.
3. Add the wine and cook for 2 minutes, to reduce slightly. Add the broth and tomatoes, plus any juice, crushing them with a fork. Tie the herbs together with string and add to the casserole.
4. Return the meat and any juices to the sauce. Cover with a lid or double layer of foil and cook in a preheated oven at 160°C for 2–3 hours, until the meat starts to pull away from the bones. Check every 30 minutes to ensure it does not dry out (top up with stock or water; no more than 1 cup extra). Remove from the oven and discard the bones and herbs. Serve with Creamy Vegetable Mash (page 150) or Soft Polenta (page 150).
5. To freeze, set aside until completely cool before spooning into rigid containers or resealable bags (flatten the bags to push out excess air before sealing). A large bag (± 2 litres) will hold enough for 4 servings.

Note

To make beef pies, use Basic Low-carb Pastry (page 148) and follow the method for chicken pies (page 128).

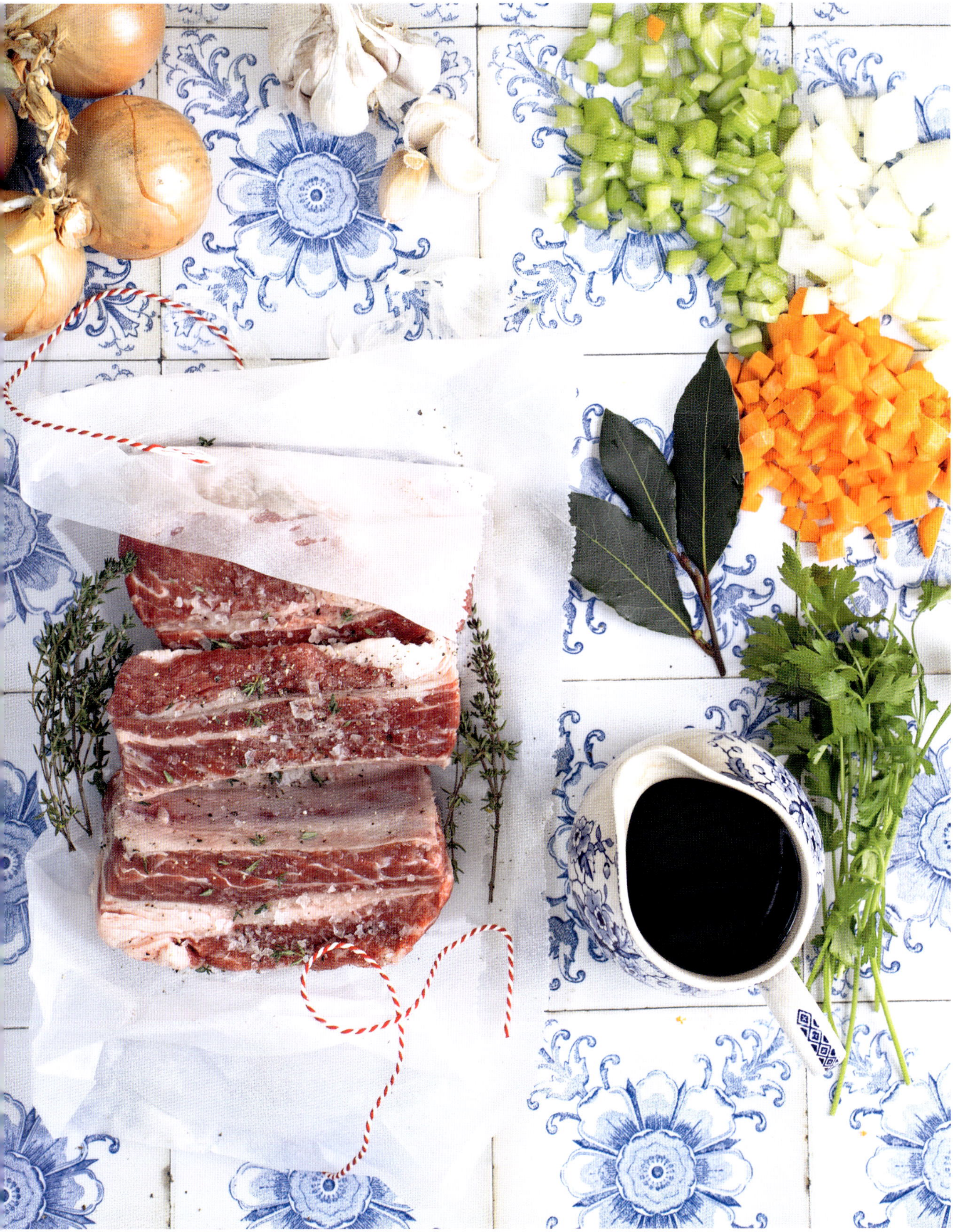

HUNGARIAN GOULASH

I make this with pork belly, because its high fat content ensures a flavourful and tender stew. The combination of sweet and smoked paprika brings authentic flavour and colour to this popular dish.

2 kg boneless pork belly

Salt to taste

2 Tbsp olive oil

2 Tbsp butter

1 large onion, peeled and finely chopped

5 cloves garlic, peeled and finely chopped

2 red peppers, seeds removed and roughly chopped

4 Tbsp (¼ cup) white wine

2 Tbsp sweet paprika

1 Tbsp smoked paprika

2 tsp caraway seeds

2 Tbsp tomato purée

1 can (400 g) whole peeled tomatoes

1 cup (250 ml) Meaty Bone Broth (page 58) or liquid beef stock

½ cup (125 ml) sour cream, for serving

MAKES 8 PORTIONS

1. If the meat has not already been trimmed, use a sharp knife to remove the skin, leaving a thin layer of fat. Discard the skin. (You can ask the butcher to do this for you.) Cut the meat into cubes (± 5 cm) and season with salt. Heat the oil and butter in a heavy-based casserole over medium heat. Brown the meat, in batches, on all sides until golden, then remove with a slotted spoon and set aside on a plate, to catch the juices.
2. Add the onion, garlic and peppers to the casserole and cook for 7–8 minutes, until soft and caramelized.
3. Add the wine and continue cooking until reduced by half.
4. Add all the paprika and the caraway seeds and cook for 1 minute, stirring, until fragrant.
5. Stir in the tomato purée and whole tomatoes, plus the juice from the can, crushing them with a fork. Add the broth or stock.
6. Return the pork cubes to the casserole, cover with a lid, reduce the heat to low and simmer for 2 hours, stirring occasionally, until the meat is tender and the sauce is rich and dark. Check every 30 minutes or so, and top up with a little water or stock if it looks too dry. Serve with baby marrow noodles or green beans, topping each serving with some sour cream.
7. To freeze, set aside until completely cool before spooning into rigid containers or resealable bags (flatten the bags to push out any excess air before sealing). A large bag (± 2 litres) will hold enough for 4 servings.

Notes

Instead of pork belly, use 2 kg pork or beef goulash cubes.

If you do not consume alcohol, replace the wine with an equal amount of clear apple juice or white grape juice.

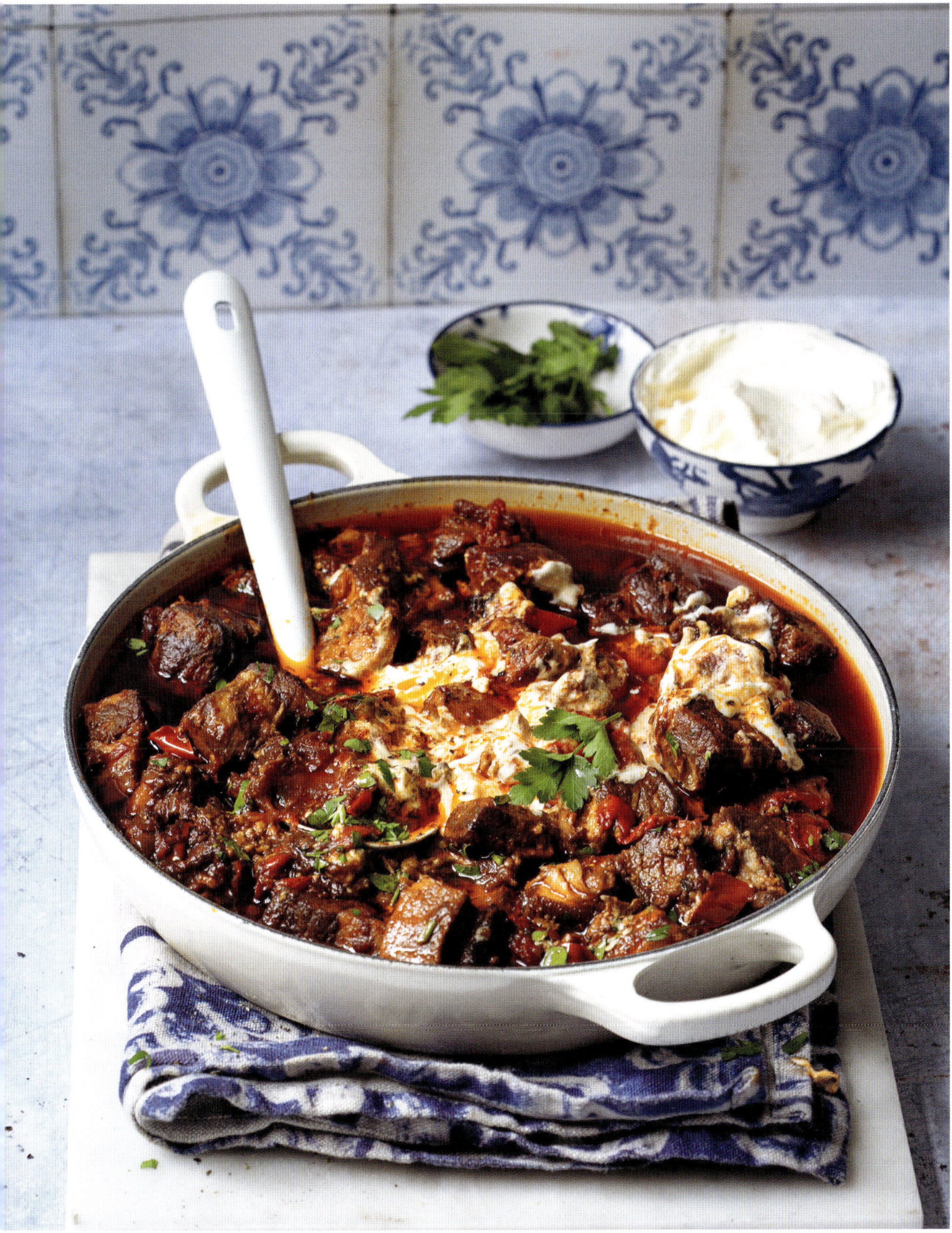

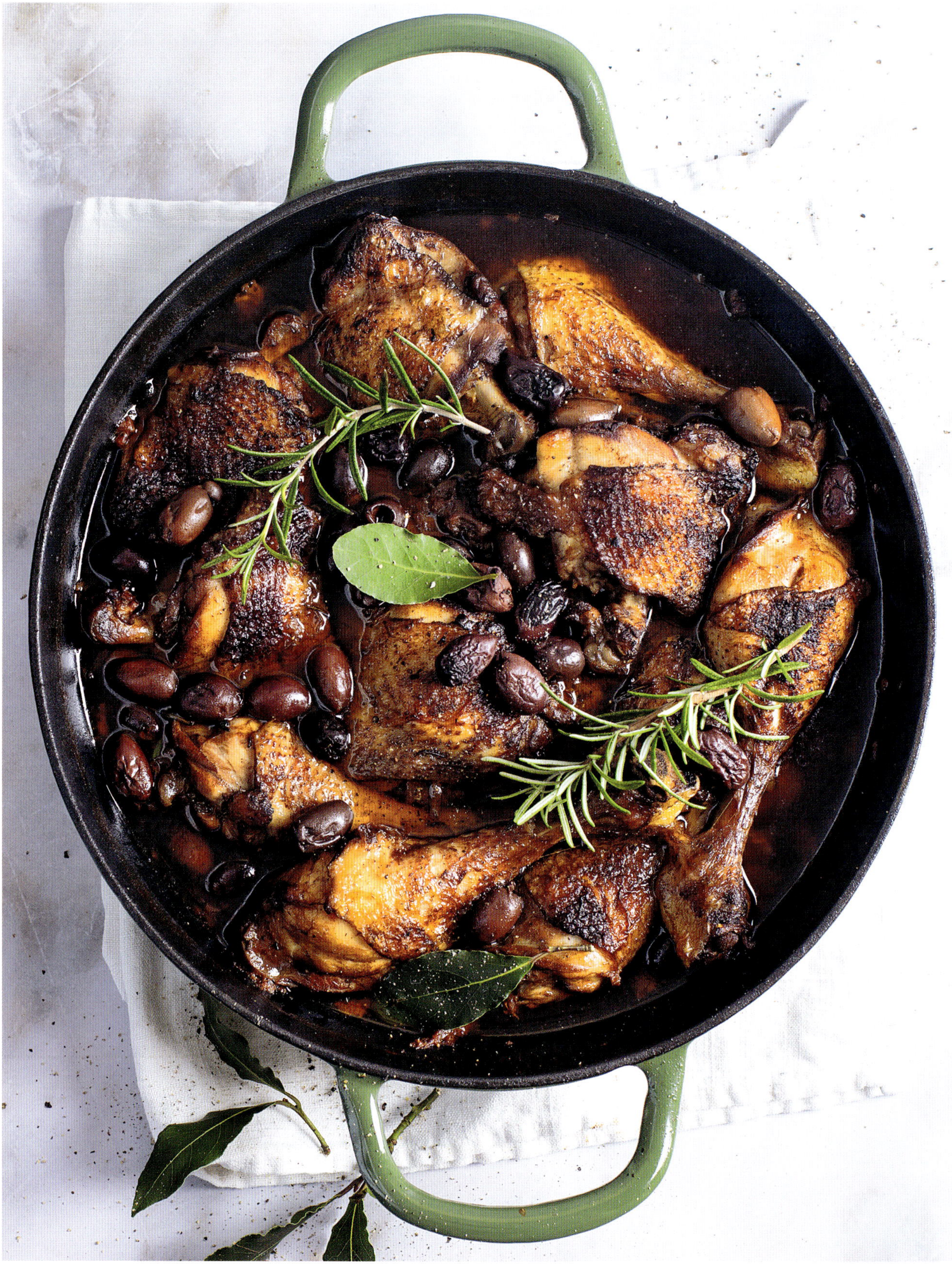

CHICKEN CACCIATORE

Prepare this 'hunter's chicken' the day before, as it benefits from marinating overnight in the fridge, although even a few hours are better than nothing. Because the chicken is marinated in wine, it may not be suitable for anyone who does not consume alcohol. This one-dish meal freezes well, making it a good choice for bulk cooking.

8 chicken legs
8 chicken thighs
Salt and black pepper to taste
8 fresh or dried bay leaves
2 sprigs rosemary
5 cloves garlic, peeled and finely chopped
1 cup (250 ml) red wine
2 Tbsp olive oil
6 anchovy fillets, chopped
½–1 cup pitted black olives
1 can (400 g) whole peeled tomatoes

MAKES 8 PORTIONS

1. Place the chicken pieces in a glass bowl and season with salt and black pepper. Add the bay leaves, rosemary sprigs, half the chopped garlic and the wine. Cover and leave to marinate for at least an hour at room temperature, or overnight in the fridge. (If marinating overnight, allow the chicken to come to room temperature before continuing with the recipe.)
2. Remove the chicken from the marinade (reserving the marinade), and pat dry with paper towel. Heat the oil in an ovenproof casserole and brown the chicken pieces until golden. Remove with a slotted spoon and set aside on a plate, to catch the juices.
3. Add the remaining garlic and fry for 1 minute, then add the anchovies, olives and tomatoes, plus any juice from the can, crushing them with a fork. Add the chicken pieces, plus any juices, and the reserved marinade (including the bay leaves and rosemary sprigs). Bring to a boil and cook for 5 minutes.
4. Remove the casserole from the heat, cover with a lid or double layer of foil, and place in a preheated oven at 200°C for 1½ hours, stirring it gently halfway through. Serve with your choice of vegetables or salad.
5. To freeze, set aside until completely cool before spooning into rigid containers or resealable bags.

FISHERMAN'S STEW

I use fresh seafood for this dish, but a combination of fresh and frozen fish and seafood will be just as good. Frozen mussels do not have to be cooked first; simply add them at the same time as the prawns and fish.

4 Tbsp olive oil

700 g uncooked whole black mussels

½ cup (125 ml) white wine or orange juice

1 onion, peeled and roughly chopped

1 fennel bulb, roughly chopped

3 cloves garlic, peeled and finely chopped

1 red chilli, finely chopped

3 short celery sticks, roughly chopped

½ cup (125 ml) white wine or fish stock

2 fresh or dried bay leaves

2 cans (400 g each) whole peeled tomatoes

Salt to taste

500 g uncooked prawns (shell-on, deveined, heads removed)

1 kg hake or white fish fillets

Basil or dill, for serving

MAKES 6 PORTIONS

1. Heat 2 Tbsp olive oil in a heavy-based casserole over medium heat. Add the fresh mussels and wine or orange juice, cover with a lid and cook for 3 minutes, shaking it now and then. Drain the mussels in a colander, discarding the cooking liquid, and set aside to cool. Discard any mussels that don't open. Wipe out the casserole with paper towel to remove any trace of grit from the mussels (there is always some!).

2. Heat the remaining oil in the casserole. Add the onion, fennel, garlic, chilli and celery and cook for 3–4 minutes, until softened. Add the wine or fish stock, bay leaves and tomatoes, plus any juice from the cans, crushing them with a fork. Reduce the heat to low and simmer for 30 minutes, stirring once or twice, until you have a chunky sauce. Season to taste with salt.

3. Season the prawns and fish with salt to taste. Add to the sauce and cook for 5 minutes. Return the mussels to the casserole for a further 2 minutes to heat through. (When cooked, the prawns will turn pink, and the fish will be opaque and flake easily with a fork.) Top with basil or dill and serve warm.

Notes

This freezes well, but do not overcook the fish because it will continue to cook when reheated after defrosting.

Defrost frozen prawns overnight (or for at least 12 hours in the fridge), then rinse under cold water and pat dry before cooking. Defrost frozen mussels in a colander overnight in the fridge. Pour off any excess liquid before adding to the casserole. There is no need to defrost frozen fish.

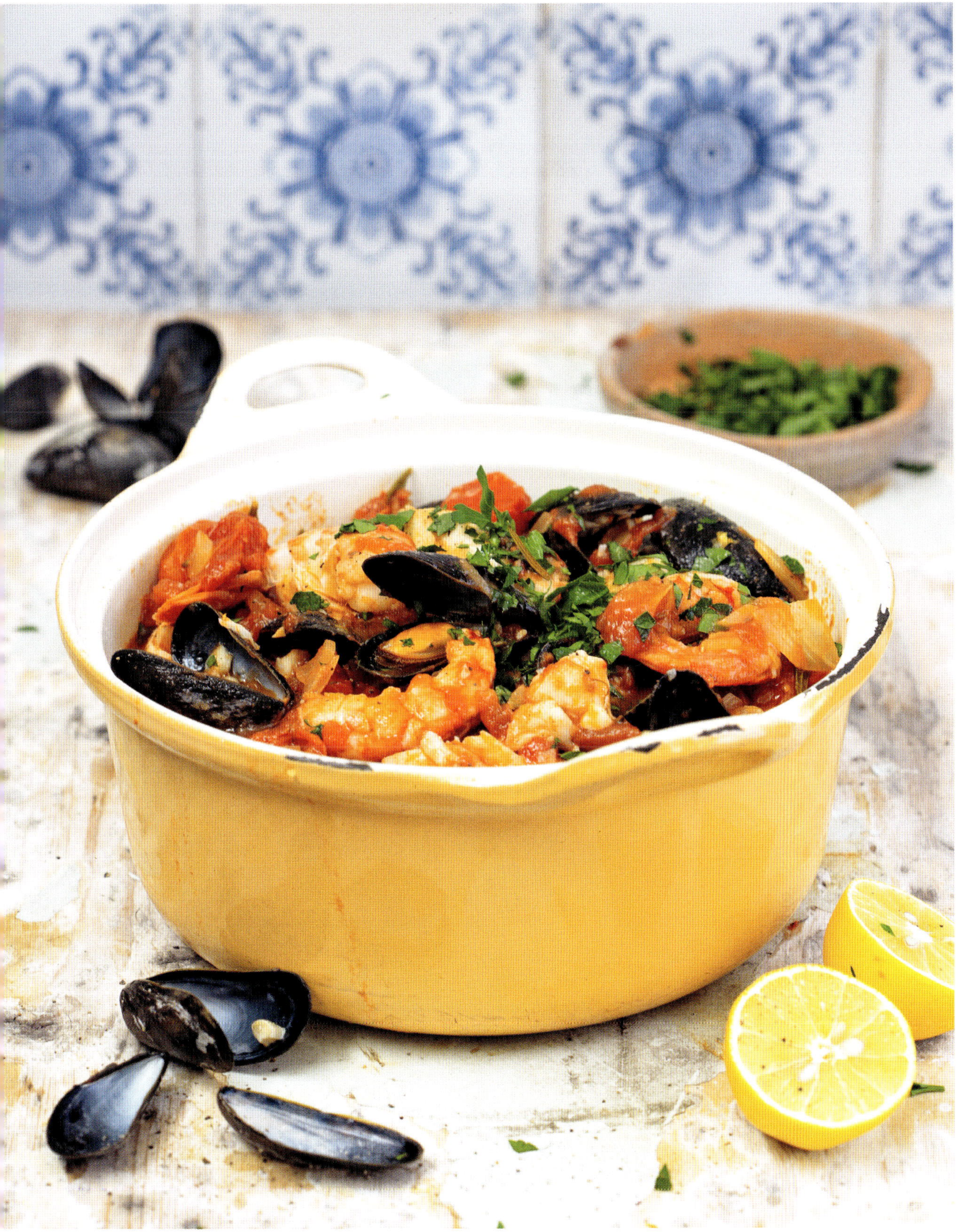

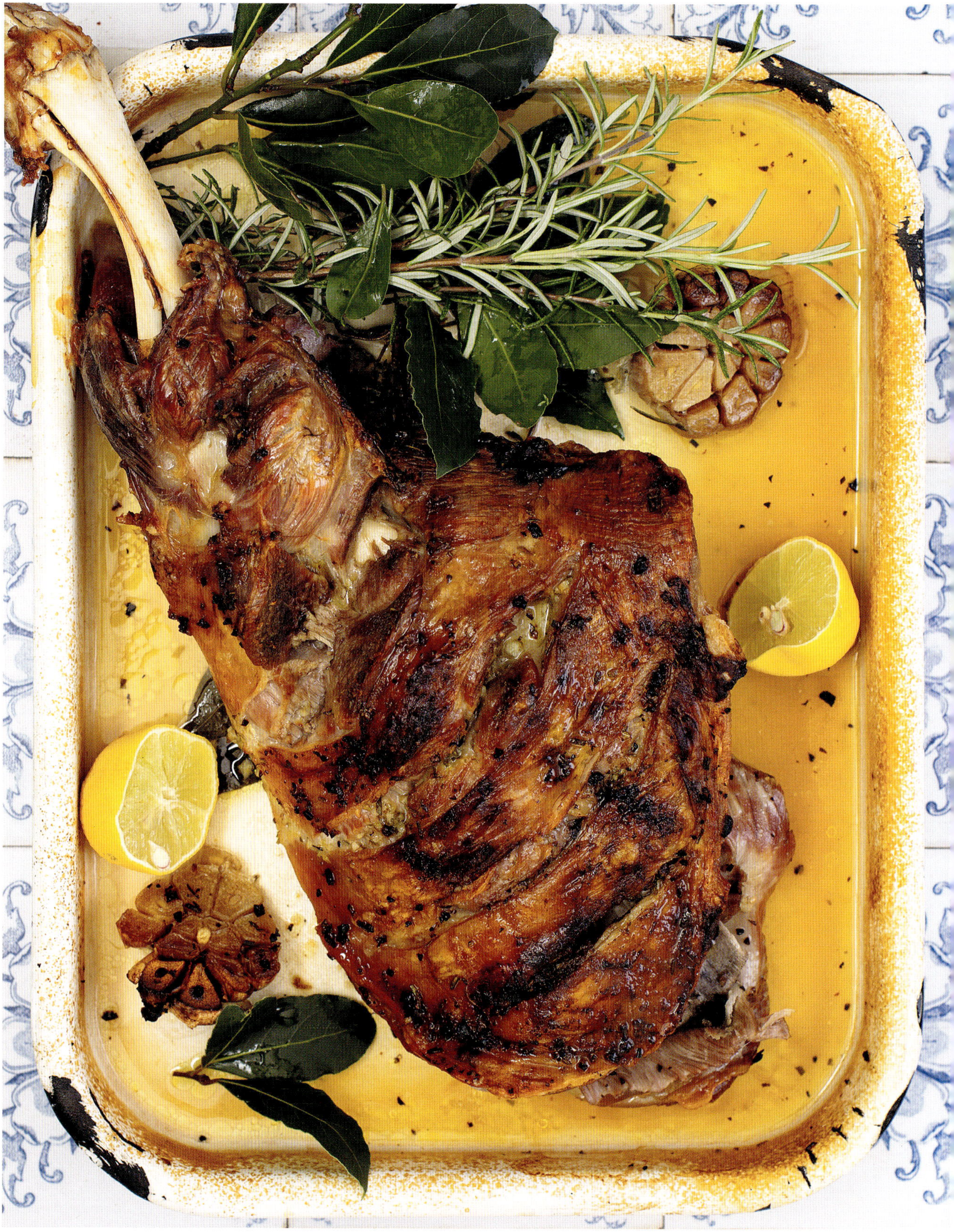

ROASTED AND PULLED LAMB

Slow-roasted lamb is tender and succulent. Use pulled meat for everyday dishes or, for a special occasion, carve the meat and serve it with Quick Pilaf (page 142) and a green salad, adding flaked almonds and pomegranate rubies for a Moroccan twist.

1 leg of lamb (1.6–2 kg)
Salt to taste
3 Tbsp olive oil
6 sprigs rosemary, leaves only
6 cloves garlic, peeled and finely chopped
Finely grated zest and juice of 1 lemon
6 fresh or dried bay leaves

MAKES 8 PORTIONS

1. Using a sharp knife, score the skin at 3 cm intervals. Season the leg with salt, rubbing it in with your hands.
2. Combine the olive oil, rosemary leaves, garlic, lemon zest and lemon juice in a small bowl. Rub the mixture all over the lamb.
3. Scatter the bay leaves over the bottom of a roasting dish and place the lamb on top. Tightly cover the dish with foil, sealing the edges. Roast in a preheated oven at 160°C for 2 hours, or until the meat starts to fall off the bone.
4. Remove the foil from the dish and increase the oven temperature to 200°C. Continue cooking for a further 40 minutes, until the surface of the meat is golden brown. Remove from the oven.
5. If serving as a roast, cover the meat lightly with foil and let it rest for up to 10 minutes, to allow the juices to settle, before carving into thick slices.
6. For pulled lamb, set aside until cool enough to handle, then use two forks to pull the meat into threads (chop any browned outer meat and incorporate it as well). Drizzle over the pan juices.
7. If not using immediately, set aside until completely cool before spooning into resealable bags (flatten the bags to push out any excess air before sealing). Freeze for up to 3 months.

Notes

You can use either a leg or shoulder of lamb for this dish.

Use pulled lamb to make Lamb, Spinach and Feta Pie (page 127) or combine it with Creamy Curry Cook-in Sauce (page 48) to make a quick curry. Pulled meat also makes a great filling for wraps, rolls and pitas.

ROASTED AND PULLED CHICKEN

I always roast two chickens, using one for dinner that day and pulling the meat off the other one to freeze for use in pies, stir-fries, sandwiches or quick curries.

2 whole chickens (±1.2–1.5 kg each)

Salt to taste

125 g flavoured butter of choice (page 32), softened

2 lemons, halved or cut into wedges

6–10 fresh or dried bay leaves

4 sprigs rosemary

8 sprigs thyme

1 head garlic, sliced open at the top and halved

4 Tbsp olive oil

MAKES 4 PORTIONS PER CHICKEN

1. Season the chicken cavities with salt and rub salt all over the skin. Using your fingers, work the softened butter under the skin of the breasts, reaching as far back as you can, but taking care not to tear the skin.
2. Insert half the lemons, bay leaves, rosemary, thyme and garlic into each cavity.
3. Place the chickens in a large roasting pan and drizzle with the olive oil. Roast in a preheated oven at 200°C for 1½ hours, or until the skin is golden and the juices run clear when you pierce the thickest part of the thigh with a metal skewer. Remove from the oven.
4. If using immediately, set aside to rest for up to 10 minutes before serving with vegetables or salad of your choice.
5. If not using immediately, set aside until cool enough to handle, then use two forks to pull the meat off the bones, and chop the skin, combining everything in a bowl to ensure the white and dark meat are mixed. Divide into portions and spoon into resealable bags (flatten the bags to push out any excess air before sealing). Freeze for up to 3 months.

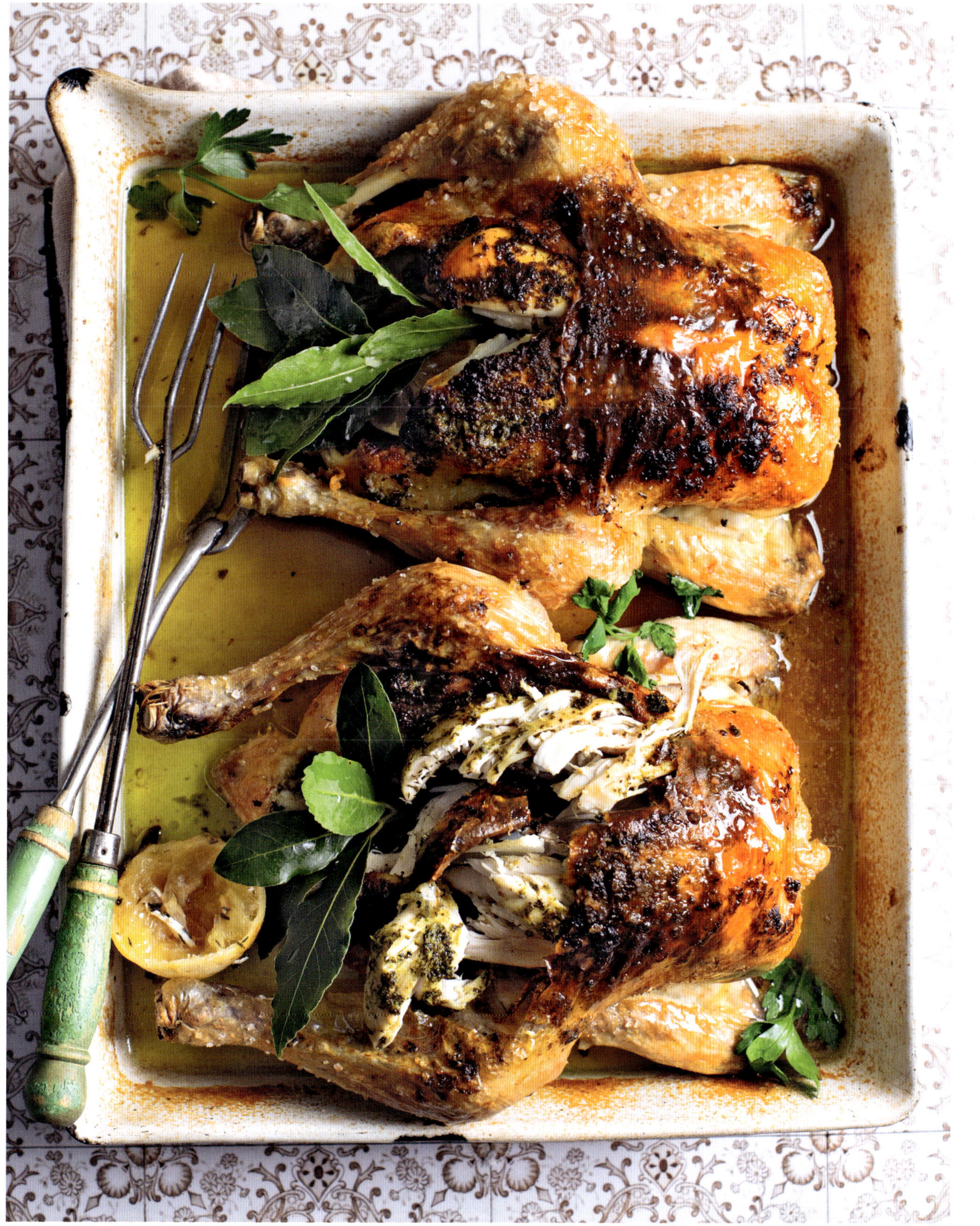

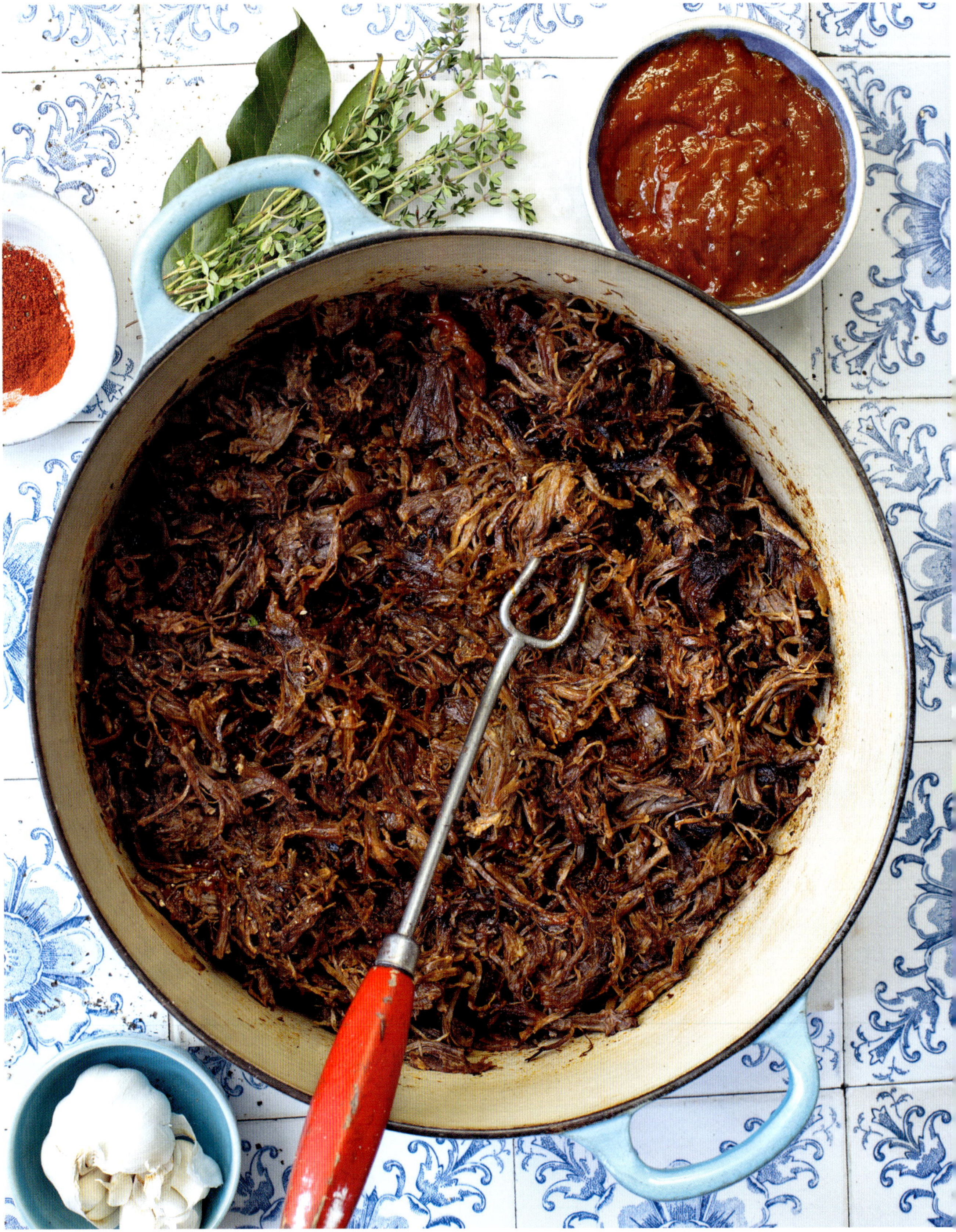

SRIRACHA PULLED BEEF

Cooking a joint of beef or lamb and pulling (shredding) it is an easy way to obtain a large amount of flavourful meat for use in pies, wraps and other dishes.

1.5 kg beef brisket or flank
Salt to taste
2 Tbsp olive oil
2 onions, peeled and sliced
¼ cup Sriracha Sauce (page 28)
2 Tbsp smoked paprika
2 Tbsp honey or maple syrup
2 tsp cumin seeds
½ cup (125 ml) tomato passata

MAKES 8 PORTIONS

1. Season the brisket well with salt. Heat the olive oil in a large ovenproof casserole and brown the meat on all sides. Using tongs, remove the meat and place in a shallow dish, to catch any juices.
2. Add the sliced onions to the casserole and cook for 2–3 minutes, until just soft.
3. Combine the Sriracha Sauce, smoked paprika, honey and cumin seeds in a small bowl. Brush the mixture all over the brisket and return it to the casserole, along with any retained juices. Pour the tomato passata around the meat.
4. Cover with a lid and cook in a preheated oven at 160°C for 2 hours, turning the meat after 1 hour (use tongs or carving forks to do this). The meat is ready when you can easily pull it apart. Remove from the oven, lift the meat out of the casserole (retain the sauce) and set aside until cool enough to handle. Using two forks, pull the meat apart. Return the pulled meat to the casserole and stir it into the sauce until well combined.
5. If not using immediately, set aside until completely cool before spooning into resealable bags (flatten the bags to push out any excess air before sealing). Freeze for up to 3 months.

Note

Use pulled beef to make homemade pizza (page 130), wraps (page 146) or burger sliders with homemade buns (page 145). It also makes a great filling for pitas.

ONE DISH

To me, 'ONE DISH' cooking means *complete meals* that can be *cooked* and served in a SINGLE PAN, OVEN TRAY or WOK. In my *meal prep*, I incorporate both *pan-cooked* and *oven-baked* recipes, because it is EASY to cook a *tray bake* or *casserole* in the OVEN at the *same time* as you prepare a *stir-fry* or make a *sauce* on the hob. I've INDICATED the *number* of *portions* each recipe *makes*, so you can decide whether to FREEZE a *full quantity* for another meal, or just *reserve* one or two portions for *lunchboxes* or a *standby meal* later in the week. As a few recipes require certain INGREDIENTS to be *precooked*, you may need to do some ADVANCE PLANNING to *ensure* that you have *everything to hand* in the fridge or freezer before you START COOKING.

CREAMY PAPRIKA CHICKEN

8 boneless and skinless chicken thighs

Salt to taste

2 Tbsp butter

3 Tbsp olive oil

½ cup (125 ml) white wine or chicken stock (see Note)

1 medium onion, peeled and chopped

1 red pepper, seeds removed and finely chopped

3 cloves garlic, peeled and finely chopped

120 g sundried tomatoes in oil, roughly chopped

1 Tbsp sweet paprika

1 cup (250 ml) cream

Basil or other leafy herbs for garnish

MAKES 8 PORTIONS

1. Cut each chicken thigh in half and season with salt. Heat the butter and 2 Tbsp olive oil in a heavy based casserole over medium heat and brown the chicken on all sides (do this in batches if necessary). Remove with a slotted spoon and set aside.
2. Deglaze the casserole with the wine or stock and simmer for 2 minutes to reduce slightly. Pour into a jug and set aside for later.
3. Add the remaining olive oil to the casserole and cook the onion, red pepper and garlic until soft and caramelized. Add the sundried tomatoes and paprika and cook for a further 2 minutes.
4. Return the chicken and wine to the casserole and heat through. Stir in the cream and simmer for 5–7 minutes, or until the chicken is cooked through and the sauce has thickened.
5. Garnish with basil and serve with low-carb noodles or baby marrow ribbons.

Note

If you don't consume alcohol, replace the wine with ½ cup (125 ml) chicken stock.

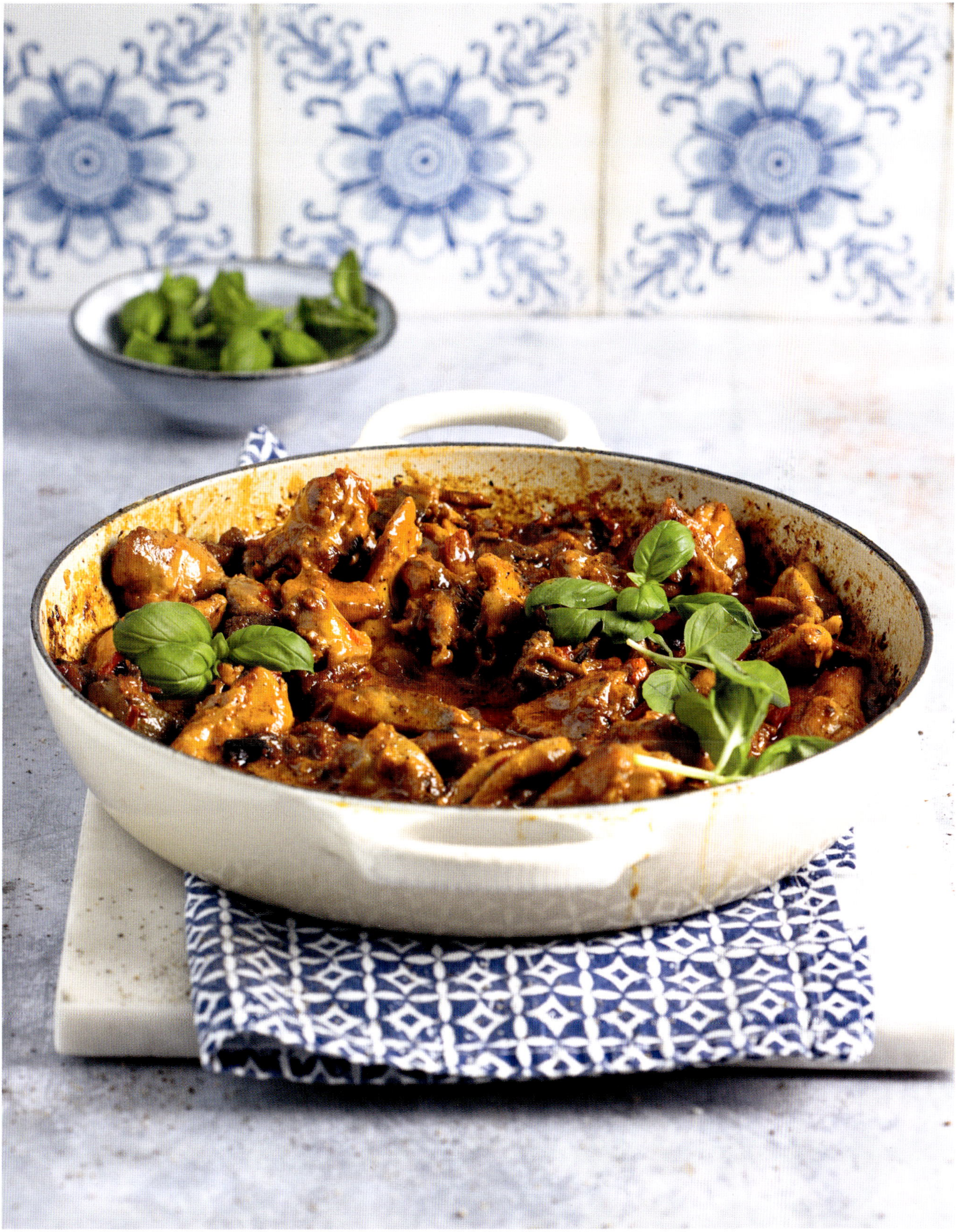

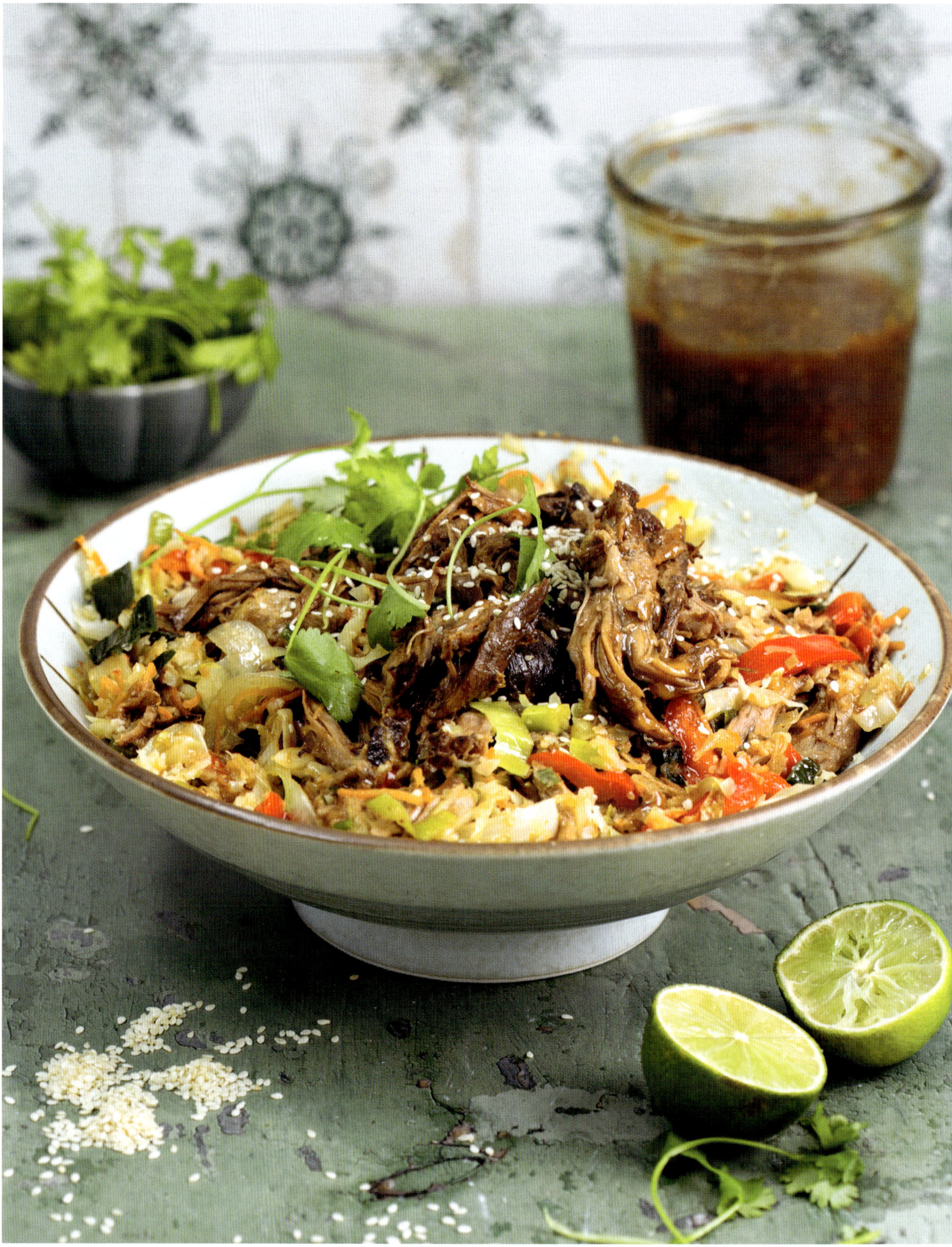

STICKY CHINESE FRIED RICE WITH PULLED BEEF

2 Tbsp olive oil

1 onion, peeled and thinly sliced

1 green pepper, thinly sliced

1 red pepper, thinly sliced

1 medium carrot, peeled and thinly sliced

2 leeks, thinly sliced

2 cloves garlic, peeled and finely chopped

6 cm fresh ginger, peeled and finely chopped

100 g shiitake mushrooms, sliced

500 g raw cauli rice *or* precooked basmati rice

½ cup (125 ml) Basic Stir-fry Sauce (page 31)

500 g Sriracha Pulled Beef (page 101)

2 Tbsp sesame seeds, for garnish

Coriander, for garnish

MAKES 6 PORTIONS

1. Heat the oil in a wok or pan over high heat. Add the onion, green and red peppers, carrot, leeks, garlic and ginger, and stir-fry for about 6 minutes, shaking the pan to prevent sticking. As soon as the veggies start to wilt and soften, add the mushrooms and cook for a further 3 minutes.
2. Lower the heat to medium. Add the uncooked cauli rice or cooked basmati rice and ¾ of the stir-fry sauce. Stir-fry for 6–7 minutes, until the vegetables and sauce are well combined.
3. Reheat the pulled beef in a separate pan with the rest of the Stir-fry Sauce. Divide the stir-fry into individual bowls and top with a portion of meat. Garnish with sesame seeds and fresh coriander and serve immediately.
4. To freeze, set aside until completely cool before spooning into resealable bags. Flatten the bags and push out any excess air before sealing. Label clearly with the date. Defrost in the fridge overnight, and reheat in a pan or wok.

RATATOUILLE FISH BAKE

2 medium brinjals, cubed
6 medium baby marrows, cubed
Salt to taste
2 red peppers, seeds removed and cubed
2 yellow peppers, seeds removed and cubed
2 red onions, peeled and cut into wedges
450 g cherry tomatoes
4–5 Tbsp olive oil
3 anchovy fillets, chopped
3 cloves garlic, peeled and finely chopped
6 white fish fillets
½ cup kalamata olives, pitted
Basil leaves, for garnish

MAKES 6 PORTIONS

1. Place the cubed brinjals and baby marrows in a colander. Sprinkle lightly with salt and toss to coat. Place a plate on top of the vegetables and weigh it down with a heavy weight. Place the colander on another plate, to catch any drips, and set aside for an hour, to draw out the juices, then pat the vegetables dry with paper towel.
2. Place the brinjals and baby marrows, peppers, onions and cherry tomatoes in a roasting dish.
3. Combine the olive oil, anchovies and garlic in a small bowl. Drizzle most of the oil over the vegetables and toss to coat. Roast in a preheated oven at 200°C for 30–40 minutes, or until the vegetables are tender and starting to brown.
4. Remove from the oven and place the fish on top of the vegetables. Season to taste with salt and drizzle over the remaining olive oil. Return to the oven for 10 minutes, or until the fish is just cooked through. Garnish with olives and fresh basil and serve immediately. (This dish is not suitable for freezing.)

Note

Salting the brinjals and baby marrows beforehand extracts any excess water and ensures that they roast well, with good caramelization. If they are not salted, they could end up 'stewing' in the natural liquid that is released as they cook.

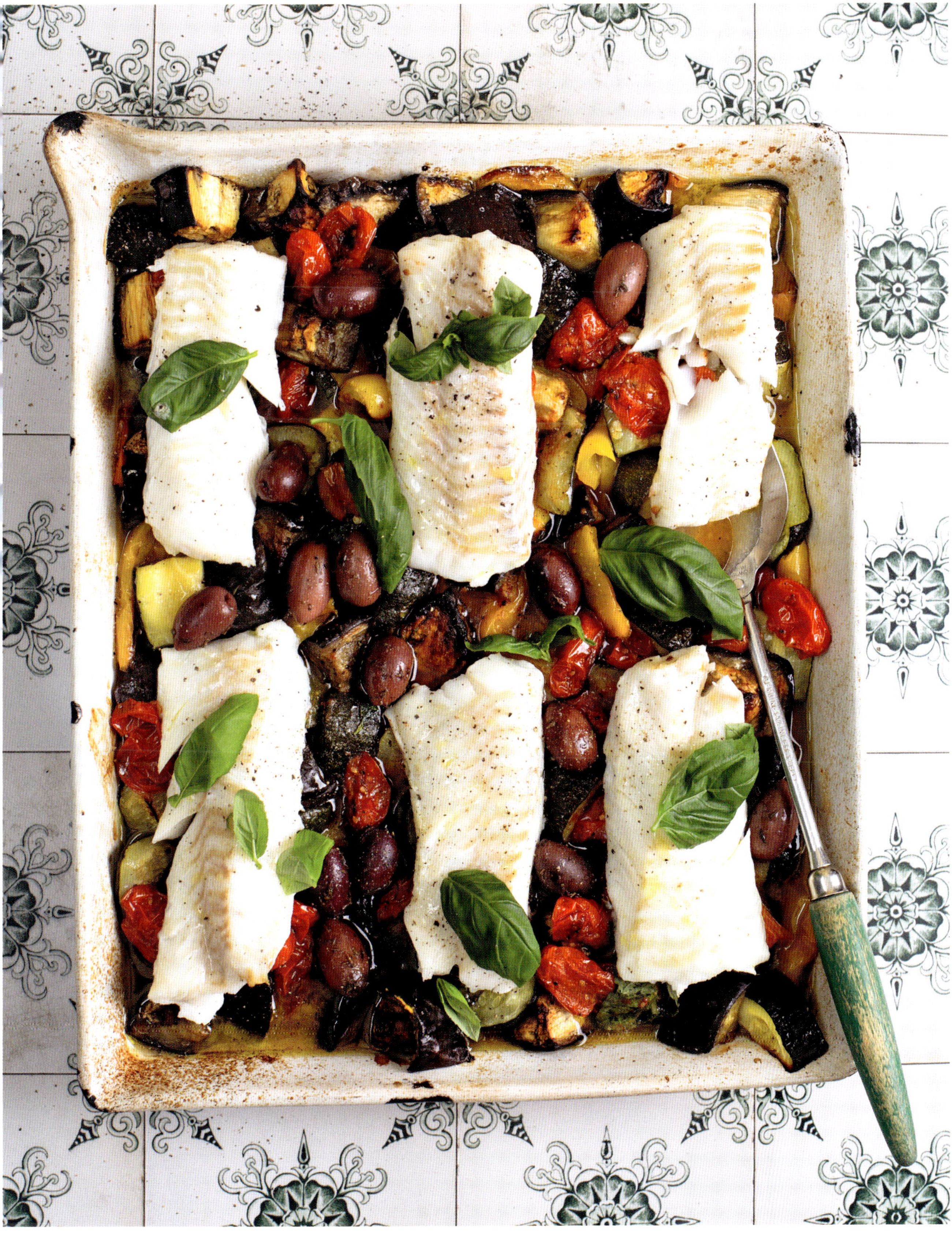

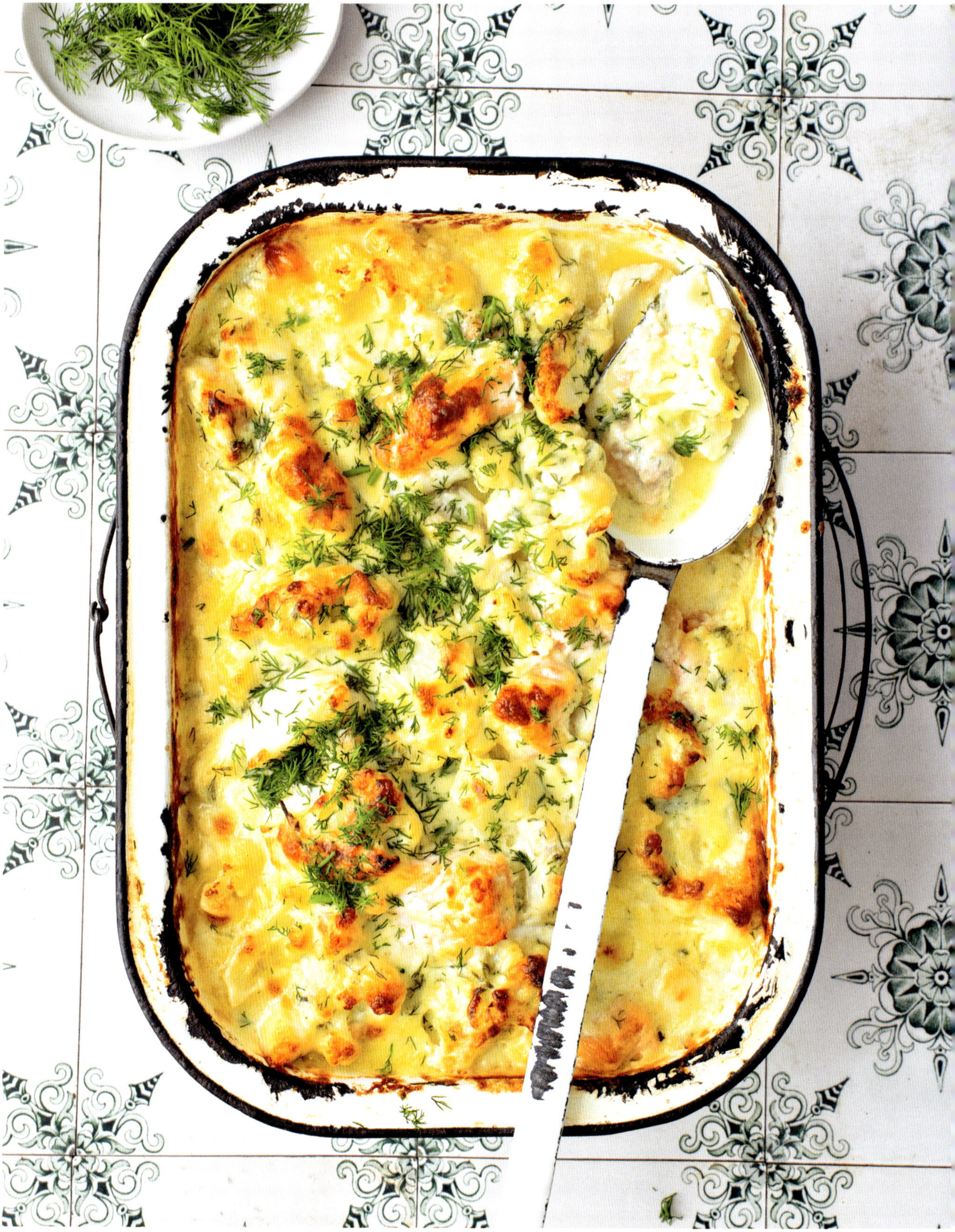

CREAMY FISH PIE

Use a combination of hake and rainbow trout for a family meal, or splash out on fresh salmon for a special occasion.

200 g fresh hake

200 g rainbow trout

Salt to taste

100 g smoked trout ribbons, cut into bite-sized pieces

500 g steamed cauliflower florets (*see Note*)

Lemon wedges, for serving

CHEESE, MUSTARD AND HERB SAUCE

3 Tbsp butter

2 cups grated Cheddar cheese

1½ cups (375 g) crème fraîche

2 Tbsp Dijon mustard

Juice and grated zest of 1 lemon

1 Tbsp finely chopped dill, plus extra for serving

1 Tbsp finely chopped parsley, plus extra for serving

2 eggs

MAKES 4 PORTIONS

Note

To steam cauliflower, place 2–3 cm water in a saucepan and bring to a boil. Place the florets into a colander or steamer basket set above the water. Cover with a lid and steam for ± 10 minutes, until the stems are tender when pierced, but still firm. Do not overcook.

1. Remove any skin from the fish and cut into bite-sized pieces. Season with salt and set aside while you steam the cauliflower and make the Cheese, Mustard and Herb Sauce (see below).
2. Combine the cubed fish, smoked trout ribbons and steamed cauliflower florets in a greased baking dish (± 30 × 20 cm, 6.5 cm deep). Pour over the sauce.
3. Cook in a preheated oven at 200°C for 20–25 minutes, until the fish is cooked through and the sauce is set and lightly golden. Remove from the oven, scatter over some fresh dill or parsley, and serve immediately with lemon wedges on the side.
4. To freeze, set aside until completely cool. Cover the whole dish with foil or cling wrap, or divide into individual portions and freeze in smaller containers. Label clearly with the date.

CHEESE, MUSTARD AND HERB SAUCE

1. Melt the butter in a saucepan over medium heat, then add the grated cheese. Stir vigorously with a spatula or wooden spoon until the cheese is completely melted. Remove from the heat and, working quickly, stir in the crème fraîche and mustard until well combined. Stir in the lemon juice, zest and fresh herbs. Set aside until cool to the touch before adding the eggs (if the sauce is too hot, the eggs could scramble). Stir the eggs into the sauce with a fork or whisk until well combined. Keep warm (the sauce is best made just before using).

BAKED LAMB CHOPS WITH PESTO, TOMATOES AND BROCCOLI

5 Tbsp olive oil

3 anchovy fillets, finely chopped

3 cloves garlic, peeled and finely chopped

Grated zest of 1 lemon

12 lamb rib chops

Salt and black pepper to taste

400 g broccoli florets

350 g cherry tomatoes

½ cup (125 ml) basil pesto

Basil leaves, for serving

BASIL PESTO

2 cups basil leaves

100 g flaked almonds

60 g freshly grated Parmesan cheese

2 cloves garlic, peeled and finely chopped

1 tsp salt

½ cup (125 ml) extra-virgin olive oil

MAKES 6 PORTIONS

1. Combine 3 Tbsp olive oil with the anchovies, garlic and lemon zest in a bowl. Season the chops with salt and add to the bowl, tossing to coat in the oil. Set aside to marinate at room temperature for 30 minutes.
2. Steam the broccoli florets until just cooked (see Note) and set aside.
3. Place the tomatoes in a roasting dish, season with salt and drizzle with the remaining olive oil. Roast in a preheated oven at 200°C for 15 minutes, or until the skins start to blister.
4. While the tomatoes are cooking, heat a pan over medium-high heat and brown the chops on both sides in the marinating oil. Remove the tomatoes from the oven. Add the chops and the steamed broccoli to the roasting dish. Pour over the pesto and stir through.
5. Return the dish to the oven for 10 minutes, or until the chops are done to your liking. Scatter over some fresh basil leaves before serving.
6. To freeze, set aside until completely cool. Cover the whole dish with foil or cling wrap, or divide into portions in smaller containers. Label clearly with the date.

BASIL PESTO

1. Combine all the ingredients, except the olive oil, in the bowl of a food processor and process until smooth. With the machine running, add the olive oil in a thin stream, until it is all absorbed. Taste, and add more salt if necessary, then scoop into a bowl and set aside. (Makes ± 1 cup)

Notes

To steam broccoli, place 2–3 cm water in a saucepan and bring to a boil. Place the florets in a colander or steamer basket set above the water. Cover with a lid and steam for ± 10 minutes, until the stems are tender when pierced, but still firm. Do not overcook.

Store fresh pesto in a sealed jar in the fridge for up to one week. (To prevent discolouration, pour a thin layer of olive oil over the surface before sealing the jar.)

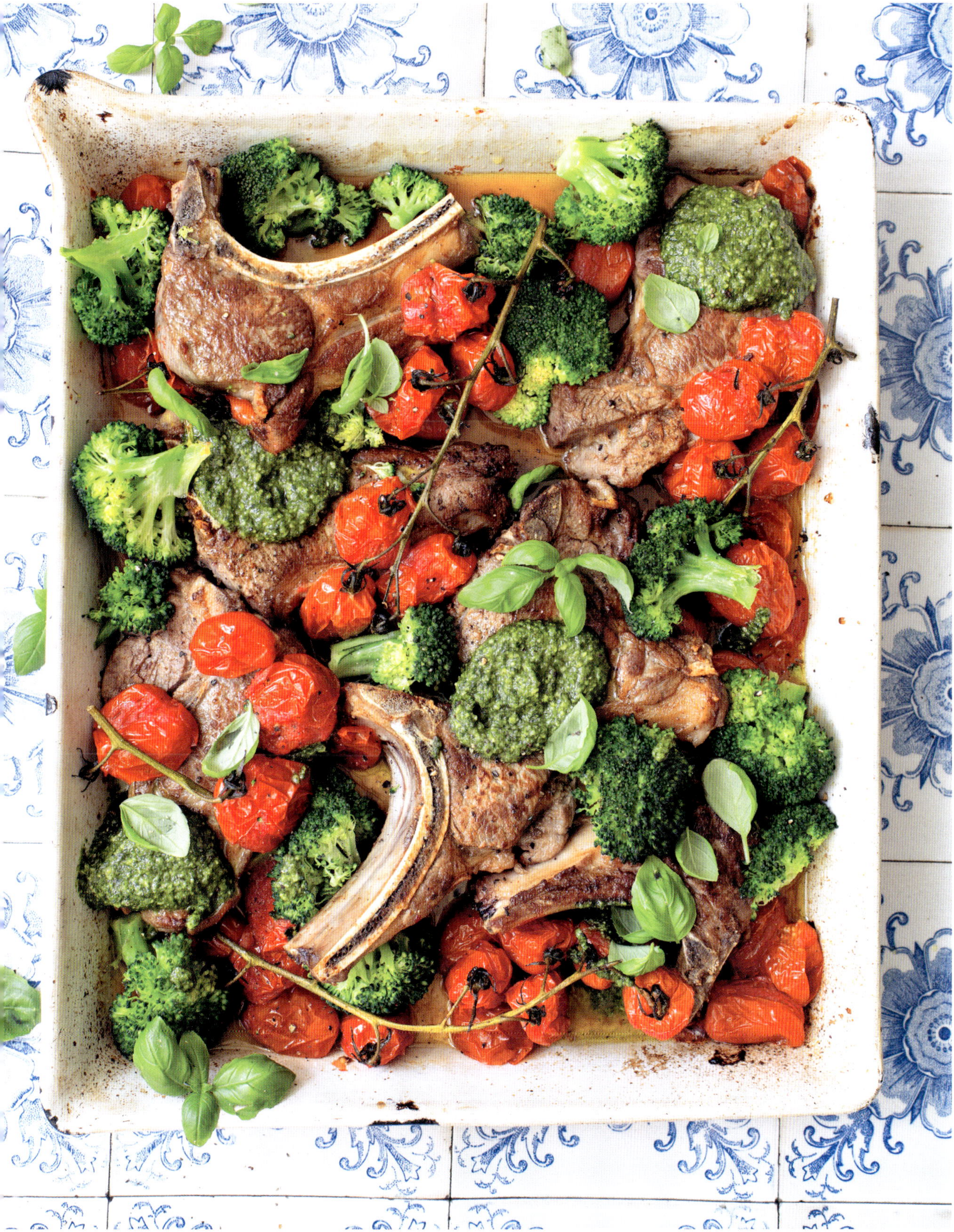

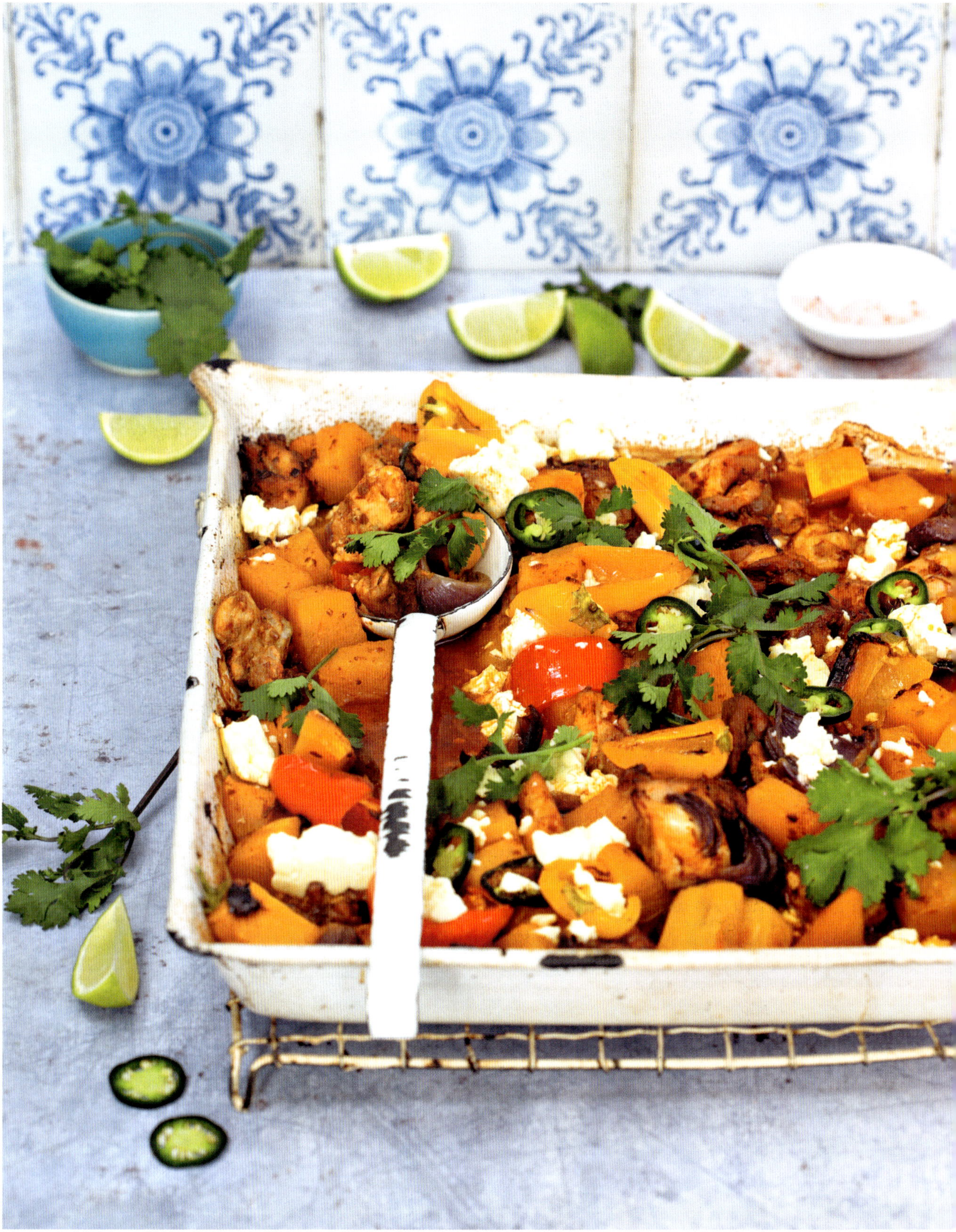

CHIPOTLE CHICKEN TRAY BAKE

1 kg boneless and skinless chicken thighs

Salt to taste

1 can (260 g) chipotle chillies in adobo sauce (*see Note*)

2 Tbsp Smoky Mexican Spice Mix (page 27)

4 Tbsp olive oil

3 cloves garlic, peeled and finely chopped

1 jalapeño chilli, finely chopped

400 g pumpkin or butternut, cubed

2 red onions, peeled and cut into wedges

1 each green, red and yellow peppers, seeds removed and roughly chopped

200 g feta cheese

Coriander leaves, for garnish

MAKES 8 PORTIONS

Notes

Chipotle chillies in adobo sauce are dried, smoked jalapeños in a slightly tart, savoury sauce that includes garlic and herbs. Find them at supermarkets or specialist food stores. You can also use homemade Spicy Chipotle Marinade (page 37).

If you intend to freeze half the batch, stir cauli rice or basmati rice into the dish before freezing. That way, you'll have a complete meal for another day.

1. Cut the chicken into bite-sized pieces and season with salt to taste. Chop the chipotle chillies and place in a bowl, along with the sauce from the can. Add the spice mix and half the olive oil and stir to combine. Add the chicken to the bowl and toss or stir to coat in the mixture, then set aside.

2. Combine the remaining olive oil with the garlic and jalapeño chilli in a small bowl.

3. Place the pumpkin or butternut cubes, onions and peppers in a roasting pan. Season with salt and drizzle over the garlic-jalapeño oil. Roast in a preheated oven at 200°C for 35 minutes, or until the pumpkin is tender.

4. Heat a pan over medium heat and pan-fry the chicken for 5–6 minutes, until golden on all sides (do this in batches if necessary).

5. Remove the roasting pan from the oven and add the cooked chicken, plus any reserved marinade, distributing the chicken among the vegetables. Crumble over most of the feta (reserving some for garnish). Return to the oven for 10 minutes, or until the feta is soft.

6. Remove from the oven, garnish with coriander leaves and the remaining feta, and serve with cauli rice or basmati rice.

7. To freeze, set aside until completely cool. Cover the dish with foil or cling wrap, or divide into smaller containers. Label clearly with the date.

GREEN CURRY SALMON BAKE

4 fresh salmon portions (± 200 g each)
Salt to taste
200 g thin asparagus spears
200 g fine green beans
100 g green peas
1 cup (250 ml) coconut cream
4 Tbsp Thai Green Curry Paste (page 20)
2 Tbsp olive oil
Juice of 1 lime
1 lime, thinly sliced, for garnish
Coriander and/or mint leaves, for garnish

MAKES 4 PORTIONS

1. Season the fish with salt and set aside.
2. Fill a saucepan with water, add a good pinch of salt and bring to a boil. Add the asparagus, green beans and peas and cook for 2 minutes. Tip into a colander and rinse under cold water. Drain and pat dry with paper towel.
3. Combine the coconut cream and green curry paste in a small bowl, mixing well. Spread the mixture over the base of a roasting dish and top with the asparagus, beans and peas.
4. Arrange the fish on top of the vegetables and drizzle with the olive oil. Cook in a preheated oven at 200°C for 10 minutes, or until the fish flakes easily. Remove from the oven and drizzle with lime juice. Garnish with lime slices and coriander and/or mint leaves and serve immediately.
5. To freeze, set aside until completely cool. Cover the whole dish with foil or cling wrap, or divide into portions in smaller containers. Label clearly with the date.

Notes

Instead of salmon, you can use fresh kingklip, hake or rainbow trout portions.

If preferred, replace the green beans with 200 g broccolini (Tenderstem® broccoli), halved lengthways if necessary. Use freshly shelled green peas if you can get them; otherwise, frozen peas are fine.

Instead of coconut cream, you can scrape the cream from a can of coconut milk (use the remaining liquid for making smoothies).

Instead of homemade green curry paste, use a good-quality store-bought curry paste.

If you intend to freeze the dish, cook the fish for less time (± 6–7 minutes), as it will continue to cook when reheated.

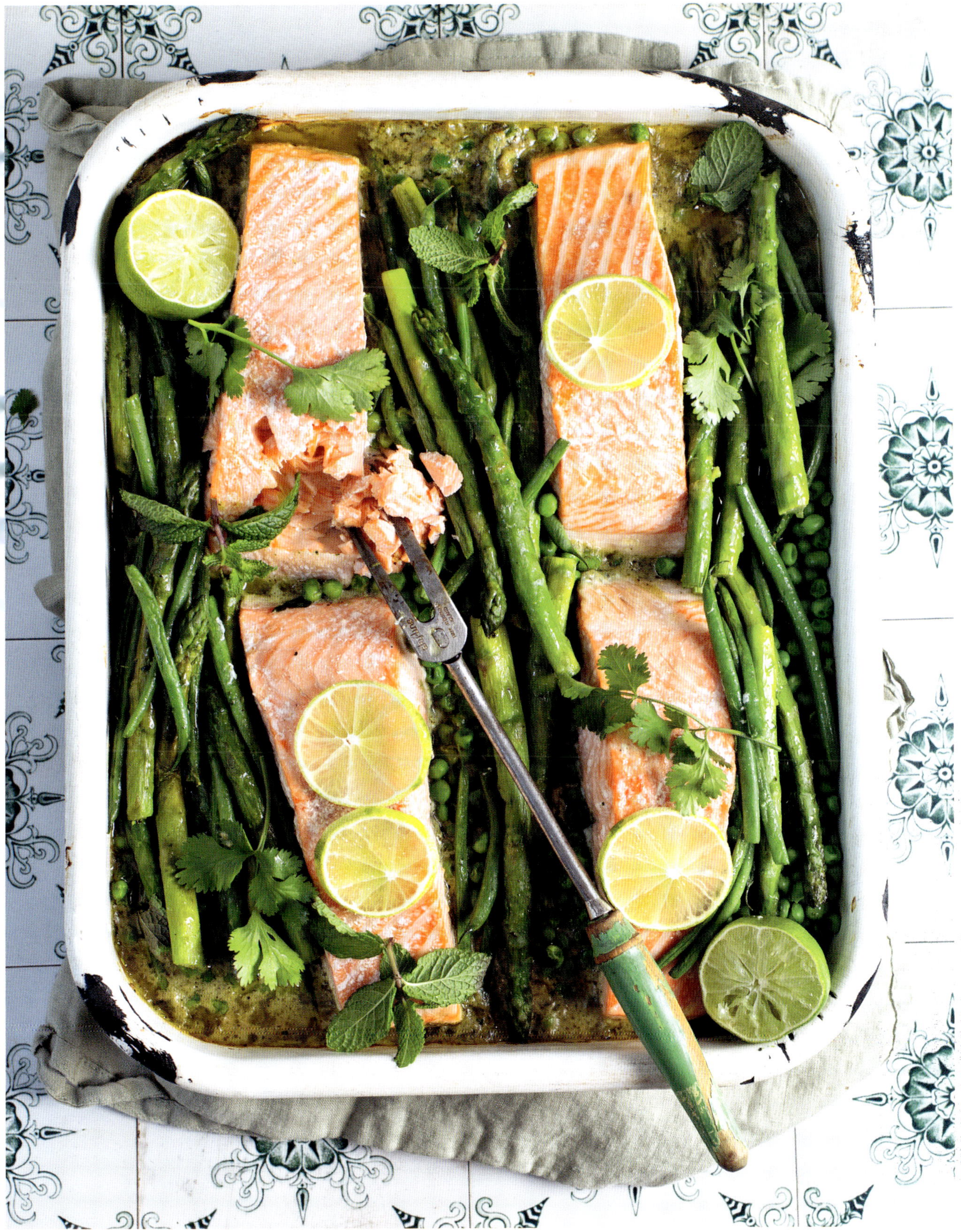

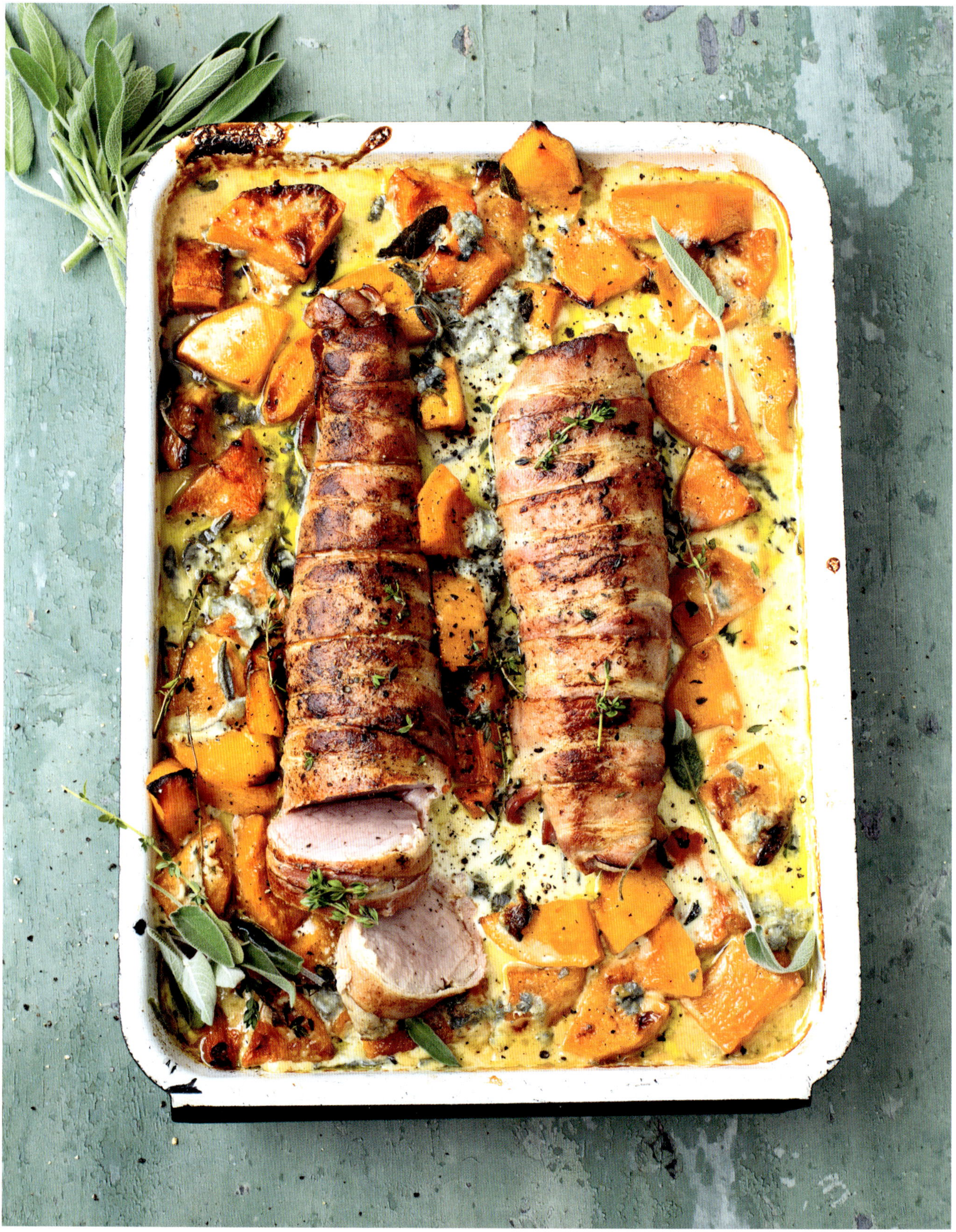

ROAST PORK FILLET WITH CREAMY BLUE CHEESE SAUCE

500 g pumpkin or butternut, cubed
Salt to taste
2 Tbsp olive oil
8–10 sage leaves, plus extra for garnish
4–5 sprigs thyme
2–3 pork fillets (±1.2 kg in total)
4 Tbsp Dijon mustard
12 rashers streaky bacon
1 cup (250 ml) cream
2 Tbsp sweet sherry or brandy
1 cup (±135 g) soft blue cheese

MAKES 6 PORTIONS

1. Place the pumpkin in a roasting dish. Season with salt, drizzle with the olive oil, and scatter over the sage leaves and thyme sprigs. Roast in a preheated oven at 200°C for 25 minutes.
2. While the pumpkin is roasting, season the pork with salt and rub with the mustard. Wrap the bacon around the fillets so they are completely covered. After 25 minutes, remove the roasting dish from the oven. Move the pumpkin to the sides to make space for the pork, placing it so the bacon is seam-side down. Return to the oven for 10 minutes, or until the bacon starts to get crispy.
3. Meanwhile, place the cream and sherry or brandy into a small pan over low heat. Crumble in the blue cheese and simmer gently until the cheese is completely melted and the sauce has thickened slightly. Pour the sauce over the pork and pumpkin and continue roasting for a further 10 minutes, or until the meat is just cooked through to the centre and the pumpkin is tender. Garnish with the extra sage leaves before serving.
4. To freeze, set aside until completely cool. Cover the dish with foil or cling wrap, or divide into portions in smaller containers. Label clearly with the date.

Notes

Choose a soft, creamy blue cheese, like Gorgonzola, Cremezola or Blue Rock, rather than a sharper-tasting cheese like Roquefort.

If you don't consume alcohol, replace the sherry or brandy with orange juice.

QUICK TOMATO BREDIE

I love tomato bredie, but traditional recipes take ages to cook. This is my stovetop shortcut for when I crave the flavours but don't have hours to cook 'slow and low'!

3–4 Tbsp olive oil

8 lamb loin chops

Salt to taste

2 onions, peeled and thinly sliced

4 cloves garlic, peeled and finely chopped

6 cm fresh ginger, peeled and finely chopped

1 tsp toasted coriander seeds

1 tsp toasted cumin seeds

1 tsp toasted fennel seeds

1 tsp ground black pepper

3 Tbsp tomato paste

2 cans (400 g each) whole peeled tomatoes

3 fresh or dried bay leaves

6 sprigs thyme

½ cup (125 ml) plain yoghurt

50 g feta cheese

50 g flaked almonds, lightly toasted

Coriander or basil leaves, for serving

MAKES 4 PORTIONS

1. Heat the oil in a large pan over high heat. Season the chops with salt and brown them on all sides, then remove with a slotted spoon and set aside. (Do this in batches if necessary.)
2. Lower the heat to medium. Add the onions, garlic, ginger, toasted spices and black pepper to the pan and fry, stirring, until the onions are soft.
3. Add the tomato paste, whole tomatoes, crushed with a fork, plus any juice from the cans, and the bay leaves and thyme sprigs. Cook for 20 minutes, until fragrant.
4. Return the chops to the sauce and cook for a further 5 minutes to heat through (the centres should still be pink).
5. Spoon over the yoghurt and crumble over the feta. Sprinkle with flaked almonds and fresh coriander or basil leaves before serving.
6. To freeze, omit the yoghurt, feta, almonds and herbs. Set aside until completely cool, then decant into suitable containers. Label clearly with the recipe name and date.

Note

To toast the seeds, place them in a preheated pan over low heat for a few minutes, shaking or stirring gently until they are fragrant. Take care not to burn them, as they can scorch easily. Allow to cool and then crush lightly before adding to the dish.

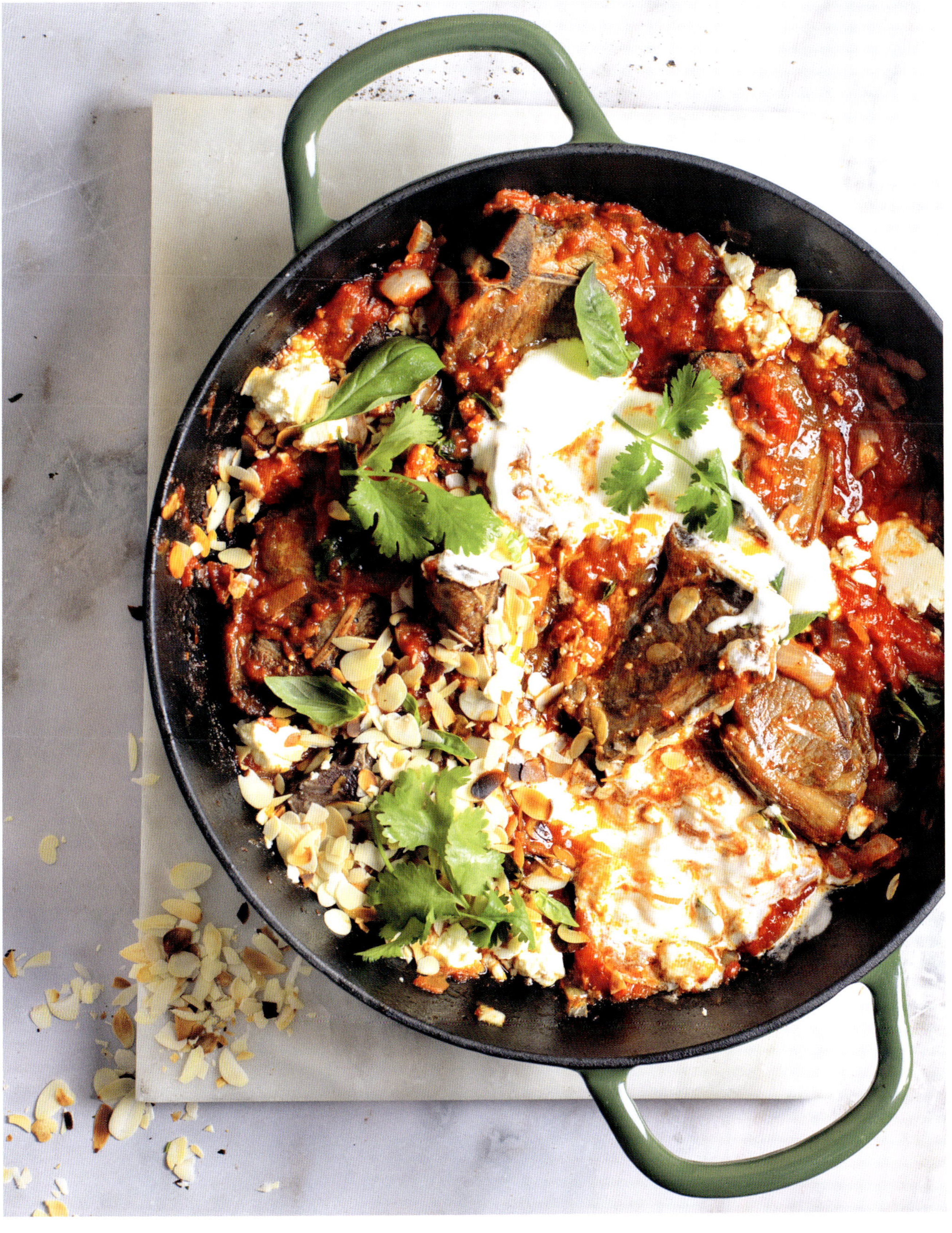

CHEESY CHICKEN AND BUTTERNUT LASAGNE

My basic white sauce is made without any flour, so it is both low-carb and gluten-free. I use it for lasagne, cauliflower cheese, and any dish where white sauce is required. Choose a mild, creamy blue cheese, like Cremezola, Blue Rock or Gorgonzola, for the sauce, and a soft, chevin-style goat's cheese for the lasagne.

3 Tbsp butter

600 g precooked chicken, cut into bite-sized pieces or shredded

6 sage leaves

1 large butternut, peeled and thinly sliced along the length into strips

Salt to taste

100 g soft, chevin-style goat's cheese

100 g grated mozzarella cheese

50 g toasted almonds or pine nuts, optional

BASIC WHITE SAUCE

3 Tbsp butter

2 cups grated Cheddar cheese

1½ cups crème fraîche

100 g mild creamy blue cheese, crumbled

1 Tbsp Dijon mustard

MAKES 6 PORTIONS

1. Prepare the white sauce (*see below*) and set aside.
2. Heat the butter in a pan over medium heat. Add the chicken and sage leaves and cook until the chicken is warm, the sage is crispy and the butter turns nutty and brown. Set aside.
3. Spread a thin layer of white sauce on the bottom of an ovenproof dish (± 20 × 27 cm). Top with a layer of butternut strips, overlapping the slices slightly. Season lightly with salt. Spread half the chicken over the butternut.
4. Top the chicken with another layer of butternut. Spoon over half of the remaining white sauce. Crumble over the goat's cheese.
5. Spoon over the remaining chicken. Top with a final layer of butternut slices and the remaining white sauce and sprinkle with the grated mozzarella.
6. Bake in a preheated oven at 190°C for 45–50 minutes, until the butternut is tender and golden. Remove from the oven, sprinkle over the toasted nuts, if using, and serve immediately.
7. To freeze, set aside until completely cool. Cover the dish with foil or cling wrap, or divide into smaller containers. Label with the recipe name and date.

BASIC WHITE SAUCE

1. Melt the butter in a saucepan over medium heat. Add the Cheddar cheese and stir for 2–3 minutes, until melted. Remove from the heat and add the crème fraîche, blue cheese and mustard, stirring well until combined. (It is important to take the saucepan off the heat before adding the crème fraîche, otherwise it will curdle and split.)

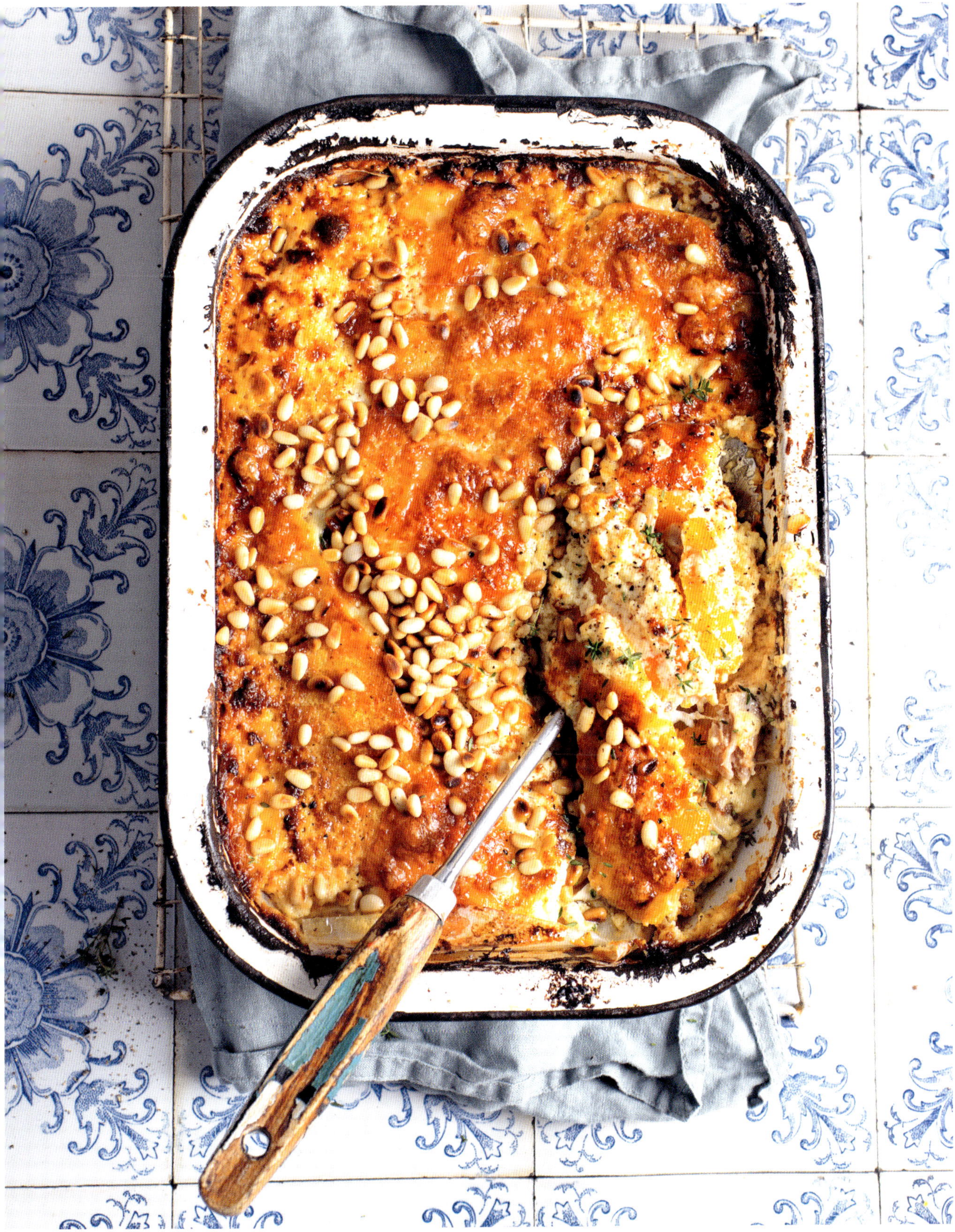

FISHCAKES

Fishcakes make a great lunchbox filler or after-school snack, so freeze them in batches of two or four for convenience, or in larger quantities for a family meal.

900 g white fish

1½ cups (375 ml) Fish Stock (page 61) or water

½ cup (125 ml) white wine

1 lemon, cut into wedges

1 fresh bay leaf

Salt to taste

2 Tbsp olive oil

2 cloves garlic, peeled and finely chopped

6 cm fresh ginger, peeled and finely grated

2 cups raw cauli rice

2 large eggs

½ cup coconut flour

2 Tbsp finely chopped parsley

2–3 spring onions, thinly sliced

Grated zest and juice of 1 lemon

2 Tbsp butter, for frying

2 Tbsp olive oil, for frying

MAKES 24 FISHCAKES

1. Remove any skin and bones from the fish. Place the stock, wine, lemon wedges and bay leaf in a pan over medium heat. Season with salt if necessary. Add the fish and poach for 4–5 minutes, until the fish turns opaque and starts to flake. Remove with a slotted spoon and set aside. Discard the liquid and wipe out the pan.
2. Heat the olive oil in the same pan over medium heat. Add the garlic and ginger and cook for 1 minute, until soft and fragrant. Add the raw cauli rice and season with salt to taste. Cook, stirring, for 10 minutes, then remove from the heat and leave to cool.
3. Flake the fish into the bowl of a food processor. Add the cooled cauli rice mixture, along with the eggs, coconut flour, parsley, spring onions and the lemon zest and juice. Pulse until the mixture is smooth and comes together.
4. Using wet hands, shape the mixture into small fishcakes (± 7 cm across) and arrange on a plate or baking tray that has been lined with greaseproof paper. Place in the fridge for 30 minutes to firm up before cooking.
5. Heat the butter and olive oil in a nonstick pan over medium heat and cook the fishcakes until golden, 2–3 minutes on each side. (To avoid overcrowding the pan, do this in batches, adding a little more oil and butter if needed.)
6. To freeze cooked fishcakes, allow them to cool completely before packing into resealable bags or containers. To freeze uncooked fishcakes, spread on a baking tray and freeze until solid before placing in resealable bags or suitable containers. (Place greaseproof paper between the patties to prevent them from sticking together.)

Notes

If you don't consume alcohol, increase the quantity of fish stock to 2 cups (500 ml).

To make tangy sauce for serving, combine 3 Tbsp Sriracha Sauce (page 28) with ½ cup mayonnaise.

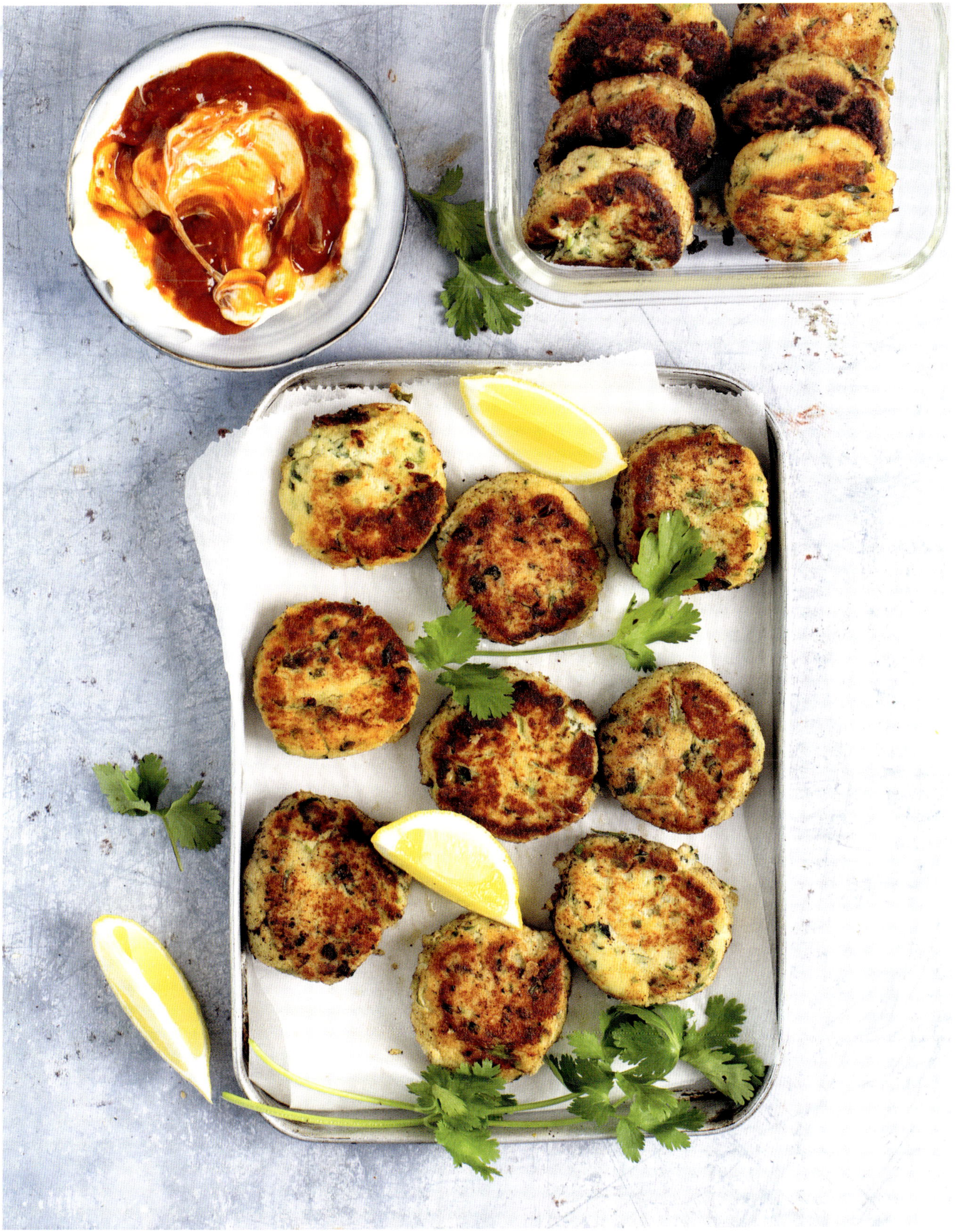

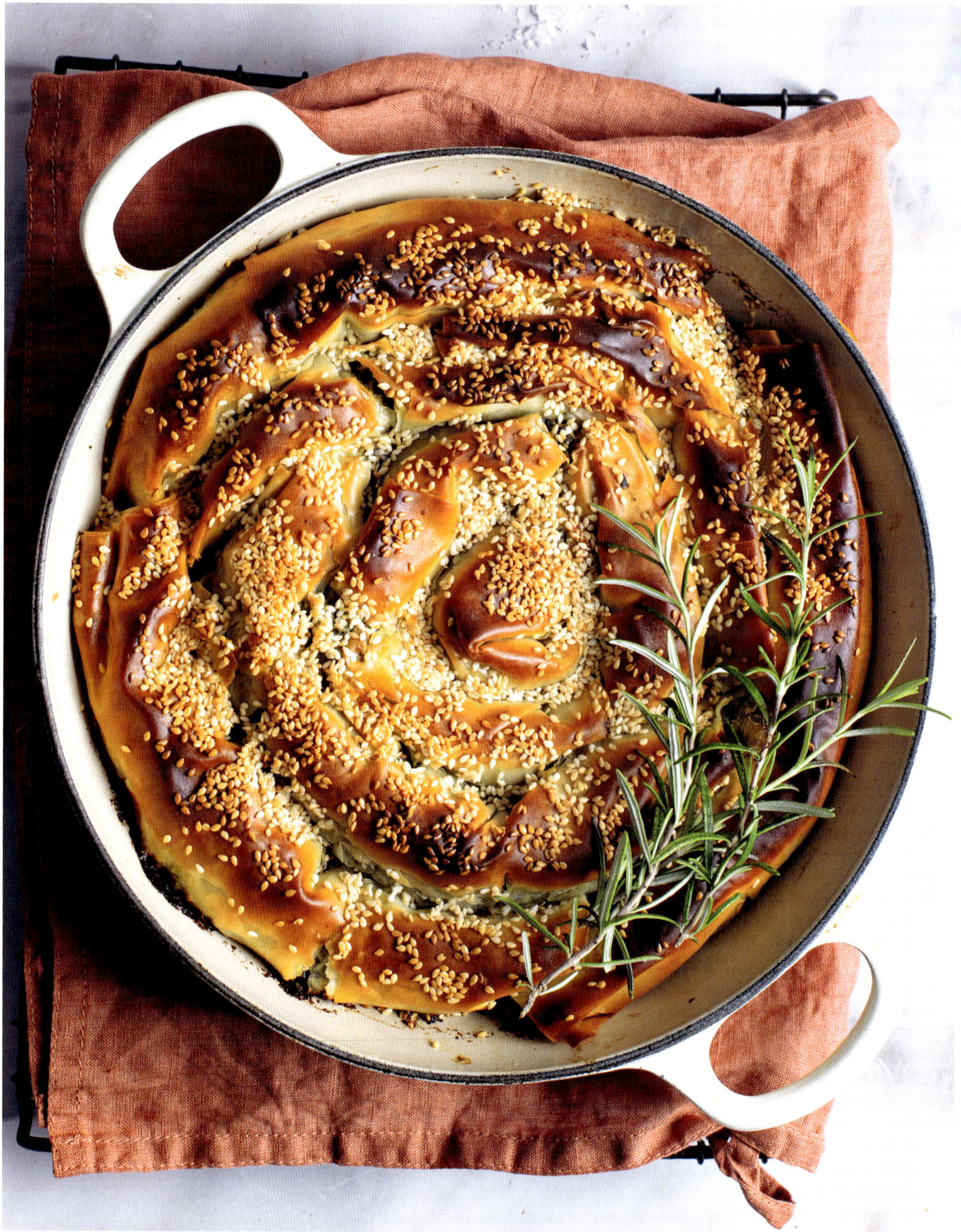

LAMB, SPINACH AND FETA PIE

Phyllo pastry is not low-carb, but because it is so thin, you use less of it. This delicious pie is easy to make if you use precooked lamb or chicken.

500 g frozen spinach
350 g Roasted and Pulled Lamb (page 97)
250 g cream cheese
100 g feta cheese, crumbled
Salt and black pepper to taste
Ground nutmeg to taste
8 sheets phyllo pastry
100 g butter, melted
2 Tbsp sesame seeds

SERVES 6

Notes

Defrost frozen phyllo pastry in its packaging for 2 hours at room temperature or overnight in the fridge. Half a 500 g pack should be sufficient for one pie.

This recipe is not suitable for freezing.

1. Place the frozen spinach in a saucepan and cook until it is defrosted. Place in a colander to drain, squeezing out any excess water with your hands.
2. Place the spinach and shredded lamb in a bowl. Add the cream cheese and feta and stir with a wooden spoon until combined. Season with salt, black pepper and ground nutmeg and set aside.
3. Place one sheet of phyllo on a clean surface. Brush all over with melted butter, then top with another sheet of phyllo, brushing it with melted butter. (To prevent the phyllo from drying out, keep the sheets covered with cling wrap and a damp cloth.)
4. Spoon one quarter of the lamb and spinach mixture along the long edge of the pastry, then roll into a cylinder, brushing the phyllo with butter as you roll. Place the roll, seam-side down, in the centre of a round ovenproof dish (±30 cm diameter) to create a tight spiral.
5. Repeat with the rest of the phyllo and lamb mixture, to make four rolls in total, coiling each roll around the previous one to complete the spiral. Tuck in any loose ends as you go.
6. Brush the pie all over with melted butter, and sprinkle with the sesame seeds. Bake in a preheated oven at 190°C for 50–60 minutes or until golden and cooked through. Cut into wedges and serve immediately, with a salad on the side.

CHICKEN, LEEK AND MUSHROOM PIES

3 Tbsp butter

3 leeks, finely chopped

2 cloves garlic, peeled and finely chopped

100 g each button and shiitake mushrooms, sliced

20 g dried porcini mushrooms, optional (see Notes)

4 sprigs thyme

2 fresh or dried bay leaves

Salt and black pepper to taste

Grated nutmeg to taste

¼ cup white wine or chicken stock

1 Tbsp Dijon mustard

400 g Roasted and Pulled Chicken (page 98)

200 g cream cheese

3–4 Tbsp finely grated Parmesan or hard cheese

1 batch Basic Low-carb Pastry (page 148) or Not So Low-carb Pastry (page 148)

1 egg, lightly beaten

Chutney, for serving

MAKES 8 INDIVIDUAL PIES

1. Heat the butter in a pan over medium heat and cook the leeks and garlic until soft (3–4 minutes).
2. Add all the mushrooms (including the porcini and their soaking liquid, if using), and the thyme and bay leaves. Season with salt, black pepper and nutmeg and cook for 5 minutes.
3. Add the wine or stock and cook until it is reduced by half. Add the mustard and stir through.
4. Add the pulled chicken, cream cheese and grated Parmesan and cook for 5 minutes, stirring, until most of the liquid has cooked away and the chicken is heated through. Remove the pan from the heat and set aside.
5. To make the pies, roll out the pastry between two sheets of baking paper, to ± 5 mm thick. Using a pastry cutter, cut eight 12-cm rounds. Place 2 heaped tablespoons of filling on one side and brush the edges with egg. Fold the pastry over the filling and press gently to enclose, then use a fork to seal the edges. Brush with egg and place on a lined baking tray. Bake in a preheated oven at 190°C for 15–20 minutes, until golden and cooked through. Serve with your choice of chutney and a salad on the side.
6. Freeze the cooked pies in a suitable container or in resealable bags.

Notes

Soften dried porcini mushrooms in water for 5 minutes, then drain, reserving the soaking liquid, and chop finely.

If you can't get shiitake mushrooms, use portabellini or brown mushrooms.

To save time, use leftover roast chicken or store-bought rotisserie chicken, shredded or finely chopped.

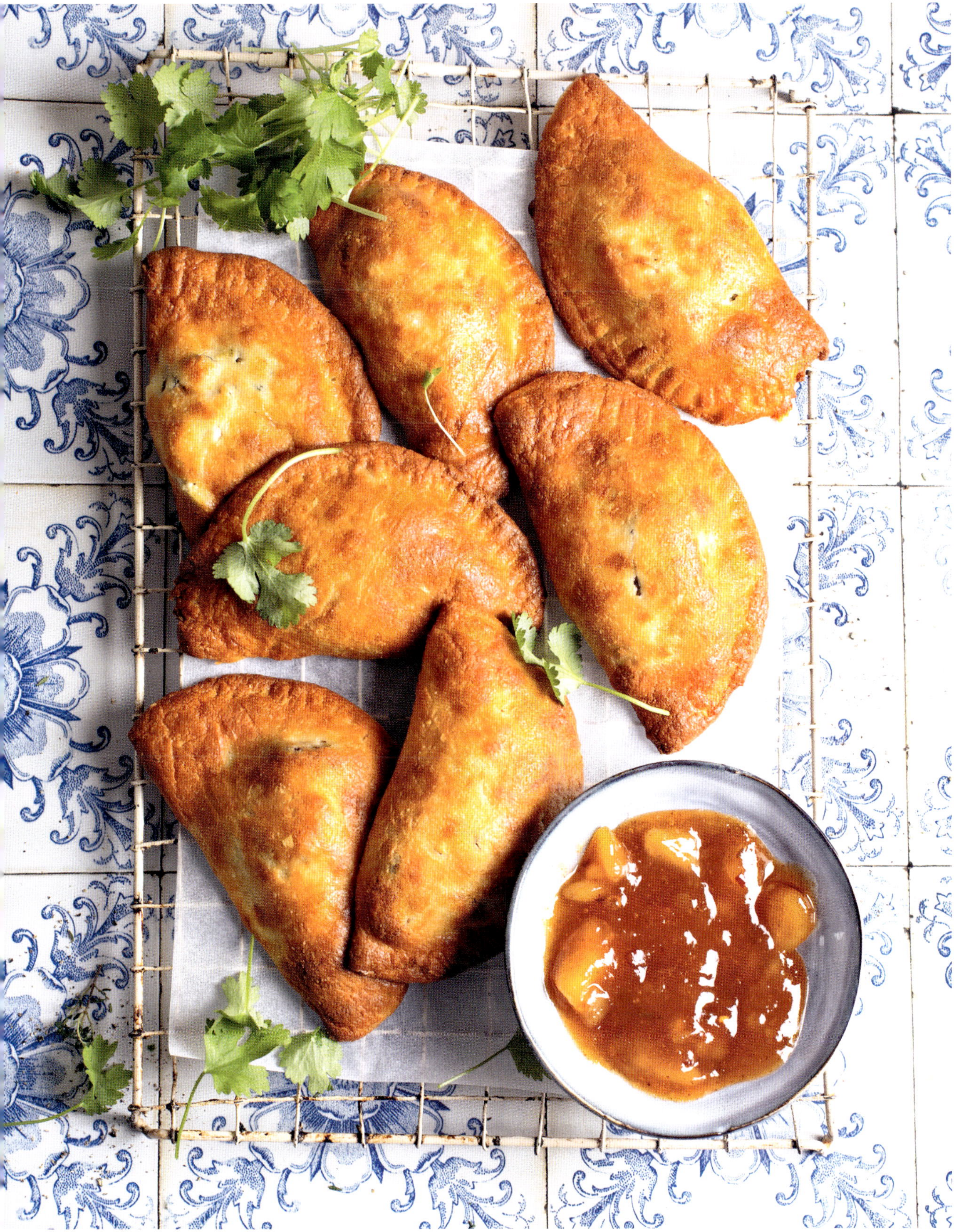

LOW-CARB PIZZA WITH SPICY CARAMELIZED ONIONS AND PULLED BEEF

SPICY CARAMELIZED ONIONS

3 Tbsp butter

2 onions, peeled and thickly sliced

2 cloves garlic, peeled and finely chopped

5 cm fresh ginger, peeled and finely chopped

2 Tbsp Masala Mix (page 26)

1 tsp coriander seeds, lightly crushed

1 tsp cumin seeds, lightly crushed

PIZZA

180 g almond flour

1 Tbsp baking powder

1 tsp fine salt

500 g grated mozzarella cheese

4 Tbsp full-cream plain yoghurt

4 eggs

2 cloves garlic, peeled and finely chopped

2 Tbsp finely chopped rosemary

2 Tbsp olive oil

Salt flakes or coarse sea salt

500 g Sriracha Pulled Beef (page 101)

150 g mozzarella balls, sliced or roughly torn

Basil leaves, for serving

MAKES 1 LARGE PIZZA, TO SERVE 4

SPICY CARAMELIZED ONIONS

1. Heat the butter in a large pan over medium heat. Add the onions, garlic, ginger, Masala Mix and crushed spices and cook for about 15 minutes, until the onions are caramelized and golden. Set aside.

PIZZA

1. Combine the almond flour, baking powder and salt in a large bowl. Set aside until needed.
2. Combine the mozzarella and yoghurt in a glass bowl. Microwave on High for 2–3 minutes, until the cheese is melted, then stir until combined. Add the eggs, garlic and rosemary and stir until well combined.
3. Scoop the mixture into the dry ingredients and mix well (it will be quite sticky). Tip out the dough onto a clean surface and knead for 3 minutes, until smooth.
4. Place the dough between two sheets of baking paper and roll it out to a thickness of 1–1½ cm. Remove the top sheet of baking paper and use the bottom sheet to lift the dough and place it on a baking tray. Using your fingers, make indentations in the dough, pressing it into the corners of the tray. Drizzle the olive oil over the surface and sprinkle with salt.
5. Bake in a preheated oven at 200°C for 10 minutes until lightly golden and starting to crisp around the edges. Remove from the oven and distribute the caramelized onions, pulled beef and mozzarella evenly over the base. Return to the oven for a further 10 minutes, or until the mozzarella has melted. Cut into portions while still in the tray. Top with fresh basil and serve immediately.

Note

If not serving immediately, allow the pizza to cool completely before cutting into squares or slices and placing in individual resealable bags. Store in the fridge for up to 4 days, or freeze.

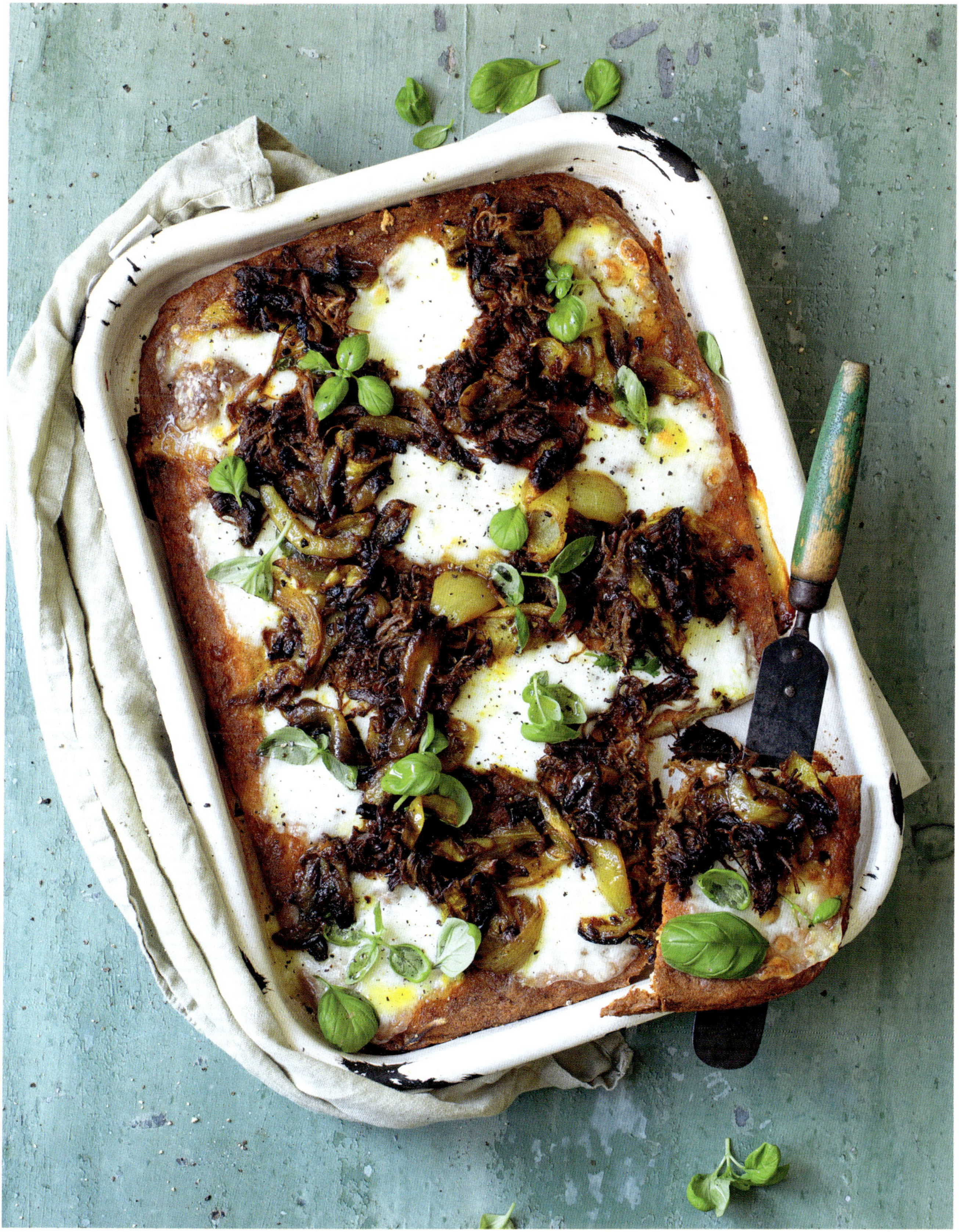

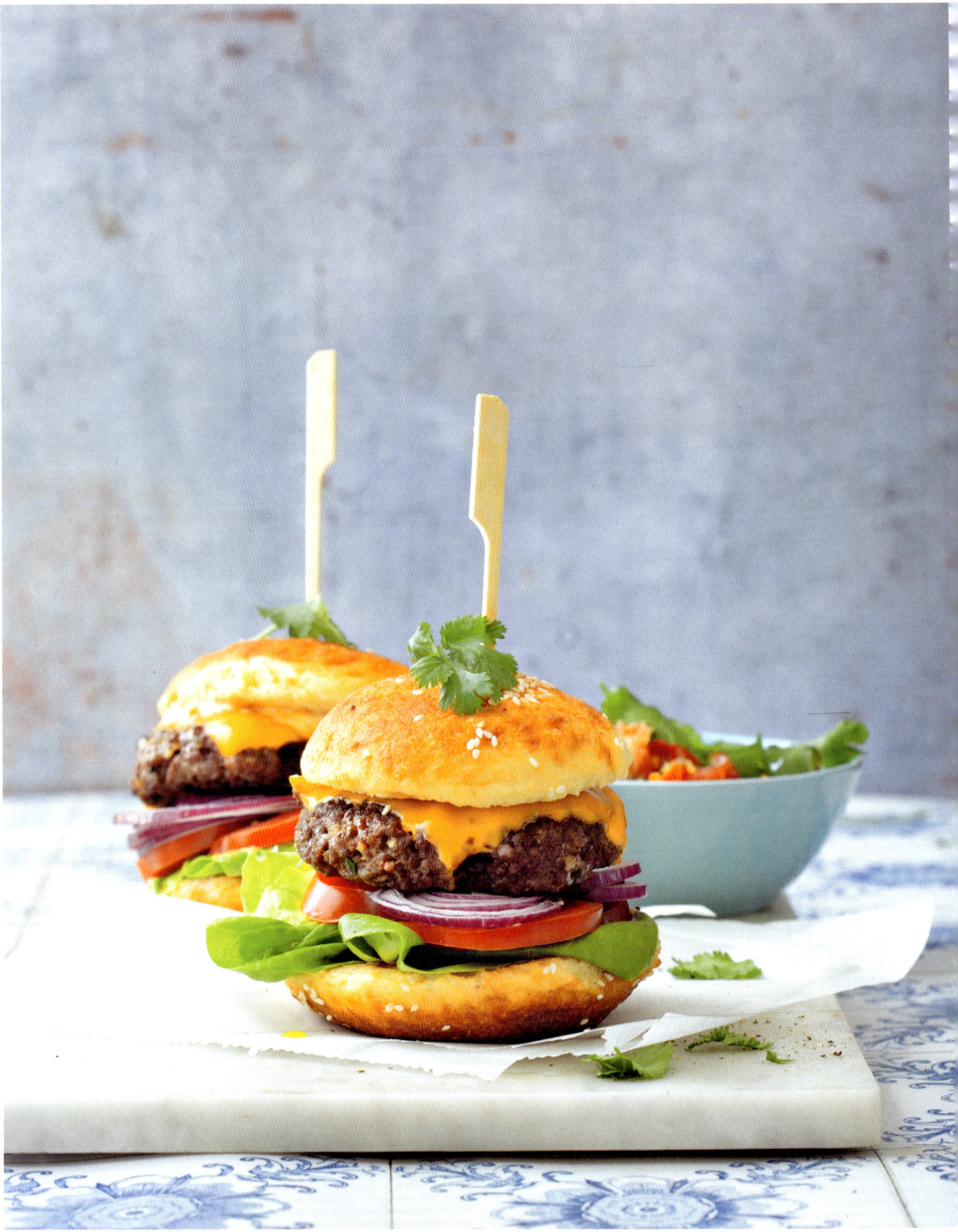

BURGER PATTIES

In order to limit the carb count, I don't add breadcrumbs to my patties. However, adding a small amount of bicarbonate of soda to the meat creates a looser texture and helps the patties brown faster.

4 cloves garlic, peeled and finely chopped
2 jalapeño chillies, finely chopped
Grated zest of 2 lemons
2 Tbsp Dijon mustard
2 kg beef mince
Salt and black pepper to taste
¼ cup full-cream plain yoghurt
100 g feta cheese, crumbled
¼ cup water
2 tsp bicarbonate of soda
2 tsp lemon juice
Olive oil, for brushing

MAKES 12 PATTIES (± 160 g EACH)

1. Place the garlic, chillies, lemon zest and mustard into a mixing bowl. Add the beef mince in batches, seasoning with salt and pepper as you go, and mix well with your hands.
2. Stir through the yoghurt and feta and continue mixing until combined.
3. Whisk together the water, bicarbonate of soda and lemon juice, and pour over the meat mixture. Using wet hands, gently mix everything until thoroughly combined. Divide the mixture equally and shape into 12 patties. If not cooking immediately, place on a plate in the fridge until required. (Separate the patties with baking paper to prevent them from sticking together).
4. Brush the patties with a little olive oil. Cook in a preheated pan on medium-high heat for 4–5 minutes per side. To braai the patties, place them on the cooking grid over direct medium-high heat and cook for 4–5 minutes per side. (To prevent the patties from breaking up, only turn them, using a spatula, when they release easily from the pan or grid.)
5. To freeze cooked patties, allow to cool before packing into resealable bags or containers. Defrost completely before reheating. To freeze uncooked patties, spread them on a baking tray and freeze until solid before placing in resealable bags or suitable freezer containers. (To prevent sticking, place baking paper between each layer of patties.) Defrost completely before cooking.

BASIC MEATBALL MIXTURE

In order to reduce the carb count, I don't add breadcrumbs to meatballs. Adding a little bicarbonate of soda ensures a looser texture and helps the meat to brown more quickly.

2 onions, peeled and finely chopped
4 cloves garlic, peeled and finely chopped
3 anchovy fillets, chopped
1 jalapeño chilli, finely chopped
1 Tbsp Dijon mustard
1 Tbsp fennel seeds
1 cup finely grated Parmesan or hard cheese
Grated zest of 1 lemon
1 kg pork mince
1 kg beef mince
Salt to taste
2 eggs
½ cup (125 ml) full-cream plain yoghurt
4 Tbsp water
2 tsp lemon juice
2 tsp bicarbonate of soda
Olive oil, for cooking

MAKES ± 50 MEATBALLS (± 40 g EACH)

1. Place the onions, garlic, anchovies, jalapeño chilli, mustard, fennel seeds, grated Parmesan and lemon zest in a large bowl. Add the mince in batches, alternating the beef and pork mince and combining it with the onion mixture before adding the next batch. Season with salt as you go.
2. Stir in the eggs and yoghurt until combined (the mixture should be quite firm at this stage).
3. In a separate bowl, whisk together the water, lemon juice and bicarbonate of soda, and pour over the meat mixture. Using your hands, gently mix everything until thoroughly combined, then continue massaging for another 2–3 minutes, until the mixture is firm enough to shape.
4. Cover the bowl and refrigerate for at least 1 hour, or overnight, to allow the flavours to come together. Using wet hands, shape small meatballs (about the size of a pingpong ball). If using immediately, heat some olive oil in a pan and brown the meatballs on all sides, 2–3 minutes (do this in batches). If making flavoured meatballs (pages 137 and 138), follow the recipe instructions for finishing the dish.
5. To freeze the cooked meatballs, allow to cool completely before packing into resealable bags or containers. To freeze uncooked meatballs, spread them on a baking tray and freeze until solid before placing in resealable bags or suitable freezer containers. (To prevent sticking, place baking paper or greaseproof paper between each layer of meatballs.)

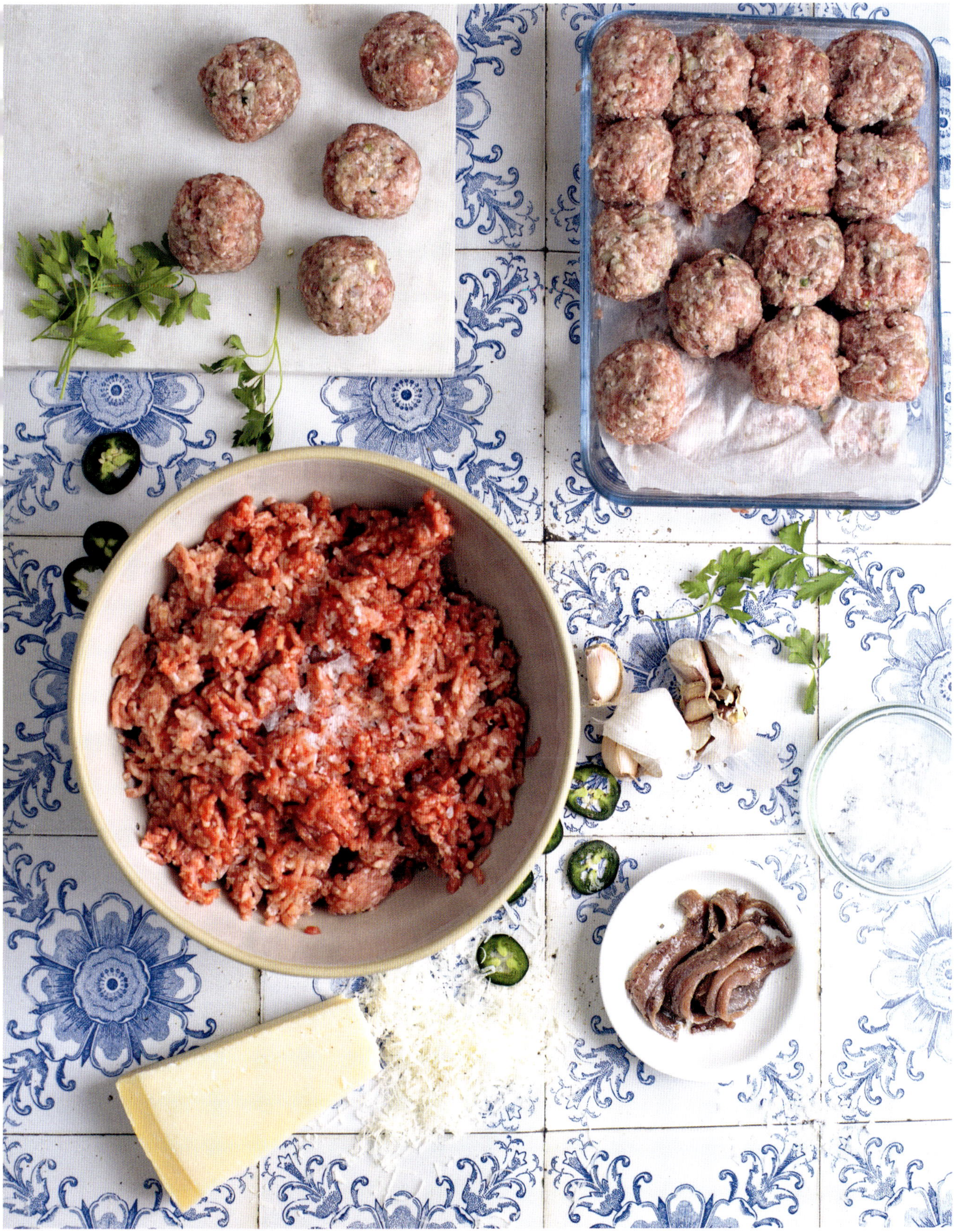

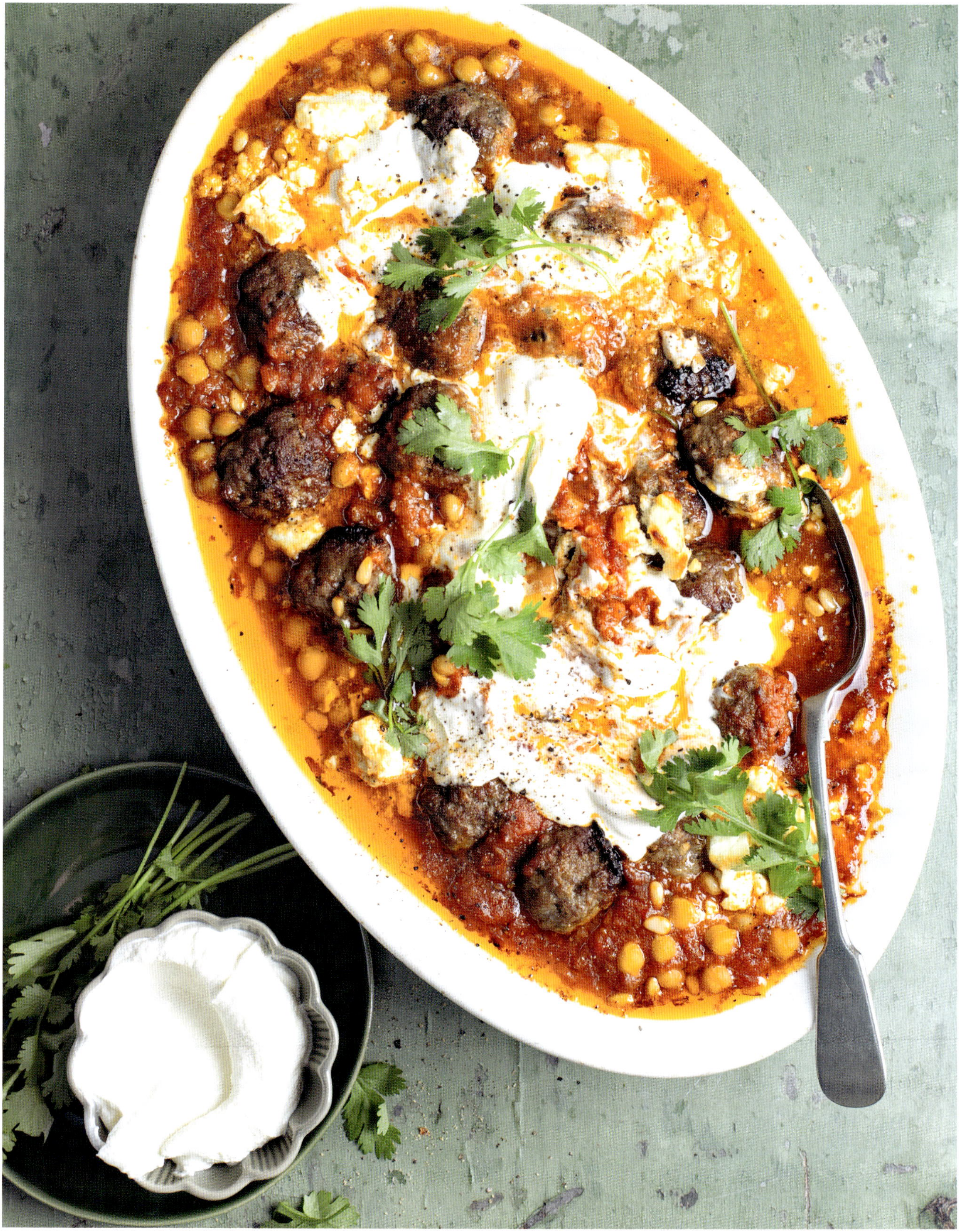

MOROCCAN MEATBALLS

2 Tbsp olive oil

24 uncooked Basic Meatballs (page 134)

1 large onion, peeled and finely chopped

1½ Tbsp Moroccan Paste (page 24; *see* Notes)

2 cloves garlic, peeled and finely chopped

2 tsp ground cumin

½ tsp chilli flakes, optional

1 cup (250 ml) Tomato Cook-in Sauce (page 44; *see* Notes)

1 can (400 g) chickpeas, drained and rinsed

½ cup (125 ml) full-cream plain yoghurt

100 g feta cheese, crumbled

Coriander leaves, for garnish

40 g lightly toasted flaked almonds, optional

MAKES 4 PORTIONS

1. Heat half the olive oil in a pan and brown the meatballs well on all sides (± 2–3 minutes; do this in batches if necessary). Set aside.
2. Add the remaining oil to the pan and fry the onion for 4–5 minutes, until golden and softened. Stir in the Moroccan Paste, garlic, cumin and chilli flakes (if using), and cook for 1 minute, until fragrant.
3. Add the tomato sauce or whole tomatoes and chickpeas. Simmer for 15–20 minutes, stirring occasionally, until you have a thick sauce.
4. Place the meatballs in the sauce (along with any pan juices). Cover the pan and simmer for 10 minutes, until they are cooked through.
5. Remove from the heat. Spoon over the yoghurt and top with the crumbled feta. Garnish with coriander and toasted almonds, if using. Serve immediately with buttered cauli rice or couscous.

Notes

If using frozen meatballs, allow them to thaw completely before using.

Instead of homemade Moroccan Paste, use 2 Tbsp store-bought harissa paste.

Replace homemade Tomato Cook-in Sauce with 1 can (400 g) whole peeled tomatoes (crushed with your hands or a fork, along with the juice from the can).

BAKED BRINJALS WITH MEATBALLS

Brinjals take the place of bread in these low-carb meatball 'subs', which are finished off with a deliciously creamy cheese topping.

6 medium brinjals
Salt to taste
4 Tbsp olive oil
24–30 uncooked Basic Meatballs (page 134)
2 cups (500 ml) Tomato Cook-in Sauce (page 44; see Note)
100 g Parmesan, finely grated
125 g mascarpone cheese
8–12 slices mozzarella cheese
Basil leaves, for garnish

MAKES 4–6 PORTIONS

1. To prepare the brinjals, halve them lengthways and lightly score the flesh. Season with salt and leave to stand for 10 minutes to extract any moisture, then pat dry with paper towel. Place on a baking tray and drizzle with 2 Tbsp olive oil. Bake in a preheated oven at 200°C for 20 minutes, until cooked but not completely soft.
2. While the brinjals are baking, heat the remaining olive oil in a pan over medium-high heat and brown the meatballs well on all sides (± 2–3 minutes). Do this in batches if necessary.
3. Return all the meatballs to the pan. Pour over the tomato sauce or passata, lower the heat and simmer for 5 minutes, until the meatballs are cooked through and the sauce has thickened.
4. Place the brinjals in an ovenproof dish and sprinkle with half the grated Parmesan. Top each brinjal with 2–3 spoonfuls of the meatball mixture, 1 spoonful of mascarpone, 1–2 slices of mozzarella and the rest of the Parmesan. Bake at 200°C for 10–12 minutes, until the cheese is melted. Top with basil leaves and serve immediately, with a green salad.

Notes

If using frozen meatballs, allow them to thaw completely before using.

Instead of homemade Tomato Cook-in Sauce, use 2 cups (500 ml) store-bought passata (Italian tomato sauce).

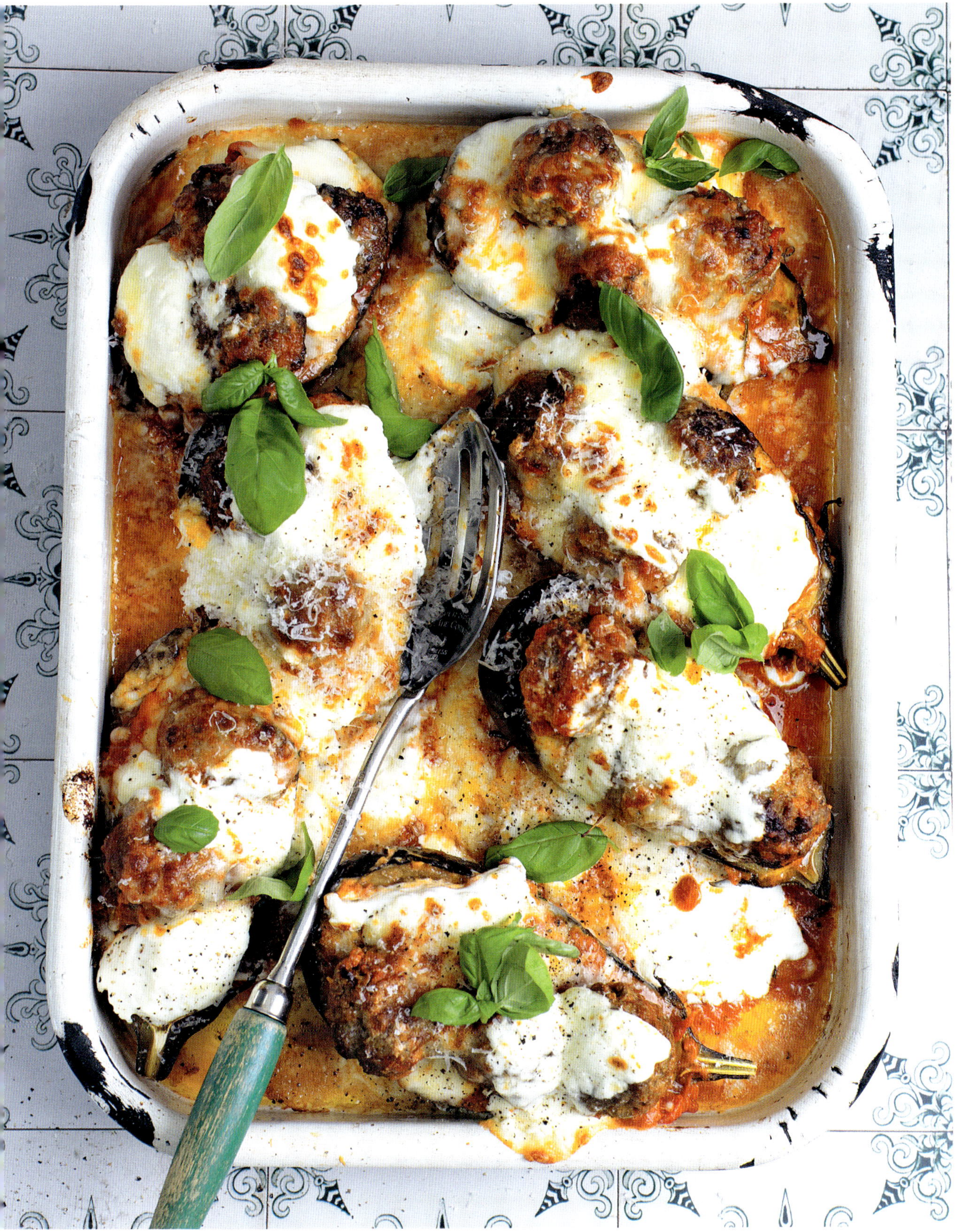

BASICS & SIDES

Because we EAT a *low-carb* diet,
I can't RELY on the AVAILABILITY of
store-bought products, so I make my own
CARB-FREE BREAD ROLLS, WRAPS
and PASTRY, and ensure I always have some
on hand in the *freezer.* This chapter includes a
few of my *family's favourite* SIDE DISHES,
which we eat on a regular basis.

QUICK PILAF

Pilaf makes a great base for stews and curries, and can be used in stir-fries as well. Because we eat a low-carb diet, I make it with cauli rice, but you can substitute basmati rice or quinoa, depending on your preferences.

2 Tbsp olive oil

2 Tbsp butter

2 medium onions, peeled and chopped

3 cloves garlic, peeled and finely chopped

6 cm fresh ginger, peeled and finely chopped

8 cardamom pods, crushed (retain the seeds and discard the husks)

2 cinnamon sticks

1 Tbsp ground turmeric

2–3 cups cauli rice (see Notes)

Salt and black pepper to taste

MAKES 4 SIDE PORTIONS

1. Heat the oil and butter in a large pan over medium heat. Add the onions and cook, stirring, for about 15 minutes, until soft and translucent. Stir in the garlic, ginger and spices, and cook for 2–3 minutes.
2. Add the cauli rice and continue cooking, stirring frequently, for 10 minutes, until tender and all the flavours have come together. Season to taste and serve warm.

Notes

To prepare homemade cauli-rice, grate a whole head of cauliflower on the coarse side of a box grater (this results in a fluffy texture). If preferred, you can use a food processor, but the texture will be more like couscous.

Instead of cauli rice, use 2 cups precooked basmati rice.

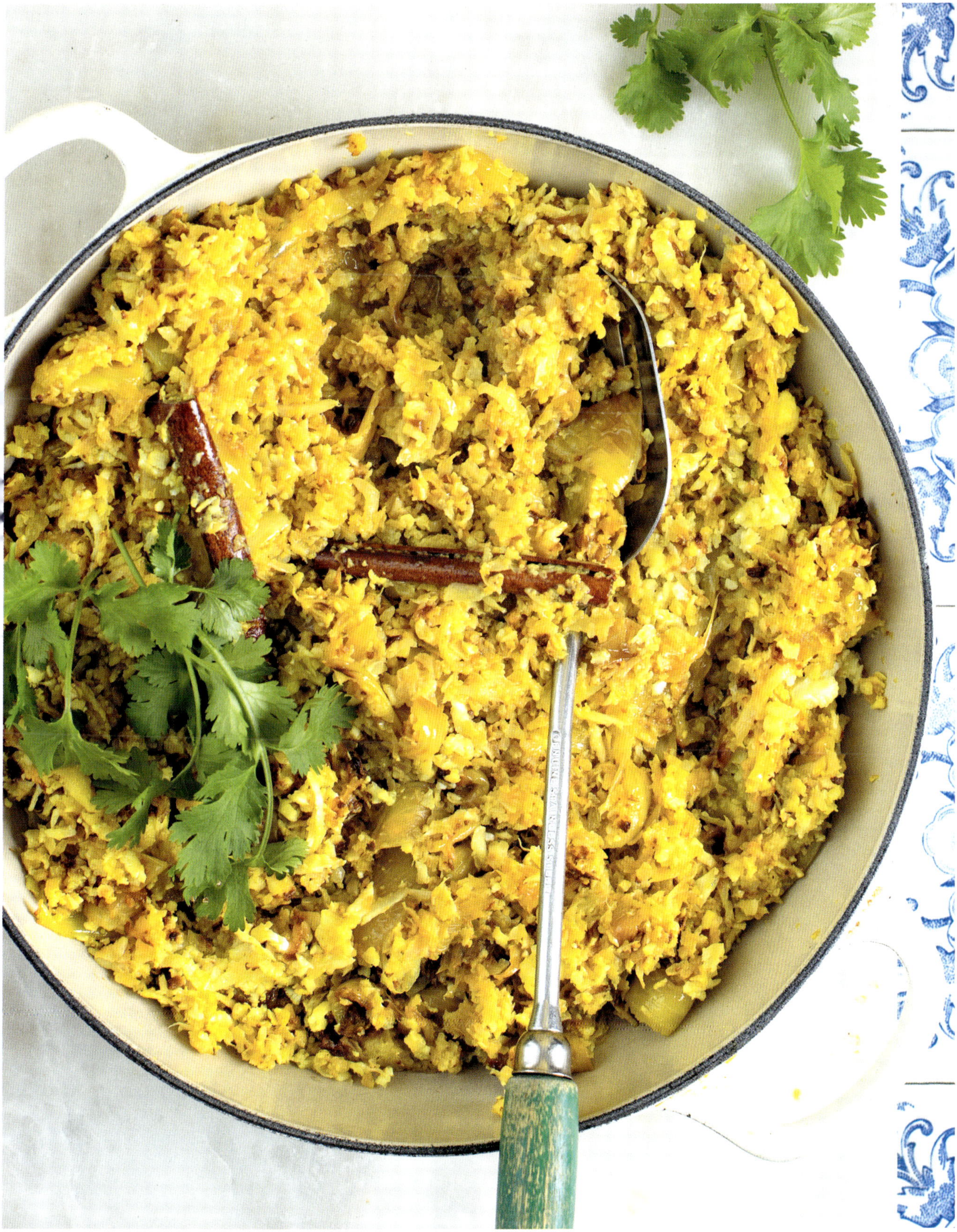

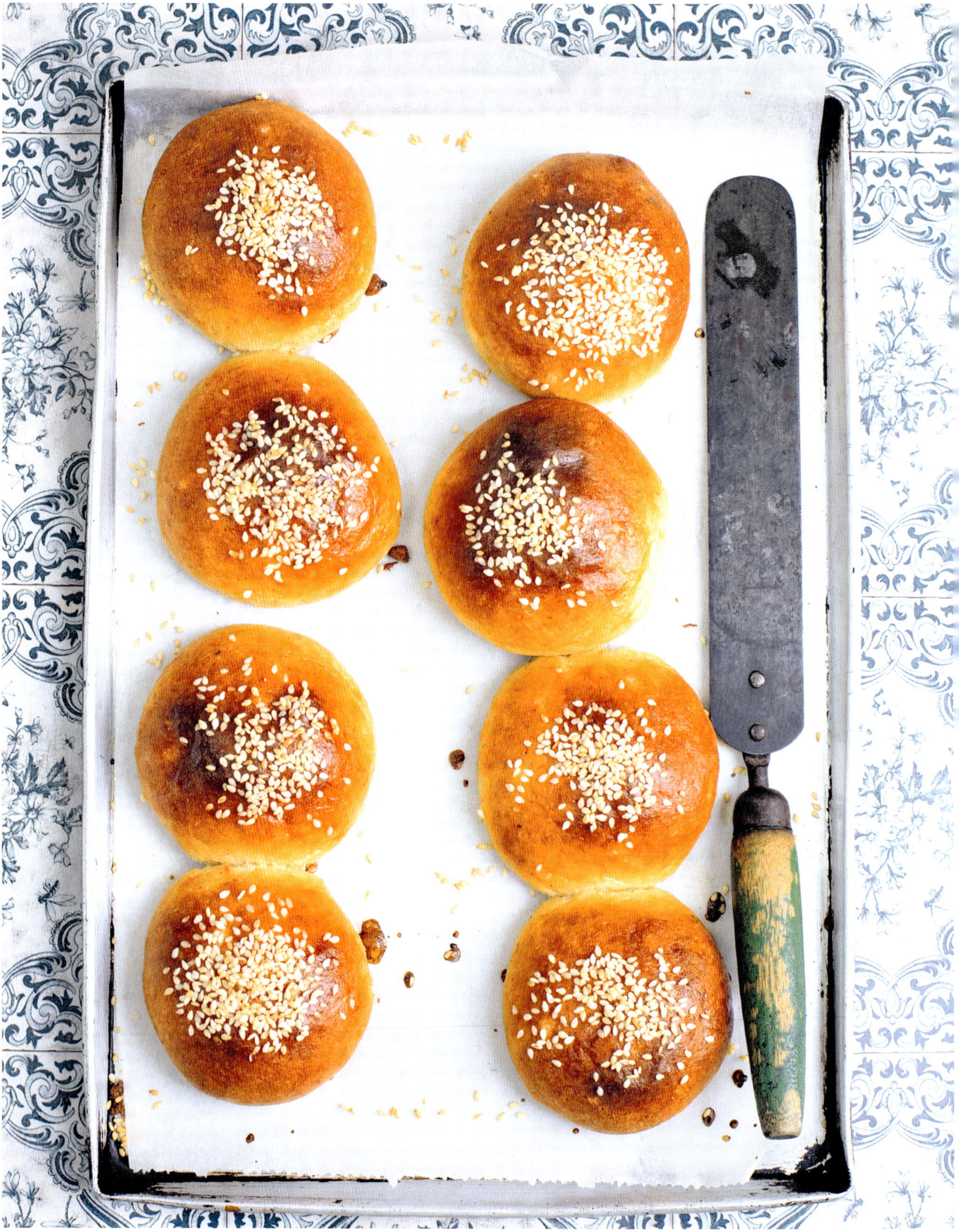

LOW-CARB BURGER BUNS

I always have a batch of these low-carb bread rolls in the freezer. Because almond flour doesn't contain any gluten, the addition of psyllium husk and gelatine gives the rolls structure, allowing them to rise.

150 g almond flour
2 tsp psyllium husk
1½ tsp baking powder
1½ tsp powdered gelatine
½ tsp salt
380 g mozzarella cheese, grated
60 g medium-fat cream cheese
2 large eggs
2 tsp apple cider vinegar
2 Tbsp sesame seeds

MAKES 8 BUNS

1. Combine the flour, psyllium husk, baking powder, powdered gelatine and salt in a mixing bowl and set aside. (Once the cheese is melted, you need to work fast, so the dry ingredients must be ready.)
2. Combine the grated mozzarella and cream cheese in a glass bowl. Microwave on High for 2–3 minutes, stirring every minute, until the cheese is completely melted. Remove and stir until combined and smooth.
3. Add the melted cheese to the dry ingredients, along with the eggs and apple cider vinegar. Stir with a wooden spoon until the mixture comes together, then knead it in the bowl with your hands until a smooth dough forms. Leave to rest for 10 minutes before dividing into 8 portions.
4. Shape the buns and place on an oven tray lined with baking paper, spacing them apart. Sprinkle with the sesame seeds. (These buns don't need to be brushed with egg wash, as the high cheese content allows them to brown easily.)
5. Bake in a preheated oven at 180°C for 20 minutes, until golden brown on top. Remove from the oven and leave to cool completely before serving, or packaging for the freezer.

Notes

Make a double batch and freeze in resealable bags (2 buns per bag, for easy defrosting).

In the absence of gluten, powdered gelatine provides structure to dough.

A version of this recipe was first published in *Lose It!* magazine, but I have adapted it since then.

MEXICAN WRAPS

We eat Mexican food every week, so always have some homemade, gluten-free tortillas in the freezer. The addition of polenta gives the wraps an authentic texture. Although it is not low-carb, the small amount used here will not raise the carb count significantly.

TORTILLAS

80 g almond flour
2 Tbsp polenta
3 Tbsp psyllium husk
½ tsp salt
1 Tbsp melted butter
½ cup (125 ml) warm water

MAKES 6 TORTILLAS

HOT GREEN SAUCE

1 cup (250 ml) buttermilk
2 avocados, roughly chopped
1½ jalapeño chillies, chopped
2 spring onions, chopped
1 clove garlic, peeled and roughly chopped
½ cup chopped coriander
½ cup chopped basil
½ cup chopped mint
2 Tbsp lime juice
½ tsp salt

MAKES 1 CUP (250 ML)

1. Place the almond flour, polenta, psyllium husk and salt in the bowl of a food processor. Add the melted butter and warm water and pulse until it forms a ball. Tip the dough onto a clean surface and lightly knead it to bring it together.
2. Divide the dough into 6 equal pieces. Place each piece between two sheets of baking paper and roll into thin, flat rounds (± 13 cm diameter).
3. Heat a small nonstick pan over medium heat (do not add any oil). Taking one tortilla, remove the top sheet of baking paper and use the bottom sheet to transfer it to the pan, flipping it over. The bottom sheet of paper will come loose as the tortilla cooks, and can be carefully removed without tearing the dough. Cook the tortilla for about 2 minutes, then turn it and cook for a further 2 minutes. It should still be soft, not crisp and dark. (Lower the heat if it cooks too fast.) Remove from the pan and keep warm while you make the remaining tortillas.
4. Fill the tortillas with Roasted and Pulled Lamb (page 97), Chipotle Chicken (page 115) or shredded rotisserie chicken. Add Hot Green Sauce or Fermented Mexican Salsa (page 55), and/or fresh coriander leaves to taste.

HOT GREEN SAUCE

1. Combine everything in a food processor and process for 1–2 minutes, until smooth, scraping down the sides as necessary. Scoop into a squeeze bottle or jar and keep in the fridge for 4–5 days. (Roughly chopping the ingredients first reduces the chance of ending up with chunks in the sauce!)

Notes

To freeze tortillas, pack into resealable bags, keeping them flat. Freeze for up to 4 weeks. Reheat from frozen in a nonstick pan over medium heat.

A version of the tortilla recipe was previously published in *Lose It!* magazine.

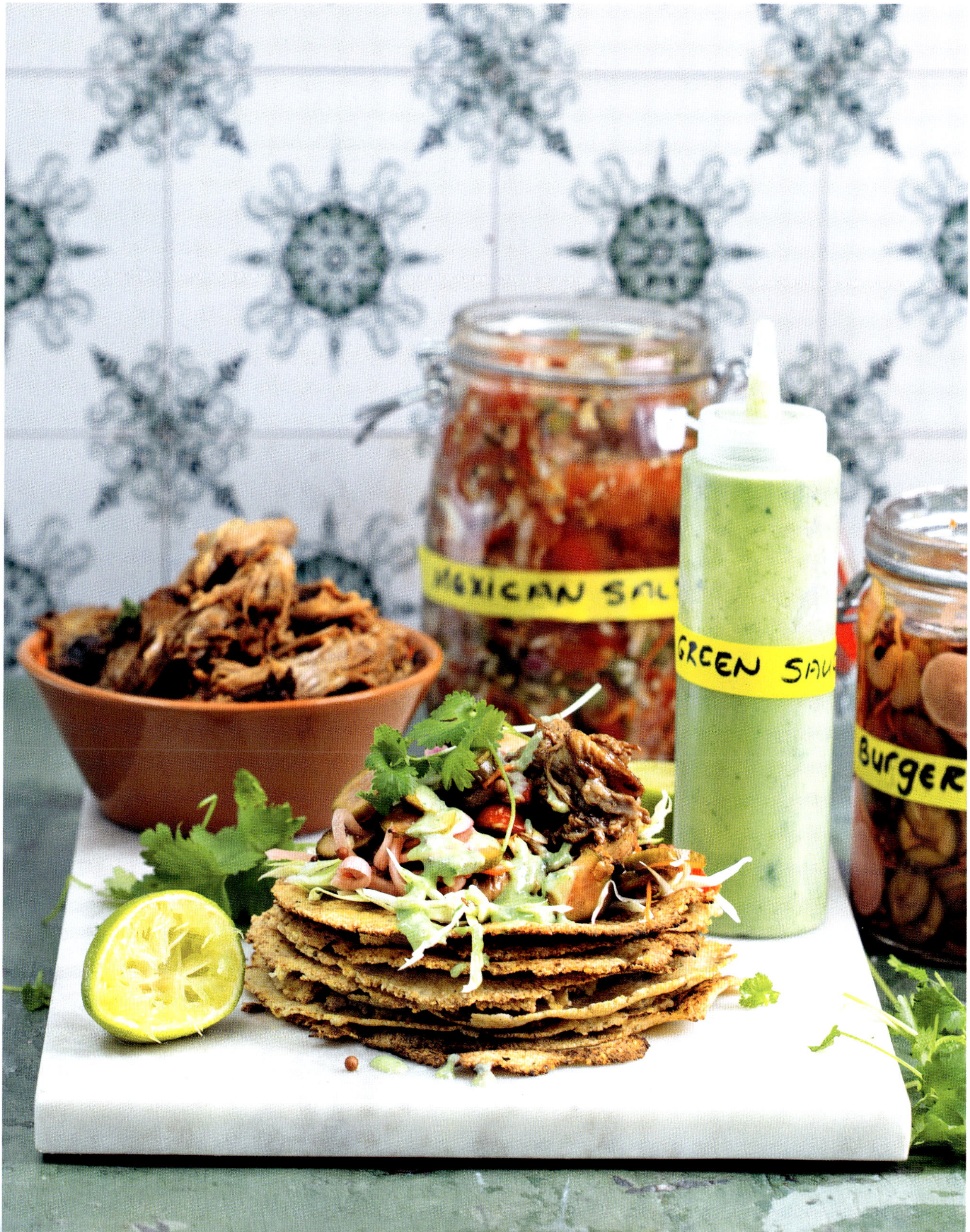
GREEN SAU
Burger

BASIC LOW-CARB PASTRY

120 g (1 cup) almond flour
2 Tbsp powdered gelatine
2 tsp baking powder
½ tsp salt
350 g mozzarella cheese, grated
2 Tbsp double-cream yoghurt
2 large eggs
2 tsp apple cider vinegar
2 cloves garlic, finely chopped

MAKES ENOUGH FOR 1 FAMILY-SIZED PIE OR 6 INDIVIDUAL PIES

Notes

The inclusion of cheese and garlic makes this pastry ideal for savoury dishes.

Because almond flour is gluten-free, powdered gelatine provides structure to dough.

The recipe is easily doubled. Divide the pastry and wrap each portion in a double layer of cling wrap. Freeze for up to 4 weeks.

1. Combine the almond flour, powdered gelatine, baking powder and salt in a bowl and set aside.
2. Place the mozzarella and yoghurt in a glass bowl and microwave on High for 2–3 minutes, until melted. Stir to combine. Add the eggs, apple cider vinegar and chopped garlic and mix well with a wooden spoon or whisk.
3. Add the cheese mixture to the dry ingredients and mix with a wooden spoon until the dough comes together in a ball. Tip out the dough onto a clean surface and knead by hand for 2–3 minutes, until smooth. (Sprinkle the dough with a little extra almond flour if it gets too sticky.)
4. Divide the dough in half and flatten into 2 discs. If not using immediately, wrap each disc in cling wrap or baking paper and place in a resealable bag. Store in the fridge for up to 3 days, or freeze for up to 4 weeks (defrost fully in the fridge or at room temperature before using).

NOT SO LOW-CARB PASTRY

120 g (1 cup) cake wheat flour
225 g cold butter, cubed
250 g medium-fat cream cheese
½ tsp salt

MAKES ENOUGH FOR 1 FAMILY-SIZED PIE OR 6 INDIVIDUAL PIES

1. Place all the ingredients in a food processor and pulse until it comes together in a ball. Tip the dough onto a work surface and lightly knead until there is no longer any visible butter or flour. Using the palm of your hand, flatten the dough into a disc. Wrap in baking paper and cling wrap, ensuring it is well sealed, and place in the fridge for 30 minutes to rest. If not using immediately, store in the fridge for up to 4 days or freeze for up to 4 weeks (defrost fully in the fridge or at room temperature before using).

LOW CARB PASTRY

SOFT POLENTA

Although this is not a low-carb recipe, I make polenta for special occasions and entertaining. It is the perfect accompaniment to slow-cooked stews.

1 litre cold tap water
2 cups (500 ml) full-cream milk
2 cups (500 ml) pouring cream
2 tsp salt
250 g polenta
½ cup finely grated Parmesan cheese
3–4 Tbsp butter, cubed

MAKES 8 PORTIONS

1. Place the water, milk and cream in a large saucepan over medium heat, and bring to a boil (there is no need to stir it). Season with the salt.
2. Add the polenta in a thin stream, while stirring. Reduce the heat to low and simmer, stirring two or three times, for 30 minutes, until all the liquid has been absorbed and the polenta has the texture of soft porridge.
3. Remove from the heat. Stir in the grated Parmesan and butter and serve immediately.

CREAMY VEGETABLE MASH

This is our low-carb alternative to mashed potatoes, which I serve with stews and ragus. You can use any combination of cauliflower, pumpkin, turnips and/or celeriac.

2–3 Tbsp butter
500 g cauliflower or pumpkin, cubed
1 tsp salt
½ cup pouring cream
½ cup finely grated Parmesan cheese

MAKES 4 PORTIONS

1. Melt the butter in a saucepan over medium heat. Add the cubed vegetables and season with the salt. Cook for 10–12 minutes, stirring often, until the vegetables start to soften and caramelize.
2. Reduce the heat to low. Add the cream and simmer until the vegetables are completely soft and all the cream has been absorbed. Remove from the heat and use a stick blender to blend to a fine purée. (For a coarser texture, mash with a potato masher or fork.) Sprinkle over the grated Parmesan and serve warm.

EVERYDAY ROCKET SALAD

We eat this simple salad almost daily, as it goes with just about everything. It is important to include leafy vegetables in your diet and this is an easy way to ensure that. Rocket, which falls under the 'bitter leaf' category, is good for your digestion.

400 g baby rocket leaves
Salt to taste
2 Tbsp olive oil
2 Tbsp balsamic vinegar
¼ cup finely grated Parmesan cheese

MAKES 4 PORTIONS

1. Place the rocket leaves in a salad bowl, season to taste with salt and drizzle with the olive oil and balsamic vinegar. Sprinkle over the Parmesan cheese and toss through.

STEAMED VEGETABLES

Green vegetables are an excellent source of fibre, and high in antioxidants and minerals. Steaming retains beneficial nutrients, but if you are cooking a big batch of vegetables, it may be easier to blanch them in rapidly boiling water (don't cover the saucepan with a lid), then refresh under cold running water and drain well. This halts the cooking process and ensures they stay crisp and green. You can also stir-fry delicate vegetables like green beans or asparagus, and add some flavoured butter just before serving.

EACH RECIPE MAKES 4 PORTIONS

STEAMED BROCCOLI AND CAULIFLOWER

- 400 g broccoli florets and/or cauliflower florets
- 2–3 Tbsp plain butter or flavoured butter (page 32)
- ½ cup finely grated Parmesan cheese, for serving

STEAMED BROCCOLI AND CAULIFLOWER

1. Fill a saucepan with lightly salted water so the base of a steamer basket is just above the level of the water. Steam the broccoli and/or cauliflower on high heat for ±10 minutes, until tender when pierced. Remove the steamer, pour out the water and return the saucepan to the heat. Tip the vegetables into the saucepan and add the butter, shaking the saucepan to coat them with butter. Sprinkle over the Parmesan and serve immediately.

ASPARAGUS AND GREEN BEANS

- 200 g fresh asparagus, trimmed
- 200 g fine green beans, trimmed
- 2–3 Tbsp plain butter or flavoured butter (page 32)

ASPARAGUS AND GREEN BEANS

1. Bring a saucepan of salted water to a boil over high heat. Plunge the asparagus and green beans into the boiling water, cook for 2–3 minutes, then drain in a colander and rinse under cold water, to stop the cooking process. Return the saucepan to the heat and melt the butter. Add the vegetables, shaking to coat in the melted butter. Serve warm.

CREAMED SPINACH

- 500 g frozen chopped spinach
- 100 g full-fat cream cheese
- ½ cup finely grated Parmesan cheese
- Freshly grated nutmeg to taste
- Ground black pepper to taste
- Pinch of salt

CREAMED SPINACH

1. Place the frozen spinach in a saucepan over low heat and cook until the water has evaporated. Stir in the cream cheese and grated Parmesan. Season to taste and serve warm.

Note

To freeze steamed vegetables, cool them completely before placing in resealable bags. Freeze for up to 4 weeks. Reheat from frozen.

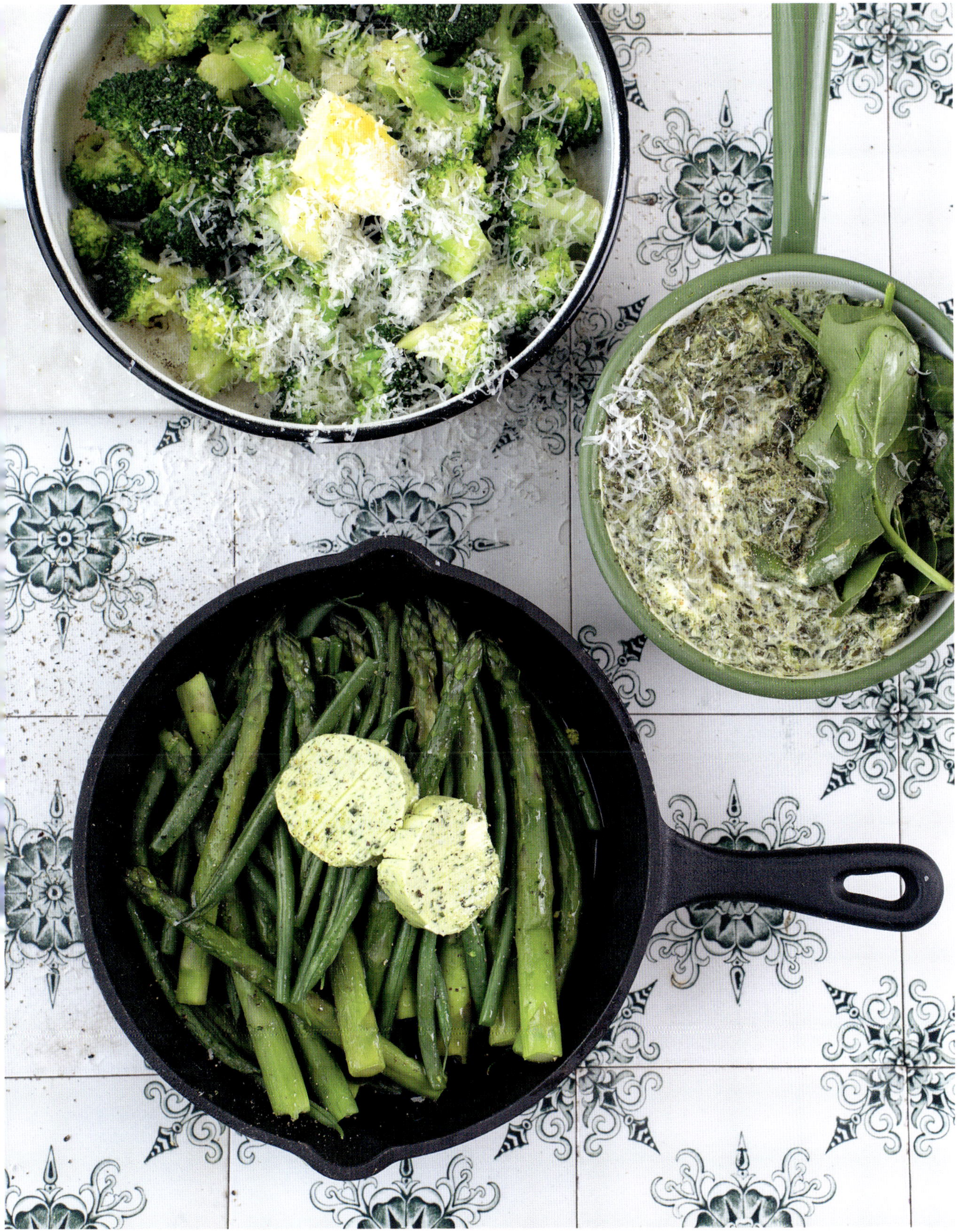

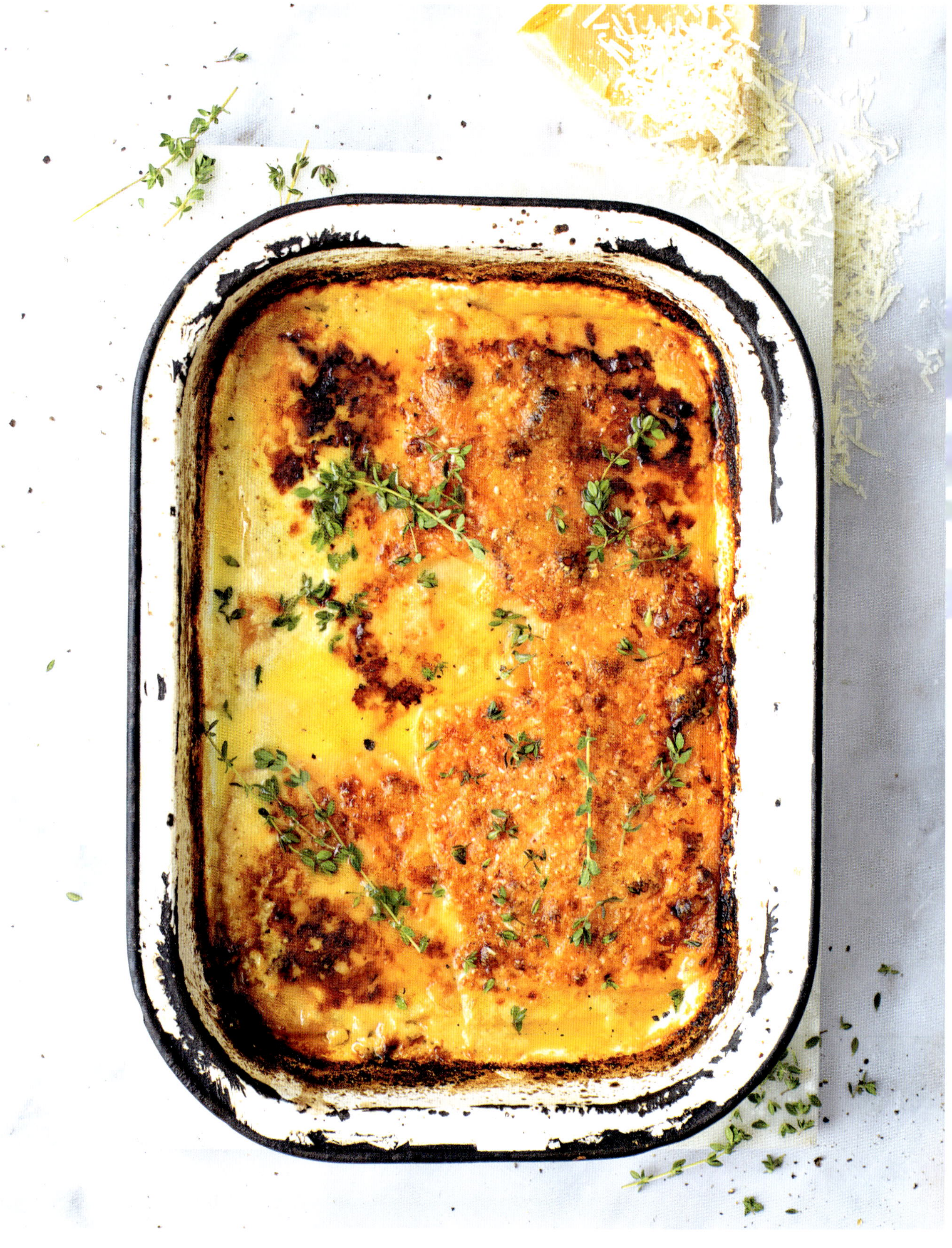

CREAMY GRATIN

I usually make this with pumpkin or celeriac, but you can use any low-carb vegetable of your choice.

1 kg pumpkin or celeriac, peeled and thinly sliced
Salt to taste
2 cups (500 ml) cream
1 cup finely grated Parmesan cheese
6 anchovy fillets, finely chopped
1 Tbsp Dijon mustard
Fresh thyme, for serving

MAKES 6–8 PORTIONS

1. Layer the pumpkin or celeriac in a deep ovenproof dish (30 × 20 cm), seasoning each layer lightly with salt (remember that the anchovies will be salty). Combine the cream, half the grated Parmesan, anchovies, mustard in a small bowl or jug and pour over the vegetables.
2. Cover the dish with foil and place in a preheated oven at 200°C. Bake for 30 minutes, then remove and sprinkle the remaining Parmesan evenly over the surface. Return, uncovered, to the oven for 20–30 minutes, until the vegetables are cooked through and the topping is golden. Scatter over some fresh thyme and serve warm.

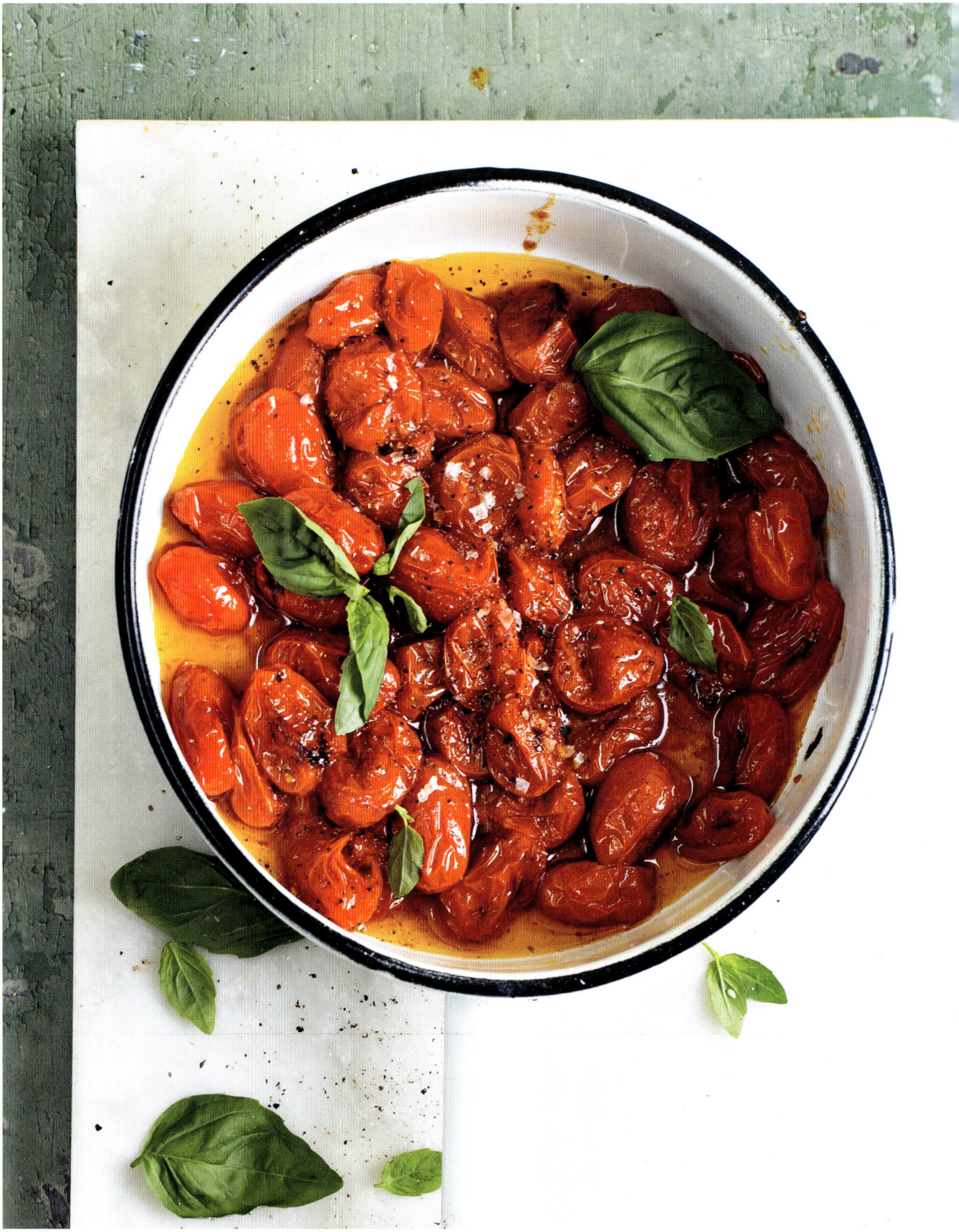

PAN-FRIED CHERRY TOMATOES WITH ANCHOVIES

These delicious tomatoes go well with grilled steak or roasted chicken. I sometimes add blanched green beans, and scatter over basil or rocket leaves just before serving.

2 Tbsp olive oil
6 anchovy fillets
500 g cherry tomatoes
Salt flakes to taste (see Note)

MAKES 4 PORTIONS

1. Heat the olive oil in a pan over medium heat. Add the anchovies, squashing them gently with a wooden spoon. (They will melt into the oil, but they can splatter, so be careful.)
2. Add the tomatoes and season with salt flakes. Cook, shaking the pan now and then, until the skins start to blister. Reduce the heat and simmer for a further 5–6 minutes, until the tomatoes caramelize and become 'saucy'. Remove from the heat and serve warm.

Note

Use salt flakes if you have them, as they help the tomatoes to blister nicely.

INDEX

A, B
Aubergine, see Brinjals
Baked brinjals with meatballs 138
Baked lamb chops with pesto, tomatoes and broccoli 112
Barbecue basting sauce 29
Basic low-carb pastry 148
Basic white sauce 122
Basil pesto 112
Beef
    Bolognaise 86
    Brisket, pulled 101
    Broth 58
    Burger patties 133
    Chinese fried rice 107
    Lentil soup 69
    Oxtail ramen soup 66
    Pizza 130
    Short ribs stew 88
    Sriracha pulled beef 101
    Stew with red wine 88
Beef and lentil soup 69
Beef and red wine stew 88
Bobotie, lamb shank 84
Bolognaise, oven-baked 86
Bouillabaisse 74
Bouquet garni 44
Bourbon 29
Brinjals, baked 138
Broth
    Chicken 62
    Green curry 70
    Meaty bone 58

Burger buns 145
Burger patties 133
Butter
    Lemon and garlic 32
    Sundried tomato and herbs 32

C
Caramelized onions 130
Cass Abrahams' masala mix 26
Cauli rice 142
Cheese, mustard and herb sauce 111
Cheesy chicken and butternut lasagne 122
Chicken
    Broth 62
    Cacciatore 93
    Chipotle tray bake 115
    Creamy paprika 104
    Lasagne 122
    Leek and mushroom pies 128
    Quick curry 82
    Roasted and pulled 98
Chicken cacciatore 93
Chicken, leek and mushroom pies 128
Chinese fried rice 107
Chipotle chicken tray bake 115
Confit
    Garlic 38
    Onion 43
    Tomato 40

Cook-in sauce
    Curry 48
    Mexican 51
    Mushroom 47
    Tomato 44
Creamy curry cook-in sauce 48
Creamy fish pie 111
Creamy gratin 155
Creamy paprika chicken 104
Creamy pumpkin and salmon soup 65
Creamy vegetable mash 150
Curry
    Cook-in sauce 48
    Green curry paste 20
    Green curry salmon bake 116
    Lamb shank 81
    Masala curry paste 22
    Quick fish 48

D, E
Dal makhani 82
Everyday rocket salad 151

F
Fermentation 52
    Burger pickle 52
    Mexican salsa 55
Fish
    Fishcakes 124
    Green curry salmon bake 116
    Pie 111

Quick curry 48
Ratatouille bake 108
Salmon and pumpkin soup 65
Stew 94
Stock 61
Fishcakes 124
Fisherman's Stew 94
Flavour bases
   Meaty stews and broths 35
   Seafood and fish 35
Flavour pastes
   Masala 22
   Moroccan 24
   Thai green curry 20
   Umami 23
Flavoured butters 32
Flavourings 14
Fragrant lamb shank curry 81
Freezing foods 9, 10, 12, 13
Fried rice 107

G
Garlic confit 38
Goulash, Hungarian 90
Gratin, pumpkin 155
Gravy 23
Green curry broth 70
Green curry paste 70
Green curry salmon bake 116

H
Honey and mustard marinade 37
Hot green sauce 146
Hungarian goulash 90
Hunter's chicken 93

I, J
Indian marinade 36
Jalapeño and lime marinade 36

L
Lamb
   Bobotie 84
   Chops, baked 112
   Lamb shank curry 81
   Pie with spinach and feta 127
   Roasted and pulled 97
   Tomato bredie 120
Lamb shank bobotie 84
Lamb, spinach and feta pie 127
Lasagne, chicken and butternut 122
Lentils, Dal makhani 82
Low-carb burger buns 145

M
Maiale al latte 78
Marinades
   Chipotle 37
   Honey and mustard 37
   Indian 36
   Jalapeño and lime 36
Masala curry paste 22
Masala spice mix 26
Meal prep 6, 8, 16, 19
Meatballs, Moroccan 137
   With baked brinjals 138
Meatballs 134
Menu plan 16–17
Mexican cook-in sauce 51
Mexican salsa 55
Mexican spice mix 26
Mexican wraps 146
Mire poix, *see* Flavour base
Moroccan meatballs 137
Moroccan paste 24, 73
Moroccan tomato soup 73
Mushroom cook-in sauce 47

N, O
Natural flavourings 14
Not so low-carb pastry 148
Omega-3 65
Onion confit 43
Oven-baked bolognaise 86
Oxtail ramen soup 66

P
Pan-fried cherry tomatoes with anchovies 157
Pastes, *see* Flavour pastes
Pastry 148
Pastry, Phyllo 127
Pesto, basil 112
Phyllo pastry 127
Pickle, burger 52
Pie
   Chicken, leek and mushroom 128
   Lamb, spinach and feta 127
Pilaf 142
Pizza base 130

Pizza with pulled beef
    and spicy caramelized
    onions 130
Polenta 150
Pork, Boneless belly 90
    Hungarian goulash 90
    Neck cooked in milk 78
    Roast fillet 119
Pork neck cooked in milk 78
Pulled, Beef 101
    Chicken 98
    Lamb 97

Q, R

Quick tomato bredie 120
Ratatouille fish bake 108
Rice, Chinese fried 107
Roast pork fillet with blue
    cheese sauce 119
Roasted, Beef brisket 101
    Chicken 98
    Lamb 97
Rocket salad 151
Rolls, see Buns
Rouille 74

S

Salad, rocket 151
Salsa, Mexican 55
Sauces
    Barbecue 29
    Cheese, mustard
        and herb 111
    Hot green 146
    Sriracha 28
    Stir-fry 31
    White 122

Seafood
    Bouillabaisse 74
    Fisherman's stew 94
Seeds, toasted 120
Seven-day meal plan 16–17
Slow-cooking 77
Smoky Mexican spice
    mix 26
Soft polenta 150
Soup
    Beef and lentil 69
    Bouillabaisse 74
    Green curry broth 70
    Moroccan tomato 73
    Oxtail ramen 66
    Pumpkin and salmon 65
    see also Broth
Spice mix
    Masala 26
    Mexican 26
Spicy chipotle marinade 37
Sriracha pulled beef 101
Sriracha sauce 28
Steamed vegetables 152
Sterilizing containers 13
Sticky Chinese fried rice
    with pulled beef 107
Stir-fry sauce 31, 107
Stock, chicken 62
Stock, fish 61

T

Thai green curry paste 20
Tomato bredie 120
Tomato confit 40
Tomato cook-in sauce 44

Tomatoes
    Moroccan soup 73
    Pan-fried 157
Tortillas 146

U, V

Umami paste 23
Vegetables
    Asparagus and green
        beans 152
    Brinjals, baked 138
    Broccoli 152
    Broccoli, steaming 112
    Caramelized onions 130
    Cauli rice pilaf 142
    Cauliflower 152
    Cauliflower mash 150
    Cauliflower, steaming 111
    Cherry tomatoes,
        pan-fried 157
    Fried rice 107
    Pumpkin gratin 155
    Ratatouille 108
    Red pepper rouille 74
    Spinach, creamed 152
    Steamed 152
    Rocket salad 151

W, X

White sauce 122
Wraps, Mexican 146
Xanthan gum 28